~ BEYOND SEDUCTION ~

THE

MACK'S BIBLE

How To Have More Women And Take Back Your Manhood

By W. James Dennis

NOTE OF WARNING

The information presented in this book is for reference purposes only. The author and publisher do not in any way endorse nor condone any illegal activity, malicious or vicious acts against another person that may be depicted in the following pages. Therefore, the author and the publisher disclaim any liability and assume no responsibility for the use or misuses of the information herein.

THE MACK'S BIBLE

How To Have More Women And Take Back Your Manhood

First Edition

ISBN – 978-0-9915587-6-6 (ebk)
ISBN – 978-0-9915587-7-3 (paperback)

Cover Design Consultation by Bryan R. Lewis

THE KNOWLEDGE, WISDOM AND UNDERSTANDING ABOUT WOMEN KNOWN ONLY TO AN ELITE FEW, NOW REVEALED...

The Game between Men and woman is as old as time itself. A Mack plays this Game with strength, finesse and unrivaled mastery. He becomes who other males desire to be – and who women desire to be with. He is the ultimate gentleman that wields the irresistible force of raw manhood.

INITIATE YOURSELF INTO THE HIDDEN WORLD OF THE MODERN MACK

A Book Over 15 Years in the Making

There are many, many books written about the subject of seduction but most of them lack true REAL GAME. They have bits and pieces of it, but I can say with confidence that they didn't actually learn them from certified successful Macks. I was in "the streets" for years before I became an author, teacher and lecturer.

Most authors never got first-hand information and experience. Many of these "seduction books" and courses teach you how to ACT like an attractive man – not BECOME an attractive man.

This book will separate the men from the boys.

SIGN-UP NOW FOR FREE NEWS, REPORTS, DISCOUNTS AND ADVANCED ACCESS TO FUTURE BOOKS AND PRODUCTS – ALL FOR FREE

TO LEARN MORE VISIT:
http://www.wjamesd.com/free-stuff

TABLE OF CONTENTS

WHAT YOU NEED TO KNOW
<u>PLEASE READ THIS FIRST!</u>

First and foremost, this book is not politically correct!

If you're looking for a nice, friendly "dating guide" then please look elsewhere.

This book is based on personal experience and the knowledge, wisdom and understanding I was given many years ago.

Some may find this material offensive or even chauvinistic but I can say with no hesitation that a true Mack has the utmost respect for women. However, a real Mack doesn't look at women in the same fashion as most people do.

Many images of the modern Mack are incorrect and exaggerated. Macking has become a ridiculous spectacle instead of what it was designed to be – a man that has accepted a high level of manhood and lives within this manhood at all times.

This book was not written to disrespect or "bash" women. Quite the contrary. This book was written to get scared males to leave their childish ways behind and become the best man that they are capable of being.

Macking begins as an inward journey to clean-up a lot of mess in the average males head about himself and women.

The average male spends a large part of their life trying to "figure out" women. And they usually fail miserably. I have taken it upon myself to give this layer of the Game the proper attention and respect it deserves.

Many people talk about it, about but no one has ever plainly laid out the modern Mack Game as I will in these pages.

Within this book I will be separating the male species into two classes.

(1) Male (males in plural) and;
(2) Man (men in plural)

A *male* is a simply a boy who has grown up. He doesn't understand manhood or his role as a man in everyday life. And he especially doesn't understand his role as a man when it comes to women.

A *man* is a male that has claimed his manhood. He is Responsible, confident, a leader and problem-solver. He is everything he was "created" to be, for lack of a better way to say it.

Macking has changed over the years but the real, true tenets of this layer of Game remain the same. Macking on the "street level" is the perfect balance between the Pimp and the Hustler. Beyond the streets (where Macking should be in this modern day and time) a Mack is a man who rules every aspect of his life with strong Standards, Principles, integrity and focus.

He is forever the ultimate gentleman and a woman's best companion. He understands her and himself on a level far beyond average.

This is part of a Mack's power and appeal. This is also part of his mystery and mystique.

This book was written to educate; not to advocate any particular lifestyle. As you become more familiar with this book, you'll find it a great reference guide.

If you have an open mind, you'll find a lot of wisdom in these pages. But as always, this information will only benefit those that are truly ready to receive it.

THE OUTLOOK
A Forward by the Author

When I look at the abundance of information in the arena of seduction I see some good information but also a lot of misinformation.

The Game of meeting, seducing and holding women has been watered down. Although the principles of manhood are still pushed to the forefront, there are huge gaps in what people are now calling "Game". Game has turned into how to sleep with women as fast as possible. To a Mack, women have a much higher value than what's in-between their legs. And this is a huge area that modern "Game" doesn't teach because many don't have the necessary information. In this book, you will be given that information.

The foundation of what I'm about to share with you was passed on to me by a great teacher. He was a very powerful and imposing man. I wouldn't go so far as to call him a mentor, but I learned a ton from him and he help shape the man I am today.

Some males are good at business, or have mastered a skill, trade or sport. But when it comes to women, they are clueless. On the opposite side of that coin, some males are extremely good with women but are very bad at managing other areas of their life. My teacher however, was a multi-millionaire business man *and* an expert with women. He was the total package (for lack of a better term).

What he shared many years ago with us young males concerning women was mind-blowing to me back then. At the time my mind wasn't too focused on women to really appreciate it, but as I mastered the financial side of life, dealing with women became a fairly high priority.

This man never considered himself a "Player" or "Mack" but you couldn't deny that if there was a definition of one, he was it. One of the first things that I remember he said about women was this:

"When dealing with women, you have to have the mentality of a pimp."

This is a powerful statement, but… only if you understand what the mentality of a Pimp actually is.

Let me clarify. Macks are NOT Pimps. Pimps have prostitutes (hoes) and make money in their particular layer of the sex industry. A Mack on the other hand doesn't have hoes (although some Macks did) and is usually not involved in the sex industry in any capacity.

A Mack is a refined gentleman that brings women into his life to build something for the future. He is both a ladies' man *and* a business man. He has a grip on these two areas of life. He walks the fine line between Hustler (entrepreneur) and Pimp.

This book is not about the financial aspects of Macking. I have given some of that information in another book entitled, *Unlocking the Small Business Game*. This book is about unraveling the misconceptions, mystery and harmful Perspectives you've been taught concerning women.

It's these backward Perspectives that have left many of you unsure, undecided and overwhelmed when you even think about approaching attractive women. These thoughts break your confidence and therefore weaken your manhood.

This book is the culmination of what I was taught and what I learned by actually *using* that information. I made a lot of mistakes, bad judgment calls and lost many good women – but you won't have to go through much of that because I'm going to give you what I didn't have. A clear guide.

It's been close to 20 years since I was first taught about this layer of the Game and it's just as relevant now as it was back then; in many regards, even more-so. Men are not men anymore. They are just "grown-up boys" with no back-bone, no integrity, lacking Standards and Principles. They're used by women – often toyed and played with. If this applies to you and you're fed up with it, then this is the knowledge you've been seeking.

When I make the claim that this information has only been passed along to a select few, that's the truth. That wasn't a sales pitch or an embellishment.

As you go through these pages you will come across concepts that have, to my knowledge, never been given to the general public. I made every effort to give you this layer of the Game in simplicity and without weakening it. I guarantee this book is well worth your time, money and study. As you'll soon discover, this book will "blow out of the water" any similar book on the subject.

All this is information is presented in a unique way. I will slowly introduce basic concepts and Perspectives and as you continue to read, I'll build upon them. By the end of this book everything will be put together and you'll behold something outstanding. So take your time and do the necessary work.

Don't just read this, study it! This book means absolutely nothing if you don't *use* what's in it. Don't cheat yourself, use this information and master this area of your life. You deserve it and you're worth it.

I welcome you with open arms into the power and mysteries of the modern Mack Game.

W. James Dennis – 2016

BOOK 1 – MEN, WOMEN & THE GAME

CHAPTER ONE

The Natural Order

1   According to the *original* Game, the story of Adam and Eve presented in the Old Testament of the Bible (the Torah) and the Koran, is symbolic.

2   Adam represents the mind state of strength while Eve represents the mind state of weakness.

3   Eve was easily tricked by the Serpent, who some call the Devil. He appealed to her vanity. In this story the serpent was the one with Game; and this Game came from god because god was the creator of all things.

4   The serpent was able to bypass Eve's logic and reasoning and "move" her on an emotional level. Her emotional decision caused her to do the one thing she was told not to do; eat from the Tree of Knowledge.

5   Then she brought the fruit of that tree to Adam. Appealing to Adam's weakness, he fell weak. He then ate the fruit and broke the one and only commandment.

6   This was the fall of man. Adam lost his position of authority because he listened to his "weaker state of mind". In the Game this is a strong reminder that emotional reactions are generally weak and should be constantly checked by logic and reasoning. This should be done before any firm decision is made. Again, this is all symbolism.

7   It's been said that one of man's greatest weaknesses is women (or sex) and that's not true. One of man's greatest weaknesses is the way he *thinks* about himself. This reflects in the way he thinks about himself in relation to women.

8   He has also been taught that in order to get women he needs to be physically attractive, have money, nice possessions and also make sacrifices for her.

9   This is his Perspective about women. The way you perceive something produces emotional responses, a male often makes bad decisions when it involves women; giving up his all important manhood in the process.

10   With no (or limited) knowledge about what manhood really is, he's susceptible to listening to his woman and doing what she wants versus what he knows is best (or better) for himself.

11   What most males have been taught that women want isn't true. And sadly, what most women have been taught they *should* want isn't true either.

12   When we talk about the "Game of the Sexes" we have to go far beyond the outward appearance of things and look at what's really going on inside a person's very nature.

13   The Game itself deals heavily in human nature. It's part psychology, sociology but yet something more.

14   The Game is an anomaly. It can't be defined by normal description or rules. It's not something you can put in a single category and label.

15   Although this book is not about the *original* Game, you have to understand what the Game is in order to understand what is going on "behind the scenes" between males and females.

16   The way I teach The Game is in 9 Principles. These are the foundations on which every Game in existence is built upon.

17   I'll briefly give you those here because you'll need these vital points as we continue to explore just who and what a Mack is.

You may want to bookmark this because I'll be making many references back to them throughout this book.

The 9 Principles of the Original Game

18   **Principle One – Justice:** *Justice is word for word, action for action and thought for thought. What comes back to the initiator is not just what they've done, but also everything that grows out of what they've done.*

19   **Principle Two – Purpose:** *The cause you choose must be higher than yourself. A purpose is the end destination of a journey. You must always know where you are headed or you will never get there.*

20   **Principle Three – Reciprocation:** *You must give in order to receive. You cannot get something for nothing and truly call it yours. You must earn the right to have or possess anything in your life.*

21   **Principle Four – Perception:** *Perception is King and emotion is Queen. How you look at things and events will determine what they mean to you. Perception can open and close doors.*

22   **Principle Five – Value:** *The idea of value is one of life's most powerful motivators. When you value something you will go through more trials to have it and accept more from it. If you do not value yourself, no one will value you.*

23   **Principle Six – Advancement/Growth:** *Anything that does not grow and changes, dies. In life you should be constantly progressing, learning and experiencing new things. Advancement is growth into bigger and better situations in life.*

24   **Principle Seven – Responsibility:** *You can only be accountable for yourself; you are responsible for everything you know and every possession in your life. You must be self-reliant.*

25   **Principle Eight – Contrast/Duality:** *Everything is opposite. There are two extremes and a middle ground where the extremes meet. When*

you bring something into your life it comes with both the good and the bad. These two are an unbreakable pair.

26 **Principle Nine – Use:** *Everything has a use. Everything is a tool that has one or more specific jobs it can perform. If you do not use it, you lose it. Or if you use a tool incorrectly, it can break.*

27 These Principles apply to everything outside of you and inside of you as I'll explain as you learn about Macking. These are tools that you will put in your toolbox to build you and your manhood (Mackhood).

28 We won't be going into depth with every Principle although they're *all* relevant to becoming a Mack. However we'll spend a lot of time with the most important ones.

29 As you develop yourself, you'll start seeing the importance of the others.

30 Think of these Principles as laws of your personal government. You can stretch them a little, even bend them but you should never break them.

31 They are boundaries; lines that should never be crossed under any circumstance. You can do (and be) whatever you want inside these boundaries but violating these have some very harmful side-effects. The biggest is you'll create problems for yourself. The fewer problems in your life, the better – I'm sure we can agree on that.

32 When you strip away all the mystery and glamour of Macking, all that's left is raw manhood.

33 And what is manhood exactly? Thousands of books and songs have been written on the subject but it's still never been made completely clear. Not because people don't know it but because they're afraid to say it. It's not considered "politically correct". But here it is, as simple and as plain as I can make it:

34   When you conquer the feminine aspects of your behavior, you become a man. This is because you polarize to become a woman's exact opposite.

35   As many of you are already aware, women are more emotional than men, while men are naturally more logical. There's nothing wrong with women being emotional. Honestly, it's a beautiful thing and it will work to your advantage. They're that way for a reason which I'll reveal to you later.

36   If what I just said is true, then to truly become a man, you have to understand exactly what a woman's *nature* is. This will give you an Aura of power that will make you naturally attractive to women.

37   Women who are sincerely attracted to males, want men. They don't want a male who behaves and thinks like a woman.

38   Have you ever really listened to the way women talk about other women?

39   Women seldom trust other women. They're also very judgmental of other women. They comment on their clothes, their bodies, their physical appearance, how they talk and how they carry themselves. This stems from a woman's natural insecurities and jealousies. These are traits that a real man should never have.

40   At the same time, which may sound like a contradiction right now, women are very easily influenced by other women. We'll explore this later in more depth as well.

41   For now you have to understand how the Game works because you're going to set up what's called a Program. It's through this Program that you'll be able to attract women in your life; and more importantly hold them.

42   The "street term" for holding a woman is "locking" or "handcuffing". As a Mack it's not about just sleeping with women (although you'll have more than enough power to do so), it's also about locking down women in your life for the long-term. You should want to grow and build something meaningful with them.

43   So, what is The Game? The Game is a structure of power. It's the pyramid structure. The one with power sits at the very top, the capstone, and this power is secured by everyone beneath him.

44   Think of any form of government, past or present. They run on this structure. The rulers (by whatever name you wish to call them) make decisions that dictate how those below them live and function.

45   Think of any corporation in the world. They also run on this structure.

46   You have the President/CEO who has the vision of the company. He's seldom seen but his rules and regulations are followed without questions by those below him.

47   As long as those below him agree to follow his lead, he'll remain at the top of his pyramid and continue to wield power.

48   Below the President you have many levels of management – Vice-President, Chief Executive Officer, Regional Vice Presidents, etc.

49   Its management's job to enforce the rules set forth by the President. They're also there to keep those employees at the very bottom of the pyramid in line.

50   How can this "king" lose power? If all the employees were to suddenly quit, the company could not produce what it needs for their customers.

51   Also, if all the customers stopped buying what the company produces, there's no cash flow and therefore no "life-blood" for the business to survive.

52   In the Pimp Game, the Pimp is the President/CEO of his company; the king of his kingdom if you will. He has a bottom woman (bottom bitch) who functions as middle management. It's her job to train and keep the other prostitutes (hoes) in line and make sure they're following the Pimp's Program at all times.

53   What does a Pimp produce and sell? Sex. And the person who buys sex is called a "trick", or "john". Without the trick, there's no business. If there's no business there's no reason for the prostitute. They're selling something no one is buying.

54   With no reason for the prostitute there's no reason for management. This means there's no reason for the Pimp.

55   In other words, this pyramid structure of power will have **no power**. There's nothing being consumed so there's no point in producing anything for sale. Meaning, there's no reason for the "company" to exist.

56   Think about you as an individual for a moment.

57   Do you sacrifice to buy the latest electronic gadgets, clothes and other "hot" new items on the market? If so, you're a trick. You're buying what someone else's power structure is producing.

58   At your job, do you buy into the company Mission Statement? Do you abide by their rules and policies without question? Are you motivated by those company "pep-talks"? If so, you're a ho. You're part of someone else's power structure and your time and energy are being used to keep that structure intact.

56   Now you may be asking, what does this have to do with Macking and manhood?

57   Macking is a layer of the Game itself. The Game has many layers, different Games played in different ways with different rules and regulations. But regardless of what a particular Game may look like on the outside, every Game is built on the pyramid structure on the inside.

58   At the top are those in power (pimps), kept there by those below them (hoes) and those that consume what they produce (tricks).

59   As I mentioned earlier, every real concept and Principle of the Game works both *outside* of you and *inside* of you at the same time. This is one way you can differentiate **real Game** from **fake Game**.

60   And you are now the owner of some authentic **real Game**. But we're just getting started.

61   Back to the question… Since Macking is based on The Game itself and the essence of Macking is manhood then you must realize that what you must become is the king of your own kingdom. The most powerful and dominating force in your own life.

62   When you take this "throne" as a man, the women who accept you in that position immediately give you power; power over what you can "touch" (your Purpose and/or goals). Because of this, it's your Responsibility (Principle number 7 of the 9 Principles) to wield that power correctly. You must become a knowledgeable, wise, understanding and indomitable leader.

63   This is one of the most attractive traits that women respond to in men. It's the cornerstone of becoming irresistible to women. Women are naturally good administrators. They can manage life fairly well because of their inherent survival instincts. But she will submit to a man who is capable of leading and teaching her.

64   But before you learn to wield this power *outside* of yourself, you must first learn to wield this power *inside* of yourself. You must be able to lead yourself before you lead others. Every great leader is forever a great student – you must never stop learning, growing and developing.

65   Realize this: Everything begins and ends with you because you are at the center of your own little world.

66   I mean this figuratively and literally. Look up from this book for a moment. Everything in physical existence is a certain distance from you. And it has always has been.

67   Your reality is literally revolving around you. You are its very center.

68   If your Inner Game is weak, your Outer Game will be weak. So we'll first develop your Inner Game and then we'll develop your Outer Game. Your outer results with women are a direct reflection of your inner thoughts and beliefs about yourself in relation to them.

69   Some people that teach on this subject will urge you to become more arrogant, bolder, more selfish and in some cases a certified asshole.

70   A Mack however is the ultimate gentleman. He respects women because he understands them better than they might understand themselves. He can be caught pulling out chairs, opening doors and standing up for his woman all the while never looking like a weak insecure spineless punk. She respects him to the fullest. But how does this work?

71   The strength and coldness of a Mack doesn't come from his aggressive tone or from his overly inflated (and often false) ego.

72   A Mack's strength is his willingness to never, under any circumstance, violate the Standards and Principles he sets for himself (I'll teach you how to develop these in Book 2).

73   He will not violate these even if it means losing the woman in the process. This is a hard pill for some to swallow but this is what manhood is all about; having character and integrity and the power to stand on them despite losing something because of them.

74   This is real strength; a strength that women, males and men respect because most people lack it. Again, what's inside radiating to what's outside; everything begins and ends with you.

75   Before we begin to explore the very nature of males and females you first need to grasp the concept of the Game that's being played "behind the scenes" – the Game of the Sexes.

76   It's quite simple really. A woman will constantly test a male's *inner* strength. She does this because she must feel confident in her choice of man. This is part of her survival instincts. Why risk her life and the life of her children by choosing a mate as weak (or weaker) than herself?

77   Despite what you've been taught, women are **not** made up of sugar, spice and everything nice.

78   Women are **not** naïve, weak or helpless.

79   Women will lie, cheat, deceive and create scenarios and situations to manipulate things in their favor. That includes the male in her life she chooses as a mate. She's usually very indirect about what she does and how she does it; and some women are very skilled in this area. Without the knowledge of this part of The Game, you'll never see it coming.

80   A woman will constantly look for areas of weakness in a male so she can find points of leverage (advantage) against him. These

points of leverage are what she uses to manipulate the males in her life. Not just her boyfriend or husband, but any male she can.

81   The reason why a Mack can be a gentleman and be respected and loved by women, while the average male can do the exact same things and be treated like a sucker, is because of what a Mack understands.

82   A Mack understands that he has boundaries; the Standards and Principles he will not violate. These are not something he just says, he lives them and teaches these to the women he invites into his life.

83   This is one area where weak males fall short. Weak males hope and wish for things. They hope a woman will understand him. They wish a woman would finally stop rejecting him and give him sex. They fantasize that an attractive woman will give him the time of day. They dream that their woman will grow to respect him because she says she loves him.

84   A Mack does none of these things. He doesn't wish, hope and dream that these things will happen; he makes them happen.

85   A Mack, as the leader of himself and king of his kingdom, or President of his company (use the analogy that makes the most sense to you), makes sure his intentions are known and understood. He instructs his women about his Standards and Principles and explains why he thinks this way and why he has them.

86   His boundaries must be respected and his boundaries become her boundaries if she's to be with him. This is one of his requirements. He sticks to them no matter where he is; at home, at work or anywhere in public.

87   The average male is too afraid to share these things with his woman because he fears running her away. So by not doing these

things he may get her, but he'll lose the most important thing in the process – her respect.

88   A woman likes boundaries and she respects them if she feels they're reasonable. If a male doesn't have any of his own, she'll implement hers into their relationship. This allows her to take the "throne" so to speak, and the weak male now exists in *her* kingdom instead of her existing in *his*. Remember how the pyramid structure of The Game works?

89   This is the "Game of the Sexes" – and although there's a lot more involved with this, the basic understanding of the subtle power struggle must be realized.

90   Let me emphasize, a Mack thinks **highly** of women. He shouldn't feel like a woman doesn't deserve equal rights in society. He shouldn't feel like women are beneath him or unworthy of simple respect. Macks are not sexist chauvinists, despite what you may have been led to believe.

91   A Mack understands women, himself as a man, and would rather lead than follow. Any woman that disagrees is not the woman for him. He'll leave her be and move on to find the right woman for him.

92   Let's look at cats and dogs. I know, sounds strange, but we're talking about the nature of things and this coincides with the Game you must have.

93   A dog will bend to his masters will. He'll wait for his master to bathe him, feed him, walk him, play with him and show him affection.

94   A dog will risk his life to protect his master and his master's home and possessions if need be.

95   A cat on the other hand does almost none of those things. Cats are very independent and seldom wait on their masters to do anything for them (unless they're highly domesticated).

96   A Mack is similar to a feline in this regard. And a lion is also a feline. A lion is one of the most respected and feared animals in the animal kingdom. Yet you've been taught that felines are weaker than canines. Again, you've been given the wrong information.

97   A male lion conquers territory and gathers a pride, a group of lionesses (female lions). These lionesses do the majority of the hunting and return with the spoils. They often give this to the male lion and usually allow him to eat first.

98   In return the male lion fornicates, sleeps and protects his pride from any invaders or other threats.

99   Don't misinterpret what I'm sharing with you. We're human beings, not lions. But again, we're talking about the nature of things. When we talk about the nature of things we're also talking about the *natural order* of things.

100   A Mack establishes his own kingdom (company) with its own laws, rules and policies. This is the natural order of things. His structure (Game) must be strong from the foundation so that he can maintain his power on top.

101   Like a king (President of a company), who in reality is nothing but a high level manager, he must not allow anything to threaten this position. Whether from the outside or from any weakness he has within himself.

102   Going back to Adam and Eve, Adam representing the strong frame of mind and Eve representing the weaker frame of mind, you cannot fall victim to a weaker state of mind and "eat the fruit". When this happens, your kingdom (company) will be

destined to fall apart. To put it simply, don't cross your boundaries and break your own "commandments".

103   With women, what you present yourself as must be what you are. A woman will test this constantly. She has to know that she chose wisely. Women never want to look foolish to other women and to other people they care about.

104   When she discovers the image you presented to her was a lie, you deserve the results of what you earned; her disrespect and her distrust. There's no one to blame but yourself. Yet, weaker males think this is the best way to get women.

105   There's some truth to what you were taught. You should be yourself with women. But if who you are is not getting you the results you want, then it's time to learn how to improve yourself.

106   This improvement starts with the fourth Principle of the Game (the way I teach it) and that Principle is Perspective.

107   Let's shatter your negative and weak Perspectives and replace them with ones that'll be more beneficial when dealing with women (and life in general).

CHAPTER TWO

The Mack's Perspective

1   As we grow up and are inundated with movies, cartoons, stories and music our Perspectives on life are programmed.

2   The way you perceive something, determines how you react to something. I'll give you a simple example:

3   Let's say you're downtown in a large city. As you're walking you see a man handcuffed on the ground. He's sweating, bleeding from one cheek and his hair is in disarray. There are two policemen standing over him. They're calling in codes on their radios and keeping onlookers at a distance.

4   What are your initial thoughts about this man on the ground?

5   You most likely assume that this man got caught stealing or something else that was criminal.

6   As you continue observing you see a woman run up to the police. She has tears streaming down her face and her tone is one of fear and anguish. You also notice she's pregnant.

7   Through all her crying and heavy breathing you can hear her pleading with the police to let her husband out of the handcuffs. She's telling the story about how he was trying to protect her from a couple of men who attempted to snatch her purse. These men also pushed her to the ground in the process.

8   Now, has the way you viewed the man handcuffed on the ground changed? Has your Perspective of the entire situation changed?

9 Like many of you, I learned a lot about women from all the movies, television shows, music and books I was exposed to growing up.

10 My mother also tried to teach me about women. But learning about women from women is a terrible way to become educated about the topic. Mainly because a woman will only explain the "good guy" traits she likes in men. Even if she, herself, is attracted to men with "bad boy" traits. She wants a gentleman, but not a weak male. She can't explain it, but instinctively she knows it.

11 Where does all this confusion come from? It comes from Social Conditioning. This conditioning is perpetuated by all those movies, televisions shows, songs, etc. that I mentioned earlier.

12 Social Conditioning (or socialization) is not necessarily a bad thing. It's the act of people wanting to be liked and accepted by others. This is how a society functions. We want to be around people who understand our ways of doing things and have a similar culture and background.

13 We want to identify with the crowd and for the crowd to identify with us. This is human nature and there's no changing it.

14 The problem comes in when what's taught through socialization is wrong and/or manipulative. People just accept it and live it although it keeps them from what they really want. Only a few people stop to examine that what they were taught may be wrong to begin with.

15 Like most young boys, you were probably taught that to think sexually about girls was wrong and disrespectful. Yet as you got older you couldn't stop some of those thought even if you wanted to.

16 Those thoughts broke your Social Conditioning (programming) and you probably felt a sense of shame or embarrassment.

17   You were taught not to stare at women's breasts although they wore low-cut tops with bras that pushed up and squeezed their cleavage together.

18   You may have been taught that you shouldn't look at a half naked woman – like a woman in her underwear for instance. You should turn your head because she's not dressed "decently". Yet, you can go to the beach and see crowds of women in bikinis which cover up just as much flesh (sometimes less) than what a pair of underwear would cover up. Where's the logic and reasoning in that?

19   You were probably taught that women shouldn't be looked at as just sexual objects. But when you turn on the television, surf the internet, or look at music videos there are many women blatantly (or indirectly) making sexual gestures and movements.

20   What you've learned sub-consciously through Social Conditioning is that it's OK for a woman to exude a certain amount of "sex appeal". But, it's improper to notice it and make comments about it. For example: It's OK for women to use sex to sell products and services in advertisements, but it's wrong for a man to pay too much attention to them.

21   In other words, it's OK for a woman to be sexualized but not for a man to find that attractive. It's also OK for a woman to act very "feminine" but not for a man to act too "masculine".

22   The fact is because of this type of Social Conditioning you have been stripped of your manhood. This is because Western society is built to cater to women. And since this is the "status-quo", you also feel it's *your* duty to cater to women.

23   Although some women would argue and disagree with this point, let's look at some realities.

23 A woman can have one or more children out of wedlock and receive assistance from her family, her friends and the government. But a single father in a similar situation probably wouldn't.

24 A woman's car can break down on the side of the road and a male will stop and go out of his way to run in and rescue her. But if a male was in a similar situation, the chances of a woman stopping to help him are nearly one-in-a-thousand. Sometimes other males won't even stop to help.

25 You were taught that women are weak and often times helpless and that they must be saved.

26 In the older action movies, the man had to go make plans, kill people, risk his life and at the end of the movie he *finally* got to sleep with the woman.

27 In video games it's the same thing. In novels it's often the same thing. And the constant reinforcement of this idea is what has created your Perspective of you as a male and how you should relate to women.

28 You're under the impression that women need to be rescued, saved, protected and catered to.

29 You're under the impression that it's OK if a woman makes many mistakes but a man can't make any.

30 You've been programmed to think that being attracted to beautiful women is something to be ashamed of and something that shouldn't be talked about in public.

31 You've been programmed to think that a woman must be earned and that you must have some magical quality to even be worthy of her time and attention.

32   You've been led to believe that you need to make personal sacrifices to please women, because again, you have to do something worthy of earning her.

33   This all breaks down to Value (Principle number 5 of the 9 Principles). All things in *every* Game spin around Value. Without Value on the table, there really is no reason to play the Game to win. There's no prize important enough to be won so there's no real motivation.

34   Since Western society caters to women, they naturally assume that they're more valuable than males. They accept that they're automatically worth being protected, sacrificed for, forgiven for their mistakes and allowed to display their bodies without expecting the same consequences as males.

35   Males put up with this Social Conditioning because he places entirely way too much Value on a women's vagina.

36   Value works like this: When you Value something you'll sacrifice for it, accept more from it and often times put aside your own needs because of it.

37   A woman's vagina is one of her greatest weapons against males. Like a dog, she can make a male wait and string him along. During all this "waiting" he must accept all of her moods, changes of mind and unacceptable behavior. All the woman has to do is create the *illusion* that she'll eventually have sex with him; and sex itself rarely happens.

38   The Value of a woman's vagina is only a Perspective. It only has the Value you choose to place on it. To a Mack, a woman's vagina has little Value. A Mack demands more from a woman than just her sex. A Mack wants the woman in her entirety – **mind, heart, body and soul**.

39   To re-emphasize, a Mack wants *all* of the woman – not just her sex. When you get *all* of the woman, everything she has in her

possession comes with her. She can't just leave her vagina locked up somewhere; she has to bring that with her too.

40   When a Mack gets the whole woman he gets every material possession she has, every thought she has, every choice she makes, every ounce of love she can give, every dollar she earns, all of her moods, all of her emotions and yes, also her vagina.

41   **Mind, heart, body and soul** – the good comes along with the bad and a Mack accepts it all.

42   Going back to Social Conditioning, the sad truth is not only have *you* been made to think women are more valuable than you, women *also* think they're more valuable than you.

43   Women have been conditioned this way, so this is what they think a male is supposed to be – someone that holds less Value than them. But this confuses the average woman because she's not attracted to males that think that way. The male that **over values** her, she'll often see as weak.

44   As once explained by legendary ex-Pimp, Andre Taylor, formally known as *Gorgeous Dre*, you can put this concept of Value to the test. Simply ask a woman if she would allow her boyfriend or husband to sleep with another woman. She would say, "No!" without hesitation.

45   Next ask her this question: If she had the chance to sleep with her favorite actor, musician or sports figure even if he was married, would she do it? Most women would say, "Yes," with some hesitation. Why the double standard?

46   She responds this way because in her mind, this actor, musician or sports figure is more valuable than her. And because of that, she will accept more from them and sacrifice her own needs to have that experience.

47 When Value is on the table, the lines of what is right and wrong become very blurred. What seems like an impossibility suddenly becomes a possibility.

48 Now you can take on the Perspective that all of this is wrong and fight against it, or you can use these things to your advantage.

49 A Mack uses these things to his advantage (some of them, not all of them). He uses pieces of this erroneous Social Conditioning to help push his agenda with the women he wants. It's not always necessary to fight against the grain. Water can wear down rock over time just by staying in constant motion.

50 Once you understand Social Conditioning, where it comes from and its effects, then you can remove it from yourself by changing your Perspectives.

51 Knowledge of something, gives you power over that thing. Or as they say, "Knowledge is power". For example: If you have extensive knowledge about food and spices and know how to combine them, you can become a great chef. Your knowledge over cooking gives you power in the kitchen. All you need are the right ingredients and the right utensils (tools).

52 Once you pull yourself away from this Social Conditioning you gain power over it. It's no longer this great unfair force working against you. It becomes another tool in your toolbox to be taken out and used when necessary.

53 What I've just given you is the Perspective of a Mack. They see through the lies and live in the truth. Game recognizes Game.

54 What gives the Mack an advantage with women is that he knows she expects the fairy-tale gentleman, but he also knows what she *really* wants; and he gives her both.

55 He is the "fantasy man" that she has been Socially Conditioned to want but at the same time he can touch her at her

deepest natural and psychological levels. He's irresistible because he has the knowledge, wisdom and understanding which you are now beginning to learn.

56   This is also where many seduction artists and pick-up artists have major leaks (weak areas) in their Game. They try to stand against this Social Conditioning instead of using it to their benefit.

57   You would probably be shocked to hear that many Pimps use Social Conditioning to their advantage as well. Although to a slightly different degree because a relationship between a Pimp and ho is very unique.

58   This is one reason, in my opinion, why you need **Real Game** for successful longevity with women.

59   It's like that old line, "Men want a woman in the streets and a freak in the bed," well women want a gentleman who cherishes her, but not more than he cherishes himself as a man. She needs to feel that he is following and guided by something greater than himself; and these are his Standards and Principles.

60   To give you a visual I recommend watching the movie, *Bram Stoker's Dracula*. The part to pay close attention to is when Dracula takes on his younger persona in London and begins to seduce the main female character, Mina.

61   Although highly stylized and fictional this will help you get this idea of becoming the ultimate gentleman in your mind. Then add this to your Perspectives as a Mack. I'm not saying take everything verbatim; no top-hats and canes needed. Just peep the Game of how Dracula used what she was conditioned to want (and expect) to "open her up" to seduction.

62   Your Perspective is your lens on life. It's how you look at the World and everything in it. Most importantly it's how you look at yourself.

63   Think of it like looking through the view-finder of a camera. When you look through it, you'll only see where you're pointing it; it's the only thing in the frame at that moment. And when you snap the picture, that's all the camera is going to capture. Everything in that picture is all that exists because that's what you thought should be photographed.

64   I'll be talking a lot about Perspective as we continue. In fact this entire book is about changing your Perspective about yourself, life and women.

65   Perspectives can benefit you, and they can also be harmful. You may lack confidence when it comes to women and much of that stems from the disempowering Perspectives you've been programmed with through Social Conditioning.

66   Confidence is vitally important to attracting women and it's something that you already naturally posses. It's just covered up by false information, weakening Perspectives and other garbage you've picked up throughout your life.

67   People speak and act the way they think. And if you think something is not possible, it won't be for *you*. But the next person may think it's possible and for *them* it will be.

69   Two different people can be faced with the same exact circumstances. And because of the difference in the way they think, one person will avoid the circumstances and the other person will deal with the circumstances and find a way to make them beneficial.

70   Your thoughts form your Perspectives. When you change the way you think, you'll change the way you look at things. When you change the way you look at things, you'll change the way you react to them.

71   **Thoughts equal Perspective, and Perspective influences behavior.**

72   Social Conditioning is nothing but thoughts that have been programmed into you from your culture, family, friends and media. They may not really be YOU. You have just accepted them and made them you.

73   For example: A male can see an attractive woman. She has on tight short pants, a tight low-cut shirt and her cleavage is exposed. He is immediately stimulated by the sight of her body.

74   Males, after all, are creatures of sight.

75   He doesn't know anything about this woman but he finds her physically attractive. If he is moved by the sight of her cleavage, his first impulse is sexual. Yet, he can't approach this woman and be completely honest.

76   He can't say, "I saw you from across the street. You have beautiful legs and I love the way your cleavage looks in your shirt."

77   He will be looked at as some type of pervert or highly-sexed freak. But her body is what initially made him feel an attraction.

78   This is Social Conditioning – the thoughts and Perspectives of culture and society. As I said before, it's OK for a woman to dress sexy and exude sexuality. In modern society, that's just being "feminine". But a male is supposed to ignore his sexual impulses because that's just not socially acceptable.

79   She can be "herself" but a male cannot be "himself".

80   So, the male has to play a game. A game of: "I'm physically attracted to you, but I can't say it. You will judge me based on your Social Conditioning. Being honest will scare you away and then I'll never get the chance to have sex with you."

81   The irony is, a woman will be the first one to say she wants honesty in a man. But if every male were brutally honest, she would be in for a rude awakening; a reality she wouldn't be able to handle.

82   Women do want honesty but not at the extent of it breaking her Perspective of reality which was programmed through Social Conditioning. In truth, every human being avoids anything that could break their Perspective of reality. But what is reality?

83   Some of you may know males who seem naturally good with women. They always have women around to date and have sex with. Their reality is probably much different than yours.

84   Then you look at the "street Games" like Pimping (and to a lesser extent Macking) you see males with three, four or five women.

85   In the Pimp Game, a ho (prostitute) is a Pimp's woman. They have a romantic relationship (to an extent) although you have been made to believe different.

86   How can a man have multiple women that all accept this *one* man as *their* man? You have been programmed to believe something like that shouldn't be possible.

87   You have been conditioned to believe that every woman on the planet would raise hell if her man was with another woman at the same time he was with her. Yet there are males that live that way so the truth is, it is possible.

87   A Pimp's reality is much different than yours.

88   And in some cultures around the World, a man having multiple wives is nothing out of the ordinary. In these cultures a male holds more Value than a female. Their reality is different than yours.

89   So isn't it possible that many Perspectives of reality that you've accepted may be wrong? Or at the very least, may be wrong for *some* people?

90   It's extremely important as a Mack that you accept reality. You don't live in a fantasy world. At the same time, you have to separate socialization's concepts of reality from your own.

91   If you ask the average Social Conditioned male what he wants in a woman, he will run down a list of personality traits and probably physical traits. Pretty standard.

92   But every male is scared to say what he *really* wants from a woman. It's considered wrong and socially unacceptable.

93   What do you really want from a woman? Be honest with yourself. If you can't be honest with yourself there is nothing I can teach you in this book that's going to help you. "Man-up" and be brutally honest with yourself.

94   What you really want from a woman is (1) for her to respect you; (2) for her to admire you; and (3) for her to cater to you as a man.

95   Stop playing games and quit lying to yourself. How far has that gotten you with women?

96   I'm not saying that a woman should be some type of slave – that she must do everything you say, when you say it and how you say it. If you feel that way then there's some insecurity within yourself that you have to deal with.

97   By catering to you as a man, I mean that she *wants* to please you. She *wants* to give you her admiration, respect and devotion. She should want to freely give these to you – she doesn't need to be tricked, manipulated or forced. If it has to be forced, then it's not real. A Mack deals with what's real.

98   These are things that you must earn from a woman. You have to give what is necessary to get what you want. This is the Principle of Reciprocation (Principle number 3 of the 9 Principles)

99   To clarify, you don't need to earn (or "save") a woman to get one. It's her complete submission to you that needs to be worked for.

100   Weak males try to earn women. They show-off, brag about their money and possessions; they spend money on expensive clothes, shoes and jewelry. A Mack however understands that having women is the natural order of things.

101   A male is already, by nature, what a woman wants and it's his natural right to have them (thank you, *W. Anton*).

102   *Getting* a woman is one thing. It's not difficult. Having her *submit* to you is another matter entirely. There are millions of males who have a woman but this woman shows him very little respect, admiration and refuses to cater to him.

103   This book will guide you step-by-step into making a new reality for yourself when it comes to women. But first you need to understand their very nature.

CHAPTER THREE

The Nature of Women (The Basics)

1   I'm now going to reveal what was given to me by a great teacher of mine. When you really understand this (and use it), you will be able to charm, seduce and hold (handcuff) any woman who is into you.

2   The following will help you to continue developing your Inner Game and change your Perspectives into something more beneficial than the Perspectives you currently have.

3   Since you now know that women have an idea of a gentleman in their heads (thanks to Social Conditioning); you also need to know what it is she *really* wants in a man.

4   I'm going to give you "the 5 plus 1" concept. There are 5 basic psychological needs of a woman and 1 greater need that will keep her motivated to please you.

5   After I share these, we'll explore how they work in relation to a woman's very nature. Remember, when you have knowledge of something, you have power over it. This chapter will help you develop more power over women because you'll know them better than they might know themselves.

6   Through these 5 plus 1 "important needs" you'll become that fantasy gentleman and never be seen as weak; she'll give you her utmost respect. One thing that turns a woman on is when they deal with a man that understands them.

7   When you can consistently touch these 5 plus 1 needs in a woman she'll be drawn to you. It doesn't matter her race, her social status, her financial level, her upbringing, her culture or whether she's a 10 on the beauty scale. These needs are hard-wired

into her very nature. Most women don't even know them but, when these are triggered, she'll find herself feeling deep levels of attraction.

8   Never forget this important piece of Game: **The way you start with a woman is the way you must continue with a woman**. First, let's go through the 5 important needs of a woman then we'll talk about the "plus 1". The 5 needs of a woman in order of importance are:

9   **(1) COMMUNICATION** – Men are creatures of sight. Women are creatures of sound. Since women are social creatures and often express themselves verbally, you need to engage a woman's interest by being a proficient communicator.

Women love to talk. In fact, a woman's favorite subject is herself. She loves to talk about what she did, what she wants to do and what she's doing; she also loves to talk about how she's feeling and what she's thinking. If you doubt me, listen very closely the next time a woman is talking to another woman. No matter what subjects come up, they'll eventually lead to them talking about themselves. Take note of this and learn to use it to your advantage.

When you first meet a woman, you can get an idea of her comfort level with you simply by paying attention to how much she talks about herself. The more comfortable she is, the more she'll talk and reveal things about herself. Be mindful about what you say to a woman because she'll probably remember it even if you don't; especially if it involves her.

10   **(2) SECURITY** – A woman must feel that all areas of her life are stable and secure; although in reality nothing is secure. At any moment something can happen that lays the best plans to waste. Although women are generally good at managing crises, she would prefer not having to.

In a romantic relationship, it's extremely important a woman feels secure about how her man feels about her and about their relationship. Even if the relationship is based on sex (which a Mack should never involve himself in), she'll accept this just as long as it's stable.

Women are insecure about many things, mostly her self-image. To compensate, she has a drive to make sure her relationships, friendships and living situation are secure. Any woman who forsakes these is a woman out of touch with her feminine nature; not worthy of a Mack's time. A Mack is not a savior of women although if she respects him and submits to his Program he will consider a place for her – until then, a distance must be kept.

Security is psychological for a woman. **Consistency** in her life and in the man she chooses is the ultimate security every woman is looking for.

11   **(3) PROVIDING** – A woman likes to feel as though she is being provided for. Don't think of providing as strictly material things such as buying homes, fancy cars, jewelry, clothes and expensive furniture. That's how a male thinks – not a real man or a Mack. Yes material provisions are important but there are other ways a woman must be provided for.

You should provide emotional stability for a woman. She needs to know that you'll be strong when she's at her weakest (a highly emotional state). You should provide plans to improve your lives, motivation, a shoulder to cry on and boundaries. Women also respect men that can solve problems before she figures out how to. As you can probably tell, providing involves a lot of attention to detail and can be viewed as a burden. But as a Mack, you must take on this burden. A woman who has to bear these burdens will lose respect for you and come to the correct conclusion that she doesn't need you.

If you're the leader, this is part of the leader's Responsibility. Are you going to take the "throne" or is she? When it's all said and done, one of the most powerful ways to provide for a woman is to give her your time, energy, affection and attention.

12 **(4) SEX** – Despite what you may have been led to believe, sex is just as important to women as it is to males (and men). Although the importance of this need differs from woman to woman, she will not tolerate being completely dissatisfied in this area for long. If you're not skilled in the bedroom, you must develop in this area. Don't be ashamed and feel insecure to admit this to a woman. Never forget, what you claim to be to a woman must be true. She would rather be told the truth and be given the choice than to be lied to. Weak males lie, men don't.

For some women, this need may be more important than **PROVIDING**. You'll be able to determine this by how comfortable she is with her sexuality and how openly she talks about sex. As a Mack, it's your job to learn your woman in and out; backwards and forwards.

Both women and males/men are emotionally vulnerable during sex. A Mack takes this time to talk to his woman and enjoy her while she enjoys him. No matter how "tight" or "loose" a woman is, you must explore her sexuality. This should be implemented as soon as possible. Why is this important? Because it marks moments that only you two will share; she will never forget them for the rest of her life.

13 **(5) ENTERTAINMENT** – Women thrive off of external stimulus. Whereas most males could sit on a sofa by themselves and watch television, a woman needs more than that. Women love to enjoy themselves just as much as they enjoy talking about themselves. She wants to explore and experience new things.

Entertaining a woman doesn't mean you're her personal clown or comedian (although humor breaks down a women's guard); it means that you need to constantly stimulate her senses (sight, sound, taste, smell and feel). This can be done by going places and doing things outside the house. For some women it can be as simple as dinner and a movie. For other women, they may need a constant change of environment, such as travelling the country or simply spending a weekend with family; or alone with you at a hotel across town.

Women need to be constantly looking forward to something. This helps keep her motivated and functioning within your structure (Game). A good way to do this is to keep her looking forward to entertaining and fun times with you. Be careful here – the way you start is the way you must continue. If you start taking a woman out every weekend, this will become what she expects and when this stops, she'll bring it to your attention as a problem.

Do what is capable for you to do, no less no more. Doing something new and different once a month is perfectly acceptable in most cases. You must plan these events, she more than likely won't and you shouldn't expect her to. Yet another Responsibility you must take on as a Mack.

14   What was just given are the bare-bone basics, but enough Game for you to expand on and base around your personality. Mix all these needs together and you'll come up with ideas to help establish your Game.

15   The following graphic is a visual representation and easy way to remember these 5 needs of a woman as they were told to me.

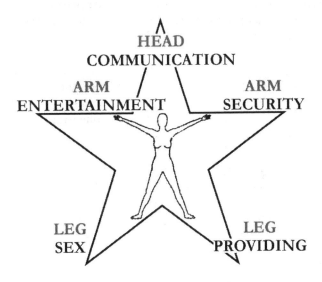

16 By remembering a 5-pointed star it will help keep the important needs in mind. Now let me reveal to you the **Real Game** that many weak males and pseudo-ladies' men lack.

17 The process of Macking a woman begins in her mind through COMMUNICATION. The two arms are her two wrists. This is where you place your "handcuffs". These allow you to limit the "reach" of a woman. This simply means that you take the position of authority and leadership. You lock her wrists by giving her a sense of SECURITY (making her feel secure and stable) and ENTERTAINING her (keeping her in a positive and optimistic mood).

18 With a lot of stress and burdens removed from the woman, she'll be able to get back in touch with the feminine aspects of her nature.

19   A woman's legs and feet represent keeping a woman mentally and emotionally "grounded" by PROVIDING for her deepest needs and SEXUALLY fulfilling her.

20   Constantly and consistently "touching" these 5 needs will make a woman *want* to give you her mind, heart and body. Touching these needs aren't one-time events, you must do these almost daily.

21   The last and most important gift you want from a woman is her soul. The soul represents the very essence of her as a woman. It's the greatest endowment a woman can ever give a man. Her soul is her complete devotion and unshakable love. This is something that a real Mack does not take lightly. If you abuse this, you'll earn a woman's wrath; this wrath can be destructive and dangerous.

22   It is the "plus 1" (of the 5 plus 1) that will allow a woman to feel comfortable and confident in giving you her soul.

23   **A Word Of Caution**: If you don't feel a woman is qualified to be with you for the long-term, **never** accept her soul. You must turn this gift down and tell her to keep it for the next man she feels is worthy. Violate this at your own risk!

24   Before we get to the plus 1 and how to receive a woman's soul, let's further explore the nature of women so you get a bigger picture of how and why all this works.

25   Have you ever heard the saying, "Women and children first?"

26   This is often said when there's a situation of danger and males usher the women and children to safety before saving themselves. Although chivalrous (and necessary in some instances) there's also a lesson about women to be learned here:

27   Women have child-like qualities.

28   Think about a young child for a moment and consider some of their behavior: Children are usually possessive; don't like sharing; will throw tantrums when they don't get their way; easily become jealous; can be selfish; will make emotional decisions instead of logical ones; will say hurtful things when they're emotionally hurt; and they're usually insecure;

Children will fight to show their independence even though they don't know exactly what they're doing; they will try to cover up their mistakes and often lie to do so; they will clamor and beg for attention; they will blame others for their mistakes; will break the rules just to prove that they don't need to follow them; they will play the victim just to gain sympathy; sometimes they will act ignorant if it will keep them from getting in trouble; will test the rules laid down by their parents; they can be emotionally unstable – happy one moment and sad the next;

Also, children are curious about how things work so they ask a ton of questions; children will speak their minds whether right or wrong; they try to comfort those who are sad if they care about them; will talk down to another child to intentionally hurt that child's feelings; will avoid hard work if they can play instead; they never forget when you promise to do something "fun or interesting" with them;

And an extremely important one to remember is that children will avoid Responsibility (Principle number 7 of the 9 Principles), especially if there's someone else that can be held accountable or take the blame.

29   And some of these same attributes and patterns of behavior can be found in women; and unfortunately, weaker males.

30   A woman having child-like qualities is not a negative or despicable thing. In fact, it's a beautiful thing and something to be respected.

31 This is a necessary part of her feminine nature as the first true teacher of a child. She is capable of sympathizing, empathizing and relating to children in a way a male/man cannot. She is mentally, emotionally and instinctively "wired" to be their first nurturer and protector.

32 To evolve from a male to a man and then to a Mack, you must weed out as many of these behaviors as possible. You must polarize yourself to be the exact opposite of children and women. A man is like the trunk of a tree and women and children are like the branches of that tree. A strong wind can knock around the branches; bend them and sometimes even break them. But it takes much more than just a strong wind to uproot the trunk of a tree.

33 Since woman will pay careful attention to your behavior and judge your strength of manhood by it, you need to be what she isn't.

34 It's the *behavior* of a man that attracts a woman more than any house, car, jewelry, bank account, muscles, good hair, good teeth or anything else that males have been taught they need to attract women.

35 If you can transform your behavior and not react emotionally to situations like women do, she'll begin to recognize your manhood and respect it. Sometimes this happens very fast, sometimes not, but when you are consistent in your *behavior* she will begin to compare you to other males and recognize that you are different.

36 To a woman, it's extremely important that who you claim to be matches who you really are. If you say you're a man, then you damn well better behave like one.

37 How do you behave like a man? By not giving into your emotions. You must approach life situations and problems with reasoning and confidence. A woman is always observing how you handle life *and* handle her.

38   If a woman can ever bring you into a highly emotional state (whether negative or positive), she wins because at that point you're acting like a woman; and women can handle other women. This highly emotional state can be any emotional state; anger, joy, jealousy, envy, fear and the list goes on.

39   Not to confuse you but there are exceptions to this "rule". Since women often react from emotions, you can act in an emotional way to alter her mood. As an example, you may appear angry on the outside, but inside you're as cool as a fall breeze.

40   The key is only *you* can move yourself emotionally. She can never be allowed to move you emotionally. You must remain in control of yourself and your emotional states at all times. Nothing she says or does can have any emotional affect on you.

41   This is achieved by learning to place you first more. You must Value (Principle number 5 of the 9 Principles) yourself more than you Value her.

42   You must Value your COMMUNICATION more than hers. You must Value your SECURITY and what you're able to PROVIDE over her ideas of what they should be. Also, you must Value what you find ENTERTAINING over what she finds entertaining. And you must Value your penis more than her vagina.

42   Taken to the extreme you can become a narcissistic, arrogant chauvinist – which a Mack is not – a Mack is the ultimate gentleman. So don't take this Perspective to the extreme. Your job is to simply tell *and* show her that you think highly of yourself and there's nothing she can do or say to make you think (and feel) otherwise. If you don't place Value on yourself, why should she?

43   You could reason that this Perspective would turn a woman off, but it actually turns a woman on. Why? Because you represent something she's not and something that she can't influence.

Women can control children and other weaker women, but she doesn't want to be able to control a man; although she will constantly test to see if she can.

44   Taking your Standards and Principles seriously helps a great deal with this. But to help make this a little clearer, here are some of the most important characteristics and behaviors you must develop to properly represent yourself as a man:

45   (1) You must become less judgmental of her core *nature* – but correct her *behavior* (however she doesn't mind you judging other people she doesn't care about);

46   (2) A person who wants to thrive (improve their station in life) not just survive (just accept their station in life). You must be autonomous – free from external controls and judgments;

47   (3) A man who understand women and is able to make her feel like a woman by fulfilling her 5 main needs. This is extremely difficult for a woman to find and this elevates your Value;

48   (4) A man who is *fearless* but not *foolish*. Women are full of fears, doubts and insecurities. You have to be her rock and lead with reasoning, logic and confidence, never emotion;

49   (5) A man who plans and acts on those plans. He doesn't wait and seek permission for doing what he knows needs to be done;

50   (6) A man who understands her child-like qualities and accepts them instead of trying to rid her of them. He understands that a woman needs to stay within her womanhood;

51   (7) A man who takes Responsibility for himself and her. He takes on the blame and accountability of the relationship because this is what a leader must do in that position;

52   (8) A man who has Standards and Principles (integrity) and will not violate them for any reason or for anybody, not even for her;

53   (9) And lastly, a man who does not *behave* like a woman (or child) in any form or fashion.

54   When a woman recognizes these attributes, behaviors and is honestly attracted to a man, she will respect and Value him until he gives her reasons to doubt that decision.

55   She will be with him through sickness and health and through richer or poorer because she knows that this is the type of man that may make mistakes and fall down, but he will always pick himself back up and pick her up too.

56   To have a woman give you their soul, this is the type of man you must become.

57   The plus 1 (of the 5 plus 1 important needs) is the overriding need of *all* women. They yearn for it and when it's given to them they will find it difficult to resist. Every "test" she gives is all geared to finding a real man that makes her feel like a real woman.

58   The plus 1 is that a woman has to feel cherished by the man she cares about.

59   Cherished means to treat someone with affection and tenderness and to hold them as valuable and precious. It's the best definition I've ever found to sum up what I'm really trying to convey.

60   To a woman, she'll just call this "feeling loved" and being shown that "she matters"; that she's important to her man. A woman needs to feel included in her man's future. But here's the Game about this:

61 A woman has only 3 first "loves": (1) Her father (or father figure); (2) the male who takes her virginity; and (3) the father of her first child. She will forever have an emotional bond with these men.

62 The following three verses are not hard and fast rules. I give them to get you thinking of what may be going on inside the women you choose to date.

63 If she doesn't have a father (or father-like figure) who makes her feels cared for and important, this can create a huge *emotional* gap – a void that must be filled; a yearning for acceptance and love from a man.

64 If she didn't have an emotional attachment to the male that took her virginity (such as in the case of rape), this can create a huge *confidence* gap in her sexuality with males.

65 If the father of her first child left (physically and/or emotionally), this can create a huge *fear* of abandonment when dealing with future males. She'll never feel completely secure because she was left at a vulnerable time; a time when her fear of desertion was high and when she needed protection the most.

66 Again, these are not hard rules, just Perspectives that you should keep in mind since you must know your women inside and out; backwards and forwards.

67 A woman will give her soul (her deepest devotion, respect and love) to the man that can make her feel she is valuable, desirable and precious to him – **more valuable, desirable and precious than *other* women**.

68 But never more valuable than the man she chooses. The man always needs to place himself first.

69 This is what all women *really* want and where they place Value above their other 5 needs. They will sacrifice for these feelings,

put aside their other needs to possess them and go through trials and tribulations to make sure they won't lose them once they find them.

70 I highly recommend looking up the words valuable, desirable and precious in a dictionary if you're unfamiliar with their definitions. You should know *exactly* what they mean so that you can invoke these feelings in women.

71 A Mack PROVIDES these feelings only to the women he feels are worthy of it. He must be prepared to turn down the gift of a woman's soul if he feels she's not worth having long-term. She'll despise a Mack for this, but it's better to be despised for telling the truth than to be despised *and* be a liar.

72 She'll get over being hurt and keep respect for the Mack because of his honesty. However, she will never give respect to the Mack (or any male) that uses and lies to her.

73 Respect is a trait that should be synonymous with every man's name, especially a Mack. Respect is what your reputation as a Mack should revolve around.

74 Reputation is like an expensive fine vase. Once that vase shatters, no matter how you try to put the pieces back together, it will never look the same. A Mack's reputation should be treated like most weak males treat women – put up on a pedestal and protected from outside harm.

75 You have now been given the 5 plus 1 greatest needs of a woman. Understanding this one chapter alone will give you more confidence when dealing with women. But there's so much more to Macking than just dealing with women.

78 You have to play them into the position where you're not dealing with them but, they're dealing with you – a real man.

79   In Book 2 we'll begin to get you walking in the direction of developing that strength of manhood that's already naturally inside of you.

BOOK 2 – STANDARDS, PRINCIPLES & CONFIDENCE

CHAPTER ONE

The Most Misunderstood Principle in the Game

1   I've already mentioned the Principle of Value (Principle number 5 of the 9 Principles) many times over the last few chapters.

2   The thing about Value is that although people have a general idea of what it means; to have real Game, you need to fully understand what it is and how it works.

3   Everything, in *every* Game in existence spins around the Principle of Value. This is no different in the Game between men and women.

4   Let me define the Principle again before we break it apart. After this chapter, you'll never look at life the same way again.

5   **Principle Five – Value:** *The idea of value is one of life's most powerful motivators. When you value something you will go through more trials to have it and accept more from it. If you do not value yourself, no one will value you.*

6   Let's say you were very wealthy. It's a beautiful summer day and you're driving down the road of an affluent area in one of your expensive $150,000 "toys" and you pass a store.

7   There's a sign on the store's door that reads, "By Appointment ONLY." The store appears to be closed. The curtains are drawn shut and there doesn't appear to be anyone going in or coming out.

8   You think to yourself, 'That's odd… how does a store make money if it's not opened for business?'

9 Out of curiosity (and nothing else better to do) you park your vehicle and walk to the store's front door. You place your ear to the door and don't hear a peep from the other side.

10 You take out your cell phone and look up the store's telephone number. You find the number and dial it.

11 A polite and smooth gentleman's voice is heard on the other end of the line. You ask him questions about what the store sells and why it has an "appointment only" policy.

12 The gentleman explains that they sell the finest imported goods from around the world. Many are one-of-a-kind items. Some were created specifically to be sold inside the store.

13 You're curiosity is piqued and you ask to make an appointment. To your disappointment, the next available time is 16 months from now.

14 A little agitated you explain who you are and how much you're worth. In fact, you could go to your bank right now and take out a cashier's check worth $300,000 and you would be glad to spend most of it if you saw something that struck your fancy.

15 The gentleman politely declines your offer and explains how not only is that a violation of store policy, but it would be unfair to other people on the waiting list.

16 You re-iterate that you have money to spend – today, right now! The gentleman on the phone bids you a good day and hangs up.

17 As you turn to leave a well dressed woman approaches the door of the store. Behind her follows an extremely well-dressed couple. The woman smiles at you, does something on her cell phone and it unlocks the door.

18   The woman enters with the well-dressed couple behind her. You peer into the store and can barely make out anything because the lights are off. The door closes in your face.

19   You take a couple of steps back as the curtains of the store's windows are drawn open. The lights in the store are now on and all you see is a well furnished area with a fine desk and some expensive art on the walls. There appears to be another door near the desk.

20   The woman and the well-dressed couple seem to be chatting and laughing. The couple's heads both turn toward the window at the same time. They look at you briefly. The man smiles at you and his woman nods in a snobbish nonchalant manner.

21   Despite being the powerful person you are and having the money to spend, you're treated like an outsider. You leave feeling disenchanted...

22   This story illustrates an important lesson about Value. How do you think the well-dressed couple in the store felt in that moment? They felt privileged, powerful and in the position to do what the average person couldn't.

23   Let me share a quote of mine with you,

24   *"To see what Value is; try to borrow a person's most cherished possession. To understand the sheer power of Value, try to take that possession from them."*

25   Think about it. If you had a friend that worked hard over the last five years to finally afford a shiny new $100,000 car and you asked him to borrow it for a day. What do you think his reaction would be?

26   He would turn you down, in whatever way, to make you understand that he's not risking anything happening to something he worked hard for.

27   Take your same friend. Let's say he had the expensive new car for a week and it was suddenly stolen. What do think his reaction would be under those circumstances?

28   How about if someone kidnapped one of your children? You would probably be ready to literally kill the kidnappers if you had the opportunity.

29   The point I'm trying to make is that we protect and sacrifice for things we feel are valuable to us. And we Value things that make us look and feel a certain way.

30   Your friend, in the above example with the new car, more than likely purchased that new car to look and feel a certain way around his social circle.

31   A child on the other hand is someone that you love and know needs to be protected. And unlike a car, they cannot be replaced.

32   Is one more valuable than the other? Yes, the child should be looked at as more valuable. But how many of us place Value on replaceable things? How many of us sacrifice our needs and accept bad conditions or treatment because we look at something as valuable?

33   Value is an illusion 75% of the time. It's subjective and based completely off a person's Perspective. It's often just an ideal of what *could* be and not what *is* – a fantasy not always based in reality.

34   There are things in this World that deserve to be Valued but most of the time people place Value on things that mean very little.

35   Going back to our story at the beginning of this chapter, the couple who made it inside the store felt valuable at that moment.

Although there was nothing in reality that should have made them feel that way.

36   They waited months or years to get inside of a store and spend money. So what?

37   The store created the *illusion* of Value. They did that simply by disarming the wealthy person. How did they do that?

38   By lessening the Value of money.

40   No amount of money could get someone into that store. They don't care how much money someone has. They place more Value on their store policy, their business and being fair to their customers.

41   Because of this, they're able to cater to an inner need of the wealthy; the desire to feel that they're able to do (and have) what the average person can't.

42   Value is like a spell. **This spell can only be broken by something of equal or greater Value**.

43   Now let's bring this into the world of males and females.

44   Women have been taught that a large part of their worth is based on their physical looks. The older a woman gets, the more she's concerned about losing whatever physical attractiveness she has left.

45   Woman place Value on beauty. You'll see tons of television, internet, billboard and magazine advertisements that prove what I've just told you.

46   These advertisements are usually based around "looking younger", because youthfulness is a big aspect of beauty.

47 While a male might not feel like he's attractive because he doesn't have a good job or a fancy car; a woman will feel less attractive because of her physical appearance.

48 Since women have been taught to equate youthfulness with beauty, as a woman ages she becomes more insecure in that area. She feels that her Value to men and society in general, diminishes.

49 On the opposite side of the coin, since a male is taught that having nice possessions and a good career makes him attractive, as he grows older and acquires these things he feels his Value to women and society in general, increases.

50 Here's the issue. Why do you want to wait to have women in your life until you're older? Especially when it's not necessary.

51 A woman does lose Value as she gets older. Many males lie to themselves and try to pretend that they're not attracted to youthful looking women.

52 Attraction to youthfulness is more than just physical, it's also biological. By nature, a younger woman is able to birth more children over time and remain in a man's life longer.

53 On a deep psychological (and biological) level, women know this and understand this about males. This is one reason they place so much Value on their physical appearance (generally speaking).

54 All throughout history, women have also realized the power of their vagina and how it can be used to literally control weak males.

55 They place great Value here as well and many use it as a weapon.

56 A woman will deny her male sex in an attempt to get him to behave the way she wants him to behave. Some women will even

use it to get complete strangers to buy her drinks, take her on trips or pay her bills if she's bold enough.

57 Since Value is a Perspective and usually an illusion, if you know that women place high Value on their appearance and vagina, like the store in the story above, you can use these to disarm her – to take away two of her most powerful weapons.

58 (1) Her appearance as a means to attract a male; and (2) her vagina as the means to control him. As a Mack, you have to make these two things of little Value to you.

59 Yes, you should have as many physically attractive women as you want but, her attractiveness alone shouldn't be enough to make her qualified to be with you. You should demand more.

60 Yes, you do want sex but, her vagina shouldn't be enough to make you throw out your Standards and Principles. You should want a woman who has more to bring to the table than just her sex.

61 For many women (not all) when she's faced with a man that cares more about what she can *do* over how she *looks* and what's in-between her legs, she's immediately disarmed. She no longer has any tool or weapon to "fight" with.

62 What she's been taught to Value most about herself is now off the table.

63 What's placed back on the table is what *should* be Valued. That is you as a man and the Standards and Principles you live by. These are the requirements she must accept to be with you. However, you must always give her the choice.

64 When a woman sees that the man she's attracted to is not ruled or swayed by the physically attractiveness of other women, she's intrigued.

65   And if this man is not weak to the promise of sex from other women, she'll realize that she's not dealing with an average male.

66   To put it another way, when you no longer place so much Value on a woman's looks, body and vagina you're actually making yourself more attractive to women.

67   How does this work? Because this gives her a feeling of SECURITY in the relationship. Especially as she gets older and her physical attractiveness begins to fade.

68   If *she* has to submit to your Standards, Principles and Program (we'll discuss a Program later), then she knows that any *other* woman will have to do the same. This will be the reality no matter how attractive the other woman is – if you truly are who you claimed to be.

69   This understanding alone will aid you when giving any woman a reason to Value and respect your manhood.

70   Only a real man can make this mental transition. It's not easy to look at physically attractive women and not think about sex when you're around them.

71   The key is to Value your Standards and Principles over your lower animal instincts.

72   When Value is on the table, what seems impossible can become possible.

73   The Value you must place on the table is something that's more important to you than your sexual impulses and any woman – your manhood.

74   Standards and Principles are the core of what you'll use to represent yourself as a man. Not just to women but to every person you cross paths with in everyday life.

75   You must break the illusions of Value that women have. Let's be honest, in the grand scheme of things, there are more important things in life to be Valued other than women and sex.

76   Women will profess the same thing but yet they hold deep insecurities when it comes to their appearance and bedroom skills. They have accepted this Social Conditioning as reality.

77   One of your duties as a Mack is to take a woman out of her programmed reality and bring them into your own little world.

78   Your world is much different than the world they're used to. The life you live is different than the lives of most males she has met.

79   You become more than just a "boyfriend" or "mate" you become a teacher, leader and an actual man; what she spends a large amount of time searching for.

80   Because of this, she'll place Value on you. And like anything that's valuable to a person, she'll sacrifice her personal needs and accept more from you. At the same time you'll demand more from her than any man (or male) she has ever encountered in her life.

81   In return, she'll receive all of her biggest mental, emotional and psychological needs fulfilled (as previously explained in the last Book).

82   Even if the relationship doesn't work out and she moves on, you'll forever have a place in her heart because there's almost literally no other man out there like you. The spell of Value you weaved can only be broken by someone of equal or greater Value.

83   As a Mack, you and what you represent should be the most Valuable thing in a woman's life; with the exception of her family and children, of course.

84 This isn't something you wish and hope for, this is something you must *create* and *make* happen.

85 This isn't difficult because of the nature of Value. Let me share a secret with you.

86 Whenever someone tries to possess something of Value, it ends up possessing them instead.

87 Consider the truth of that statement. When you really place a high Value on something, you're possessed by it. You'll protect it, covet it, sacrifice for it, become selfish in regards to it and have a difficult time letting it go.

88 An easy way to see how this works is looking at your job. Although you may not like your job, it provides a paycheck and therefore a means to support your lifestyle.

89 You sacrifice your time, energy and sometimes even self-respect to keep this job. You place more Value on the paycheck you receive over the time, energy and sacrifices you have to make. You'll miss family birthday parties, special events and many of life's leisure activities to make sure you're at work at the time you're told to be there.

90 You protect your job position by doing what you're instructed and following the rules of the company. You understand that any serious violation means you'll be fired. And with that job goes your paycheck and your standard of living.

91 You work when you're told to work and stop working when you're told to stop. You have to ask permission to take a vacation and at some jobs, you even need to ask permission just to take a bathroom break.

92 Do you have a job, or does your job *have* you?

93 This is similar behavior to someone who buys an expensive item. If it costs a lot, and is of good quality, people will do similar things to protect it.

94 If it's an expensive piece of jewelry for example, people will hide it or lock it away.

95 And again this is similar behavior with a family pet (if it's valued).

96 The pet needs food, shots, time, attention, be taken out for walks, bathed, an area to sleep, be cleaned up after, and the pet does nothing more than just act according to its nature.

97 Are you the master of your pet, or are you the pet's *pet*?

98 You now have a better understanding of how Value works and as you continue we'll be exploring other aspects of it.

99 It's time to dig inside of yourself and bring out your manhood. I'm going to teach you how to develop Standards and Principles for yourself.

100 As far as Inner Game is concerned, this is the most difficult part for a lot of males. The reason is because you'll be constantly battling with yourself. You'll be trying to decide if the Standards and Principles you're setting are *really* coming from you, or are they coming from your Social Conditioning?

101 I urge you to take your time with the next chapter. If you rush through it you'll be putting yourself at a disadvantage. When we tie these in with confidence later, you'll find yourself not developing as quickly as you could be.

102 If you want to be worth (Valued) more than the average male, Standards and Principles is where it all begins.

CHAPTER TWO

Developing Standards & Principles

1   A man without Standards and Principles (plus the integrity to never break them) isn't a man — he's just a grown boy.

2   You will never truly be a Mack without these tools.

3   I won't be giving you what I think your Standards and Principles should be. These are something that you must develop for yourself and implement into your life. You know yourself much better than I do.

4   Having Standards and Principles is not always convenient. Sometimes you'll have to sacrifice gaining or having things, but this is something you must accept. **Both the good and the bad sit at the same table at all times**.

5   You may be wondering why having these are necessary to define you as a man? I think that's a fair question.

6   Not only does having Standards and Principles create boundaries that you don't cross, giving you guidelines to follow when you make decisions,

7   they also bring order to chaos, help you make sense out of non-sense and give you a "flashlight" to see in the dark. You can be and do whatever you want in your kingdom (company) just as long as you don't break the boundaries you create for yourself.

8   As you begin to bring women into your life, you're going to be put in many situations that you don't know how to handle.

9   Some of these will be the woman testing you to see how you respond; others will be regular relationship "drama moments" that must be addressed.

10   Sometimes you'll be put on the spot and have to decide the best course of action to take. Since you must take the role as leader and decision maker you need *reference points* that you can base all your decisions from.

11   Adhering strictly to your Standards and Principles makes your decision making and behavior consistent. Consistency helps give a woman the feeling of SECURITY she needs and longs for.

12   You're a stable rock in her sometimes chaotic ocean of life; something she can grab on to and feel safe when she's not sure of anything else.

13   Lastly, and just as important as the reasons I listed above, Standards and Principles put you in the seat of taking on Responsibility (Principle 7 of the 9 Principles).

14   You have to appear responsible for everything in your life. Women often times don't take responsibility for their actions, decisions and behavior so this burden falls upon you as a man.

15   Women are social creatures. As such it's important to them to look "good and right" around other women and their family.

16   Let's say that the diet of your children is important to you. You have a Standard that young children shouldn't eat too much candy and junk food.

17   Although your woman may have agreed to that, one day she comes to you with a situation. Her family wants to take the children out for Halloween. Of course this means they'll be getting a lot of candy and other sugary treats. She asks you if the children can go. What do you do?

18   You would say, "No," because this goes directly against the Standard of diet you have set for your children.

19   Your woman will probably get upset at this fact and in the act of removing Responsibility from herself, tell her family that *you* said, "No," and that *you* don't want the kids eating too much sugar.

20   The children not being able to trick-or-treat suddenly becomes *your* fault – although your woman has already agreed to a good diet for the children.

21   Now suddenly you look like the bad guy and you're to blame. And with this, she may never tell her family that she also thinks that a child eating too much junk food is bad for them. She has laid the blame and Responsibility completely on you.

22   There may also come a time when you meet a woman who claims she has a boyfriend. Yet she'll still flirt with you, communicate with you and make the occasional sexual remark.

23   What's the woman doing? She's laying the burden of having sex with her, on you. She doesn't want to make the first move because sleeping with a man while she has a boyfriend isn't socially "good and right". In society's eyes, she'll looks like a slut.

24   So now she places the Responsibility on you to seduce her. To make her feel like one day she just got caught up in the moment and had sex outside of her relationship.

25   You're to blame for her indiscretion. You seduced her and she just temporarily got lost in her emotions and ended up doing something she felt was wrong. At least that's what she'll tell some of her friends if they ever ask.

26   As a man and a Mack you'll constantly be taking on the Responsibility for your relationships with women.

27   It will be on you to approach the woman, initiate communication, ask for the first date, begin the flirting, convince her that she should be involved with your Program and create the moods that allow her to feel it's OK to have sex with you.

28   Leadership involves Responsibility and you'll often times find that women won't make concrete decisions because they don't want to be blamed if things go wrong; or end up looking "bad" or "foolish" in the eyes of other people – especially her female friends and family.

29   And what is a Mack's Perspective about this aspect of women's nature? He recognizing it and accepts it because it works to his advantage. His response? "If you're looking for somebody to blame, then blame me." Because he already knows he's going to bear the blunt of blame anyway.

30   Since women avoid Responsibility and Responsibility is an important aspect of Leadership, this gives even more power to the Mack. This power comes with a price though; the Mack is going to be blamed for a lot of things. **Both the good and the bad sit at the same table at all times**. This is just how the Game goes.

31   Let's start to build your Standards. The majority of the following exercise was taken from, *Revealing the Secrets of the Game*. I have carefully streamlined and adapted it to make it more relevant to Macking and manhood.

32   We've covered the Principle of Value (Principle number 5 of the 9 Principles) as it applies to creating self Value. But now we must discuss what the *personal* values in your life are. In other words, what's most important to you?

33   First let's discover your Likes and Dislikes. Everyone has things they absolutely can't stand, things they can't do without out and other things they could care less about.

34   This is an important exercise because you really have to know you. When you know *you*, creating Standards for yourself is much easier.

35   As I mentioned before, don't rush through this and don't push it aside like it's not important. To be a Mack, you have to be a man first. Very few *males* will ever take the time to define themselves as a *man*.

36   This will separate those that are serious from those that are curious.

37   The exercise works best when you aren't tired, sleepy or hungry. You should have no food, alcohol or other intoxicants at least two hours prior to doing this exercise. Your mind must be as sharp as possible.

Developing Your Standards

38   **(1)** Find someplace quite and free of distractions. Turn off your cell phone, your tablet, the radio and television. Send the kids and pets away and your woman too if you have one.

39   **(2)** Grab a pen (not a pencil, you're not allowed to erase anything) and a piece of paper. On one side of the paper write "Likes" at the top. On the back side of the paper write "Dislikes" at the top.

40   **(3)** Take a few deep breaths, settle your mind and just write. Don't judge anything! Don't second guess it, censor it or try to make it sound good; just write. Write down your likes on the "Likes" side of your paper and your dislikes on the "Dislikes" side of the paper.

41   **(4)** I repeat, don't judge what you write! This is very important. Just let our thoughts and feelings come out. Also don't

read what you've written until *after* the hour is over. If you run out of space, grab another sheet of paper.

42   You never need to show these lists to anyone. This is for you alone. It will help you discover the basis of you as a man.

43   After the first few minutes you may find yourself straining to find more things to write, this is normal.

44   What you're doing is gently refocusing the mind. Just keep thinking, "What do I really and honestly like, and what do I really and honestly dislike?" keep asking yourself those questions and your mind will respond. When it does, write those answers down immediately.

45   After your hour is up, go back and read over what you've written. If you took this exercise seriously, you'll discover a thing or two about yourself you didn't know before.

46   This exercise brings out deeper parts of you because when you write like this, it's the deeper parts of you being expressed; that "inner voice" inside that we rarely listen to anymore.

47   You should now have a general idea of the things you Value, because you *like* them. What you like is what brings you joy, pleasure, peace and motivation.

48   If you have the time you can continue with the next step, if not this can be done at another time when you have some peace and quiet.

49   **(5)** Grab your Likes list and a few sheets of blank paper. During this next hour you want to go over each one of your Likes, one-by-one, and ask yourself a very simple question,

"What benefit do I get from this?"

50   You should keep asking yourself this question about a single like until you can't come up with more answers.

51   **(6)** Write these answers down as they come to you. Again, don't over-think, analyze or judge them. Once you've exhausted your answers move on to the next like on the list and ask yourself the same question.

52   Repeat this until you have done this with every like on your list.

53   What's interesting about this process is that you'll come to realize that your likes alone are *not* that important. Your likes are only as important as what they give you (or bring to you).

54   You should always be moving toward your likes and away from your dislikes. Not *running* from them. You can't control everything, but you almost always have a choice.

55   Now it's time for the final part of our exercise in defining your likes. And that's to actually turn these likes into Standards – things you will "stand on" as a Mack at all costs.

56   **(7)** When you get another hour of quiet, bring out your likes list along with your answers from steps 5 and 6. We're going to break your answers apart and get them down to only *one* or *two* words that define them.

57   This isn't easy. I suggest breaking out some more paper and a dictionary and/or thesaurus if you need them.

58   The one or two words you choose are very important and you need to know *exactly* what they mean. If your woman, or anyone else for that matter, ever questions you about your Standards you'll be able to explain yourself with confidence and no hesitation.

59   Let me clarify how this works with an example: Let's say one of your likes was intelligent women. After you asked the question, "What benefit do I get from this?" You came up with a few reasons why intelligent women are good for you.

60   You may have written down that you have more meaningful conversations. You might also have that it's easier to explain your plans to them. The list might also include that intelligent women seem more reasonable and react less emotionally.

61   When you break these down and look at the core benefits of intelligent women you come up with these two answers. Each is only one or two words:

(1) **More engaging** (more worth your time)
(2) **Less difficult** (requiring less effort from you when you communicate)

62   From just these two values alone you now have requirements that you should use to *qualify* all women that you consider for a relationship.

63   One, you will only deal with intelligent women who can keep you engaged. And Two, you want women who pose little difficulty in understanding you, your life and your Program (we'll define what a Program is later).

64   Any woman who doesn't fit these criteria is not a woman you will waste your time on. They don't have the qualities you Value in a woman and therefore there's really no place for them in your life (at least in a romantic capacity).

65   As you go through all your answers you'll see many themes that relate to one another. The one or two words you come up with will often repeat themselves over and over again.

66   These are your **core** personal values, your Standards. These are what you need to "stand on" as a Mack at all times, no exceptions.

67   Knowing your Standards has tremendous benefits:

(1) It will further develop your character and integrity as a man; (2) Knowing what you Value most (and standing on it) will increase your Value to the women you date and to other people in general; (3) Many of your fears and anxieties about life will fall away because you'll have a deeper understanding of yourself; and (4) You'll develop a sense of inner strength that will be felt by those around you. This is the beginning stages of your "Aura". An energy generated by you that others will "feel" and "sense".

68   With confidence and your "Aura" (both of which we'll get into later) you'll sometimes find that you draw women to you. You'll catch them looking at you, smiling at you and going out of the way to make you notice them. Sometimes, something simple as putting themselves close enough to where you can initiate a conversation. Remember, the Responsibility is almost always left on you.

69   Knowing your Standards are one thing, living them is another. To truly be a man and a Mack, you must make these an integral part of your personality and judgments.

70   Let no female or male turn you against your own Standards. If they don't agree with them, so what? These aren't the people you want in your life anyway.

71   You're Responsible for what you *know* and knowing yourself is the greatest Responsibility of all.

72   While Standards are *reference points* to help you make decisions and judge things by, Principles are your actual patterns of behavior.

73   Standards are the blood and organs while Principles are the bones.

74   Principles are the "backbone" or "spine" that women keep saying they want in a real man.

75   Don't move onto this next exercise until you have completed defining your Standards. Your Principles will be based on your Standards. Let me give you a brief example of how these two would interplay in real life:

76   You're in a bar and you notice an attractive woman. You approach her and engage her in conversation. While you're talking to her another man approaches, sits down beside her and grabs her around her waist.

77   How do you *judge* this situation? If you had the Standard of avoiding **unnecessary drama**, you would respect another man's woman; because not doing so causes unnecessary drama. Unless *she* specifically gives you a reason to do otherwise, you would choose to leave this situation alone.

78   That's the *judgment*, the **Standard**. But what's the proper *behavior*, the **Principle** you use in this situation?

79   If you held the Principle of respecting other males, regardless of how weak or strong they may be, you would acknowledge the boyfriend, tell him you meant no disrespect and walk away gracefully.

80   This is reasoning and logic. No emotion involved. You acted according to your Standards and Principles; meaning how you think – your Perspective.

81   And you shouldn't care what anyone else would have to say about it.

82   There were many possible ways to handle that situation. Some good, others not so good, but you abided by what you thought – your Perspective. This is the foundation of manhood. This is what will give you consistency in everything you do. And this will also give you meaningful Value in the eyes of women.

83   Imagine if you told this story to a woman and she asked you why you did what you did. You could break down exactly why you chose your course of action in detail.

84   The woman might not agree, but she'll respect the fact that you operated from something "higher" than yourself – that you reasoned and thought your actions through; no emotions involved.

Developing Your Principles

85   In Book 1 – Chapter One, I gave you a list of 9 Principles of the Game. Although I highly recommend you add these to your Standards and Principles as a Mack, the final decision is yours.

86   **(1)** In another quiet hour, take out your sheets of paper that have your Standards on them. Grab something to write with and some blank sheets of paper. Also get out that dictionary and/or thesaurus.

87   **(2)** Go one-by-one through your newly found Standards and ask yourself this question:

"What behavior (actions) defines this Standard?"

88   Taking our previous example where we defined two Standards of why we Value intelligent women, we might come up with something like this:

89   **More engaging –** What action defines this Standard is excellent, above average conversation. Not only do you require

this of women you date, but you require this of yourself. You would limit your time with anyone who just wants some idle chatter.

90   Because of this you would make it a point to always talk about deeper more meaningful things. It could be politics, business, the state of the World, the unfair distribution of wealth, etc.

91   You might also not care to talk about a woman's hair and nails, but instead fashion as a whole; what interests you in that area and discover what interests her in that area.

92   The second Standard we came up with was:

93   **Less difficult** – The actions that might define this Standard are more peaceful interactions.

94   You prefer not to fuss and argue, so you don't start arguments and you don't fuss. You say what you need to say and allow the woman to say what she needs to say. You share with her the importance of speaking to one another in a non-combative civil tone.

95   Occasionally voices might get raised but you always bring it back civil. If the woman refuses to keep a civil tone with you, you hang up on her if you're on the phone or walk away if you're in her presence.

96   If she's in your house you ask her to leave and if she's in your car you immediately take her home (or give her some cab money and drop her off at the nearest safe location – a Mack is always a gentleman).

96   You tell her you'll continue the conversation when she can talk to you properly, and leave it at that.

97   This is the "coldness" of a Mack that some of you may have heard about. It's not about being aggressive and degrading a

woman by calling her a bitch or any other name. It's about not allowing her to emotionally move you enough to violate your Standards and Principles.

98   You come first. Your Standards and Principles define you as a man and you will not let your manhood be comprised. Ever!

99   Yes, she's going to be upset but you won't lose her respect. If she leaves you because you stood up for your manhood, that's all the better. That's not a woman you want in your Program to begin with. Why? Because she'll constantly try to test your manhood – a headache you can do without.

100   Remember, you must stand on your Standards and Principles even to the extent of you losing the woman. When she sees how committed you are to who you are as a man, she'll either submit to it or leave. And this is what you want – either way, you win.

101   **A Word of Caution**: Don't make this any more complicated than it needs to be! Some people think way too long and hard and end up getting frustrated, or they get lazy and write things down just to speed through the exercise.

102   This is the foundation of your manhood, treat it as important but don't let it become a chore.

103   Think about how you want your kingdom (company) to look and function. Consider what you'll tolerate and what you won't. This will help in figuring out what behavior (actions) defines your Standards.

104   If this takes you a week or two, or even a month, there's absolutely nothing wrong with that. This isn't a race; it's about you and becoming a man who is exceptional with women.

105   You'll become a man who will garner women's respect, not by begging for it or asking for it. Respect will automatically be given just by you being consistent with who you claim to be.

106   Your manhood will shine through as they observe your overall behavior and how you handle things. This eliminates any confusion or misinterpretation. Even if there is any, you can explain why you think the way you do in a simple logical fashion.

107   These exercises aren't easy, but they're worth the time. When women start commenting about the way you "carry yourself", you know that you're more than half-way there.

108   With these under your belt, let's delve into the confusing sphere of confidence. Women claim they like confident men. But what is confidence? And how does a man develop it?

109   If Principles are the bones and Standards are the internal organs, then confidence is the blood. It what keeps everything running so that you can "move and shake" with your Macking.

CHAPTER THREE

Bringing Out Your Confidence

1   There are many definitions of confidence, but let's start with the dictionary definition. Here is a couple:

(1) A feeling or consciousness of one's powers or of reliance on one's circumstances – Faith or belief that one will act in a right, proper, or effective way.
(2) The quality or state of being certain.

2   Confidence is nothing more than being completely certain that what you think, say and do will be right (proper and/or effective). And this is an acceptance of your personal power.

3   There are hundreds of books on confidence and even more articles you can find online but I'm here to tell you that you're already naturally confident.

4   Some of you may be asking yourself, "How is that?" Because you don't feel confident. You don't feel certain (or sure) in your words, actions and thoughts. Although that may be true now, this wasn't always the case.

5   When you were younger you had a certain degree of confidence. You probably spoke your mind, weren't afraid to ask questions and didn't care what other people thought of your behavior (except maybe your parents and family).

6   Over time you were taught that certain things were wrong to do and right to do. Certain things were wrong to say and right to say. And certain things were wrong to think and right to think.

7   Because of this, your natural confidence was "covered up" by the programming of Social Conditioning. If your confidence is like

a bright light, then the lack of confidence is that light being covered up by bags of garbage and debris. The light still shines but no one can see it or recognize it. And the first person that needs to notice this light of confidence is you.

8   To improve your confidence, you must begin to remove all the "bags of garbage" that's piled on top of it.

9   In other words, you must begin to remove your Social Conditioning. Since Social Conditioning are like programs running in the computer of your mind, there are some that need to be re-programmed. You must do what needs to be done so that your mental computer runs at optimum efficiency.

10   Your computer (mind) needs to be cleaned of all viruses, trojans, spyware, key-loggers and malware. If not, the operating system cannot function as it should. Sometimes the computer won't be allowed to boot-up at all – you'll get a "system error".

11   Let's use this computer analogy as I explain exactly how your mind functions in relation to information. When you grasp this concept, you'll see how the process of gaining back your confidence is possible.

12   Before we continue, let me just be clear. We're separating the *mind* from the *brain*. The brain is an organ that helps the body perform natural bodily functions such as breathing, regulating your heartbeat, giving signals for the digestion of food, etc.

13   But the mind is the ability to think; to imagine. It's in the mind where you have allowed outside "programs" to interfere with what you think and how you think; as well as what you imagine and how you imagine it.

14   Speaking of imagination… imagine your mind as a huge vault of file servers. If you're not a computer person, then imagine a huge vault of file cabinets. Every server or file cabinet stores information about a **single** subject.

15   For example, let's talk about the subject of *love*. Everything you have every been told, seen, heard, felt and taught about *love* is stored on a single file server or in a single file cabinet.

16   Whether this information came from your grandparents, parents, brothers, sisters, television, music, school, books or anywhere else; all this information about *love* is stored or filed.

17   When you think about love or someone mentions love, your mind runs a "search function". Something like an internet search engine.

18   In order to relate to the subject of *love*, your mind needs to pull this information off the server; or open the file cabinet and "pull out" the files.

19   And what's in these files? Everything you were ever taught or experienced concerning *love*.

20   If these files are "bad", "incorrect" or "dis-empowering" then this is what you think about concerning *love*, because this is what you know (or think you know) about it.

21   Here's how this works when we talk about confidence.

22   Since confidence is being **certain** in what you think, say and do, if the information on your file server (or in your file cabinet) about a situation is not to your benefit, you'll feel **uncertain** about it.

23   Also, if you have no file server (file cabinet) about a situation, there are no files to pull because there's nothing for your mind to search for. You'll have no clue of what to think, say or do.

24   Bad or incomplete information equals uncertainty. No information also equals uncertainty. And when you're not **certain**, there's no confidence.

24   Many of you reading this have no confidence in your ability to speak to attractive women. Why? Because either the information in your mind is weak or incomplete; or you have very little or no information to work with.

25   **Your mind can only work with the patterns of information it has stored or "filed"**.

26   On the other side of that coin, you probably find yourself speaking effortlessly to women you **don't** find attractive. In your mind, you're just having a regular conversation, and you have years of information filed for having regular conversations. You've been doing it most of your life. It's easy and you don't even think about it.

27   Why is it easy to hold a conversation with a woman when there's **no attraction** and you find it difficult when there **is attraction?**

28   The truth is there should be NO difference. The difference only exists in your mind. It's the way you think because that's your Perspective (Principle 4 of the 9 Principles); it's the way you're looking at it.

29   You've been taught women need to be earned and therefore, impressed. When you try to impress a woman you're attracted to, you fumble around because your mind is trying to pull information that it doesn't have! This means that you're **uncertain** and this makes you freeze up or quickly run out of conversation.

30   The program of impressing women is a file server (or file cabinet) in your mind with little or no information. Be real with yourself – do you honestly know *how* to impress a woman?

31   I'm here to tell you that you don't need these files at all! They need to be abandoned. They're incomplete and a useless waste of space. They offer you no benefit whatsoever.

32 As a man and as a Mack, you're not in the business of impressing women. You're a man and you're already by nature what women want.

33 All you have to do is be the best man you can be and represent that at all times.

34 What is another file on your file server (in your file cabinet) that's interfering with your success with women?

35 Something we've previously covered – placing too much Value on them; thinking that you have to be physically attractive to get their attention; thinking you need a lot of money; thinking that you need to cater to their every whim and desire to look like a "good catch"; thinking she'll get mad if you're honest; thinking that she must like everything about you to be attracted to you; thinking that you must "win her over" or "trick" her to have sex; and I could go on and on.

36 Where has all these programs gotten you? Probably in the friend-zone and with little or no sex.

37 The information on women needs to be purged and re-written. The files server (file cabinet) you currently have about women is filled with useless and confusion information.

38 So when you're around an attractive woman and your mind does it search for information, all you get back is information that does nothing for you.

39 You need to consciously replace the information on the "women server" (file cabinet) in your mind, and replace it with new information that will benefit you.

40 When you abandon this old, tired and dis-empowering information, your natural confidence will begin to shine through.

The muck will be cleared away and things will become much clearer.

41   The next logical question is: How is this accomplished? I'm going to give you a practical exercise but first let's cover something else you need to know about the computer called your mind.

42   The mind can process a lot of information very quickly but the best way to program information into the mind is in small "bits" or "chunks".

43   Do you know why telephone numbers are broken up by hyphens? In America phone numbers generally look like this: **(321) 555-6789**.

44   This is because of a psychological truth. Although the mind is extremely powerful, it still works in patterns. For example, when you try remembering a string of numbers, the best way to do it is to break it up into smaller pieces first. You remember these smaller bits separately and then it's easier to put them all back together.

45   Take this number for example:

2738438475678975

46   This is a 16-digit number. Just looking at it and trying to retain it is a strain on the mind. Don't believe me, try it. Maybe only 10% of the population could memorize and recall a string of numbers written like that.

47   Now look at exact same numbers broken up into smaller bits:

2738-4384-7567-8975

48   Not only is this easier for the eyes to focus on but your mind can take it in much easier as well.

49   When we deal with the mind we're going to "program" it in a way that's simple and therefore more effective.

50   People seem to be big on positive affirmations in this day and time. And some of these affirmations are multiple paragraphs long! They may make you feel good, but how long will it take you to memorize something like that word-for-word?

51   And how long will it take for your mind to absorb all of that and use it to think in that way?

52   Although we're not going to use traditional affirmations, the same concept applies. We're going to program our minds with *single* words; no long sentences and no unnecessary fluff just to sound good.

53   We're going to train our minds to pull the information we *want* and not pull what's already on the file server (or in our file cabinets).

54   This is the foundation to confidence. When you can gain control over what you think in a situation, you can be more *certain*. When you're more *certain*, you'll be more confident.

55   Please keep this in mind. It's possible to "program" your mind to pull "files" for experiences you've *never* had. To literally create new information for it to pull from a file server (or file cabinet).

56   Remember, all the mind is doing is looking for a *point of reference*. This is what it's searching for to find and pull information. It uses these *points of reference* to translate what you're experiencing. This allows you to make sense out of something (to the best of your mind's ability).

57   The next time you're face-to-face with an attractive woman, instead of the mind trying to pull information to impress her or

trying to come up with cool things to say, you can make your mind pull a file that will actually make you focus on just having a simple **regular** conversation. Something you already know how to do.

58   The following exercise takes time. You're creating new patterns in your mind; you're making new files. This doesn't happen overnight or in a week or two. It's the **repetition** of this exercise that will form a new habit for you.

59   Instead of the weak habits that breed a lack of confidence, we're "installing" new habits that will make you feel and appear confident (certain in what you think, say and do).

How to "Install" New Mental Files

60   **(1)** First things first. You need to find a *single* word. This single word is the word you're going to use to make your mind pull the new information (files) you're going to be "programming" into it.

61   The word itself is not as important as its meaning to you. It could be the word, "PULL". Or even, "FETCH". The word could even be, "MANHOOD". It's whatever you decide, but it has to be something that makes you remember what you're trying to do. That's bypassing what's already in your file servers (file cabinets) and only pulling the files *you* want.

62   We're using a single word because this is a small bit of information; easy to remember and effective. Think of it as a command, something that will force your mind to snap to attention. In fact, we're going to name this word your COMMAND WORD.

63   Think of your mind as an untrained vicious dog. This dog will wreck havoc if left unchecked. It will go anywhere and do anything it pleases.

64 This exercise is going to let you put a collar and leash around this wild animal and train it. You're going to teach it where to go and when. It's going to sit down when you say, "Sit!" and stay put when you say, "Stay!"

65 You're no longer going to let your mind run wild and think how it wants to think. You're going to take control and command it from now on.

66 **(2)** Now find someplace where you'll have about 15 to 20 minutes of peace and quiet. Get comfortable. I suggest not being intoxicated, not feel hungry, sleepy or irritable.

67 **(3)** Think of one and *only* one instance with a woman where you felt very uncomfortable and were experiencing a lack of confidence (feeling uncertain). Only a **single** instance because we want to deal with small "bits" or "chunks" of information.

68 **(4)** Play the scene out in your mind. Try your best to remember everything in vivid detail. What time of year it was, what time of day, what both the woman and you were wearing, your surroundings, etc. Everything you can use to make you feel almost like you're right back in that moment.

69 What you're doing here is forcing your mind to pull the "files" of this experience – your thoughts and feelings. This is commanding the mind and training it.

70 Files are information and patterns. In this part of the exercise we're just dealing with the information. Add in sights, sounds, smells, feelings and tastes if you can.

71 Some people might find this a little difficult. Some people might even see things in bland colors or the scene might play out in slow motion. All this is fine. Don't let this distract you from what you're doing.

72   Other people may find it hard to concentrate, their mind will start thinking about what they need to do later on, what they want to eat, what they need to do at work the next day, etc.

73   If you find this happening, all it means is that your wild dog needs a lot of training. Don't let it pull you where it wants to go. Gently, without straining, return to visualizing and playing out the scene.

74   **(5)** After the scene has played out let everything fade to black. Let the images go dark. Hold this for a few seconds. Next say your COMMAND WORD out loud. If you can't say it out loud, yell it inside your mind.

75   **(6)** Next, re-imagine the entire scene. But this time see you saying and doing things different. Imagine yourself getting the reactions and/or results you want.

76   These images need to feel strong and positive. You should see yourself as certain and sure – **confident**. No hesitation, no uncomfortableness, no awkwardness and no embarrassment.

77   If it helps, imagine yourself as a smooth ladies man from your favorite movie or television show. I don't recommend this (you should only want to be you), but you have to crawl before you can walk. If this helps you through the exercise, then use this as a "crutch" until you can walk on your own.

78   See yourself standing on your Standards and Principles. See yourself as bold and representing your manhood. See yourself being the best man you can be.

78   **(7)** After the scene is done, fade to black. Then repeat this new positive scene two more times, pausing briefly between each one.

79   What you're doing here is giving your mind new information about your self-esteem and self-image which I'll go deeper into in a moment.

80   **(8)** To complete this exercise just open your eyes and say your COMMAND WORD to yourself again. Say it out loud. Again, if you can't say it out loud, yell it in your mind. That's it, you're done.

81   This exercise needs to be repeated <u>every day</u> for at least 14 days straight (21 days if this scene is especially emotionally difficult for you). Use the same negative scene. Visualize it first and then use the exact same positive scene visualized three times after. Also make sure you use the same COMMAND WORD every time.

82   When you get better at this, you'll be able to work on multiple different scenes in a single session. And do them only in a few minutes. For now, I recommend just working on one for 14 to 21 days.

83   I'm quite sure there are a few of you reading this that will think this exercise is pointless and maybe even a waste of time. But why not try it before you judge it? You chose to read this book for a reason and this exercise is in here to help you. It's worth the time and effort, trust me.

84   When you get done with one scene after 14 or 21 days, then find another experience to work with and go through the process again.

85   Behind self-confidence are both self-esteem and self-image. Like The Wizard in the movie, *The Wizard of Oz*, they're the ones behind the curtain pulling the levers and turning the knobs.

86   **Self-esteem** is how you *feel* about yourself as a man.

87   **Self-image** is how you *think* (and see) yourself as a man.

88   Both of these need to be beneficial because they add to your overall confidence.

89   If you see yourself as weak or bad with women, you'll be bad with women because that's how you **think**.

90   If you feel you're not worth a woman's time, then you won't be worth a woman's time because that's how you **think**.

91   Learn to Value yourself more than that. Stop being ashamed to be a man that likes women; stop being scared to tell them so; stop hiding behind your insecurities and your lack of "know-how". This book will give you more than enough know-how. All you have to do is "program" this information into your mind and train your mind to access it.

92   Now that we've fed your mind new information to work with, we need to teach it to search out and pull these new and better "files" instead of the old unbeneficial ones.

93   And this is simply done by using your COMMAND WORD.

94   Whenever you have the slightest unconfident thought around a woman say to yourself, "Stop!" and then say your COMMAND WORD to yourself.

95   The command, "Stop!" will keep the mind from roaming aimlessly and from pulling random old files – it's telling the wild dog to, "sit and stay".

96   Then say your COMMAND WORD to yourself. At first you may have to repeat it three or four times before you feel a slight shift in your mind. It will seem to go still and quiet for a moment.

97   Let's say you see a gorgeous woman and have the techniques in mind that I'll share with you later for approaching women.

98   Suddenly your mind starts rambling: "What is she going to think?", "What if she turns me down?", "What if I start talking and run out of things to say?", "Can I really do this?", "Is this a good time to interrupt her?", "What if I embarrass myself?" and the list goes on.

99   When you recognize this happening, take a deep breath and as you exhale yell, "Stop!" in your mind. Repeat it a few more times if you need to.

100   Once you feel those negative dis-empowering thoughts slowing down, then say your COMMAND WORD to yourself. If your command word is, "Manhood" for example, then say that to yourself. Repeat it a few times.

101   At first you might not feel too much of anything. But over time with doing the above exercise and practicing using your COMMAND WORD in real life situations, you'll feel a kind of calmness come over you.

102   Your mind, with all its power, will start pulling the new files you made for yourself; the files containing confidence backed-up with a strong sense of self-image and self-esteem.

103   In fact, I would recommend actually repeating your COMMAND WORD to yourself as you're actually in route to approaching the woman and introducing yourself.

104   Don't worry about not having a new file made for a particular situation. As you gain more experience, you'll naturally create new files based on these new experiences. All of this is a process. This is not something that magically happens overnight.

105   The beautiful part is (if you take this serious) over the course of a year or so, you'll hardly ever need to use your COMMAND WORD. As soon as your mind recognizes it's time to approach a beautiful woman, seduce one or have sex with them, it will automatically pull the best and strongest files available.

106   You'll find yourself being more certain in uncertain situations. You'll make a decision and be confident that it's the best decision you can make at that time.

107   All the anxiety, self-doubt and self defeating thoughts will turn into a force of power; a power that will make you want to see how far you can push yourself.

108   You will develop an "Aura", a presence that women will sense long before you ever open your mouth. This Aura is almost like a super-power. It will "open-up" a woman because they'll feel your confidence and strong sense of manhood.

109   Every Mack's Aura is different because every man is not the same. Your Aura will reflect your manhood and yours alone.

110   When you finally achieve this, you'll find that women are immediately comfortable around you. They'll be more receptive to what you have to say and pay you more attention.

111   The Aura is the final level of confidence and something very few males achieve.

112   We'll get into developing your Aura in the next Book. But when you start attracting women and bringing them into your life, you need to have a reason for them to be there. The reason should never be only sex if you call yourself Macking.

113   As the king of your kingdom (owner of your company), you should have positions that need to be filled; tasks that need to be done and goals that need helping hands to becoming a reality.

114   It's time to prepare and create your **power structure** as a Mack – your actual kingdom (company). This is what separates average Game from Real Game.

BOOK 3 – YOUR PHILOSOPHY, PROGRAM & AURA

CHAPTER ONE

Solidifying Your Manhood

1   What would be your reaction if you walked onto a car lot and there were no cars there? What would be the reason for that car lot to exist? There's nothing to see, nothing to test drive and nothing to experience.

2   What could a car salesman on this lot try to sell to you? Sure, he could talk about the cars he *could* sell to you if they *were* on the lot, but he would look like fool because there's no **tangible representation** of what he's selling; nothing to see or touch.

3   This is the same thing with you as a Mack. You cannot just represent something to a woman without her being able to see it, touch it or experience it.

4   Your manhood needs a showcase; something that wraps around you and displays just what kind of man you are. Those that like what's in the showcase will "buy" it. Others may simply look. But regardless, there is actually *something* to see and experience.

5   There are many ways to showcase (display) your manhood. But as with everything in The Game, you must first start within yourself and then use that and radiate it outward.

6   Your life is a great journey. You can be anything you want to be, all it takes is for you to believe in yourself *first* and for one other person to believe in you, *second*.

7   The question is, "What does life mean to you?" Not just your life, but life in general.

8   This is a question that few people ever answer for themselves and it's a shame because it's the answer to this question that will help define you and everything around you.

9   Of course, all this is subjective. What I think life means will most likely be different than what you think life means. But, so what?

10   Whose to say that I'm right and you're wrong? In the grand scheme of things, there are only two things we know for sure; we're alive and that one day we're going to die.

11   When we talk about the Game, we talk a lot about Perspective (Principle number 4 of the 9 Principles). This is so important because it's your Perspectives that shape your own little world. Not the entire world around you, but the small piece of the world you live in.

12   As a Mack you must have strong Perspective on almost everything. You should Value **what you think** and **how you think**. Not only does this add to your confidence (being certain and sure), but it also limits confusion.

13   If you only look at things in a few ways then it's easy to make a choice about it. You can see if something is right for you or wrong for you fairly quickly.

14   This is the judgment – your Standards at work.

15   Having strong Perspectives means that you must know *exactly* what life means to you so that you can live your life in the manner you feel is best.

16   In The Game we simply call this having a philosophy; your philosophy. This is how you see life and your little world. This is the first "level" in helping represent yourself to women and showcasing your manhood.

17   In this chapter you're going to define your philosophy. You're going to nail down what life means to you. This philosophy needs to be lived and shared with every woman you consider bringing into your life for the long-term.

18   Remember, you must live the life you advocate. The way you start with a woman is the way you must continue.

19   As a Mack, you're pulling women from their little world into your little world and in your little world you are the king of your kingdom.

20   Other people can have their own little kingdoms; your main concern should be your own.

21   Hopefully you have your Standards and Principles in place. Knowing these are going to make this step of Inner Game development much easier – and also the step after, designing your Program.

22   Before we go through how to develop and create a philosophy for you, we need to define just what a philosophy is. Let's visit the dictionary definition:

(1) The rational investigation of the truths and principles of being, knowledge or conduct;
(2) A system of principles for guidance in practical affairs.

23   A philosophy is based on your life Perspectives. Remember how you look at things determine what they mean to *you*. No one else, only you.

24   Since a philosophy is essentially guidance for practical affairs, this means that it involves both your Standards and Principles. Your judgments (Standards) and behavioral actions based on those judgments (Principles).

25   Your philosophy should explain three important Perspectives:

(1) How you look at yourself and how you look at others.
(2) How you view the world in general (why the World is the way it is).
(3) The meaning of your life in general (why you're here – what you're striving for).

26   By its nature a philosophy is very logical. A philosophy should be based in logic and reason but should "move" you emotionally. It should both motivate and inspire you; although a philosophy itself is not emotional.

27   When you try to describe emotions, like love for example, people can give you many different definitions to describe it. But when you describe your philosophy, there should be very little room for different interpretations and definitions.

28   People won't always agree with you, but if you can explain your reasoning behind what you think and why you think that way, that's all that matters.

29   People usually behave (act, react, think and speak) based on their moods – emotions. Not logic or reasoning.

30   Also people filter what's going on around them by what's going on inside of them. Decisions based off emotion will be wrong 90% of the time. They're usually impulsive.

31   Since women (and weak males) are more emotional than men, they often make bad impulsive decisions. As yet another reminder, you must conquer as many of your female characteristics as possible. A philosophy helps a great deal with this because it's the complete opposite of emotion.

32   Your philosophy should not change based on how you feel. Emotional responses like that make you appear average and child-like. Women and children react out of emotion; a real man should rarely, if ever, react off emotion.

33   Think of a philosophy as a rock that can't be moved. It's a frame of mind. You must develop the ability to hold this frame of mind despite the pressures of other people's opinions and Social Conditioning.

34   **A Word of Caution Here**: Don't present your philosophy as the *only* one that exists. This will create a gap between you and the women you deal with (and people in general). A closed mind shuts people out because there's no room for them. Everyone wants to be heard.

35   However what you do need to do is present your philosophy as the only one that will exist for *you* and your own little world.

36   Let me give you a few examples of a life philosophy. The following examples are a little bit exaggerated but I've written them this way on purpose. This will help to form a new file server (file cabinet) in your mind. We'll put the "files" (information) in there a little later.

37   Example 1 - Life is a Game:

"In life there are winners and losers; there are a set of rules. There are strategies and tactics. You should practice and become skilled in the areas that mean the most to you.

If you know the rules and play hard with all your heart, you'll win more times than you'll lose.

With each victory you will get closer and closer to a life of happiness and success. Only those that get in the game and play will have an opportunity to win. But if you sit on the sidelines and only watch, you'll never win."

38   Example 2 - Life is a Grand Journey:

"We all start out at the beginning of a path. As we travel this path we'll see and experience many things.

Life is an adventure so we should experience as many things as we can. On our journey we shouldn't rush or feel hurried. It's always good to stop every once in awhile and savor the view — every moment is precious.

Every journey must come to an end so why we're on it, we shouldn't take it for granted. We've all been given a great gift and that gift is life. Why not open that gift and enjoy it?"

39 Example 3 - You Only Live Once:

"People shouldn't live their lives in fear. We can't sit there and constantly think, "What if?" People who live like that will never be satisfied.

We should grab life by the balls and kick its ass! Live every moment to the fullest, seize every opportunity and if one doesn't come, you make your own.

Either you're going to live life or life is going to live you. Take charge! Never lie on your death bed with regrets. Go out fighting 'till the last breath!"

40 Since you're literally and figuratively at the center of your own little world (everything that you can see, touch, smell and feel is a certain distance from you), it should be important to live in *your* world how *you* choose.

41 You have to know who you are *first*, and then decide where you're going, *second.*

42 Your philosophy will be based off your Standards and Principles. These are your boundaries and you should never cross those boundaries.

43 Never force your philosophy on your women. You won't need to. When they see that you think and live in a certain capacity, they'll either leave you alone or submit to it and fall in line (after testing you on it, of course). Your biggest Responsibility is to keep yourself in check. Care more about what you think — Value it and women who choose you will Value it also.

44 Choosing to commit to a way of life is what a philosophy is all about. Let it guide you and be a constant reminder of your Standards and Principles.

45 This will also help make your behavior consistent. And being consistent will help give a woman that sense of SECURITY that she needs to feel from her relationship. If the man is unstable, the relationship will be unstable.

46 Another way to look at is that companies have mission statements – your life philosophy is like your personal mission statement.

47 Your philosophy should be three to five short paragraphs. It should be easy for you to remember. We're going to fill our new file server (cabinet) with new information. And by breaking it up into smaller chunks it will be easier to "install".

48 You never have to tell any woman your entire philosophy word-for-word. But you should speak about it and be able to explain why you think this way. Women need to see the reasoning and logic in it even if they don't fully understand it.

49 Just the fact that you think so deeply about your life and who you are will be more than enough to let them know they're not dealing with an average male.

50 For those of you more familiar with The Game, your philosophy is **not** your life purpose. However, your life purpose should help determine and define your philosophy and should be included somewhere in it.

Forming Your Life Philosophy

51 **(1)** Over the next 30 days observe situations; your own personal situations and other people's situations. These should be real-life situations only! No movies, novels or television. Think about how you responded (or would respond) in those situations. Always keep in mind your Standard and Principles as you do this.

52 Also observe your emotional responses and mood changes when thinking about these situations.

53 Ask yourself why you think this way and try to trace back where this thinking came from—where this pattern started, where these "files" originated.

54 It could be from parents, family, teachers, television, the media, etc.

55 Next ask yourself, "Do I benefit from thinking and feeling this way about this situation?"

56 If you cannot find a positive (sure and/or certain) benefit, you must look for (or create) a new one. You want more thoughts, feelings, moods and behaviors that benefit you.

57 I would suggest making a journal for this 30-day observance period. This way you can always refer back to them and measure your progress over time. Use as much paper as you need per day.

58 **(2)** Write down five to seven Standards (judgments) and/or Principles (actions of behavior) you want to base your life philosophy around.

59 Consider the man you want to become, what rules about your life will you not break?

60 Example: You have the Standard, "I will only be around positive people." This means that when you have the choice, you

won't put yourself around depressed, negative, drama filled women or people. Realize what this actually means.

61   You might limit your exposure to some family members, or cut them off completely. You don't romantically date anyone that has these characteristics. You probably wouldn't choose the profession of being a counselor or a psychiatrist.

62   Realistically, you can't always avoid these situations, but when you have the option, you choose your Standards and Principles over what anyone else thinks or says.

63   You can do and become whatever you choose within these boundaries, just never cross them!

64   **(3)** You're finally ready to grab a blank sheet of paper and begin to write out your life philosophy. You may not get it correct the first time. You can always come back and make changes later. For now, just get something written down! Get those ideas, concepts and thoughts out on paper.

65   Remember, your life philosophy should explain your Perspective (and reasoning) on three main points:

(1) How you look at yourself and other people.
(2) How you view the world in general (why the World is the way it is).
(3) The meaning of your life in general (what you're striving to do – why you're here in this World).

66   And, as no surprise, you must incorporate your Standards and Principles into your philosophy as best you can.

67   Don't rush through this! A big piece to your puzzle of manhood will be rooted in your philosophy. This is extremely important in not only showcasing (displaying) your manhood, but also showcasing your Value. **Think of yourself as you want to be**.

68 If you can only make one sentence about each of the three main points above, that's a good place to start. You can "fill in the gaps" later.

69 Your goal is to have three to five short paragraphs that describe your whole philosophy. It needs to be detailed enough to make sense to you. It also needs to be short enough so that you can actually remember it. You should be able to say it, word-for-word and line-for-line.

70 This process may take a single day or a week of constant writing and re-writing but that shouldn't matter. Once it's complete you'll have a stronger sense of not only who you are, but also how you should "move and shake" through life as a man.

71 When done correctly, this will be extremely empowering and liberating. It will clear up a lot of mental confusion and place all your Perspectives into a nice little package.

72 In other words, a well thought out philosophy will give you a strong sense of clarity about you, your life and the world around you. It will define your little world and open up the thoughts of many possibilities instead of thoughts of limitations.

73 Our journey to putting your Inner Game together is almost complete. But every woman you bring into your life should have a place; a position.

74 Since you sit at the top of your own structure of power (kingdom), this is only part of being a leader to them and most importantly yourself.

75 These are all forms of management. A strong Inner Game will allow you to not only manage your thoughts and behaviors, but also give you a basis to manage women's.

CHAPTER TWO

Your World – Your Program

1   What separates a Mack from the average male and even other real men? The understanding that women feel more valuable, more desirable and more precious (the plus 1) when they feel like they're needed.

2   This is a peculiar aspect of their nature. Although most males also need to feel like they're needed in their woman's life, for women it's slightly different.

3   Remember women have child-like qualities. Young children take pride in helping out their parents for example. This makes them feel included, important and gives them a sense of joy.

4   They want to help cook, carry grocery bags, feed the family pet, watch their brothers or sisters, clean up, etc.

5   And although they may grow out of this willingness to be helpful, they'll never grow out of the need to feel included and important.

6   When a woman finds a real man to care about, this willingness to be helpful and feel needed comes back in full force.

7   Despite what you may have been conditioned to accept, a woman enjoys taking care of a real man (not a male) because a real man is *already* taking care of himself.

8   Sound confusing? Let me help unlock this door so you can open it and walk through it.

9   A real man and a Mack should be autonomous. That means that they should be independent. Not just in what and how they think, but also having the ability to take care of themselves.

10   Consider this, other than sex and maybe some companionship, what can a woman do for you that you can't do for yourself?

11   You can clean your own house, wash your own car, make your own money, cook your own food, do your own shopping, pay your own bills and so on and so on.

12   And what can a male do for a woman that she can't do for herself?

13   He can give her his seed (semen).

14   A woman cannot bring forth a child without a male. Yes, it's true that a male needs a woman to bring forth a child because he can't bear children himself but, the power resides in the male. Not the female.

15   A male could literally impregnate three women in a single day. But each of those women could only be pregnant once every nine months.

16   The procreation of the human race is dependent on the male.

17   Psychologically it's been said that a male goes through life seeking many women to fulfill his *one* need; while a woman goes through life seeking one male to fulfill her *many* needs.

18   It's within a woman's nature to **union**. This works for her on every level. She wants to be connected (linked) with her family, children, friends, co-workers and other people. This is part of her natural survival instincts.

19   She's very cautious of looking "dumb" or "stupid" in front of others. Because of this, she constantly worries about their judgments of her. If necessary she'll sacrifice her own personal desires to look "right" and "good" because she Values social acceptance so highly.

20   If she's linked with a group of women who don't think sleeping with a lot of different men is acceptable, she'll usually take on this Social Conditioning; even if she may feel different inside.

21   On the opposite of the coin, if she's linked with a group of women who are promiscuous and don't judge her and encourage "slutty" behavior, she'll usually take this Social Conditioning on also.

22   By nature a woman needs to feel this way. And it's no different with her man. Once she gives her mind, heart and body to him she wants to be connected to him. She'll take on his Standards, Principles and philosophy when she fully understands their Value.

23   At this point she'll be ready to give him her soul. The soul is just a symbol. It's symbolic of the deepest level of devotion, respect and love she's capable of.

24   Until a woman gives a man (not a male) her soul, she'll usually choose maintaining her social acceptance over her man's wants. She won't fully submit because society says it's wrong.

25   She might cook, clean, perform naughty things in the bedroom on occasion, but when confronted by the "outside" world about her behavior, she usually chooses them over him.

26   This is why a Mack lives in his own little world and brings her from her world (and the outside world) into his.

27   Once she's in the Mack's world, the rules are usually different. He doesn't look at things like everyone else and he doesn't place the same expectations on her like "normal society".

28   When she can have all of her 5 plus 1 needs fulfilled with him and no longer has to place so much concern on the "outside" world, she will eventually submit.

29   Why? Because it's easier; there's less pressure. Instead of worrying about what 100 different people think, she'll mainly be concerned with what a handful of people think; her man and her children.

30   When a woman gives a man her soul, she'll even distance herself from her own family and friends if they try to put a wedge in-between him and her.

31   This desire for union is extremely strong and you must use it wisely. Don't abuse it! Let me give you an example:

32   Let's pretend you're back in high school (if you're currently in high school this example will be even easier to understand) – and a young lady is over your house with the intention to have sex.

33   This same young lady will tell you that she doesn't like liars. But she'll call up her own parents and lie to them. She'll tell them that she's over a "girlfriend's house" and that she'll be home a little late.

34   Another example that more experienced males may have dealt with: A woman will outwardly say that she would never sleep with a man that her friend has previously slept with. But if her feelings of attraction are strong enough, she'll break this social rule.

35   She'll keep this relationship a secret for as long as possible. Her and her girlfriend will still hang out, talk, go out, and shop together. She might even be around her friend and this man at the same time.

36   If that happens her behavior will be completely normal and natural. Acting is a part of her nature. She does it every single day to continue looking socially acceptable.

37   She'll hide this taboo relationship because she values social acceptance (she doesn't want to look "slutty" or "bad"), but she'll continue sleeping with her girlfriend's ex-man because she really wants to.

38   If this secret relationship was ever discovered, she'll be outcast from her friends. But in the process she'll blame a lot of her actions on him and even on her friend for "doing him wrong".

39   Women usually avoid taking Responsibility whenever possible. They don't like being held accountable for socially unacceptable behavior.

40   The little world you live in as Mack must create a place for her. Somewhere she can be herself and not be judged too harshly for it.

41   As a Mack, you must become less judgmental of a woman's nature. You can judge her *behavior*, but be less critical of her actually *nature*.

42   When a woman sees that she can be herself around you, this is a "hook" you put into her. You use this "hook" to pull her toward you. She'll want to talk to you, spend time with you and cater to you because in your little world, there's less pressure on her. The only pressure comes from her abiding by your Standards and Principles along with your philosophy and Program.

43   What you accept and don't accept are the boundaries. As long as she can remain in your boundaries she can be herself. This sounds like a contradiction but don't forget women have child-like qualities; they respect boundaries. They like to know they exist because this gives her a sense of SECURITY; stability.

44   Your world is based on your rules. A woman that is genuinely attracted to you would rather feel free in your world with only one set of rules, than live in society under tons of rules.

45   In your world her nature is accepted and understood. You'll understand things about her better than the rest of society.

46   The allure of your world must vastly outweigh the "outside" world on both a mental and emotional level. In your world it's OK for a woman to cry; it's OK for a woman to share her insecurities; it's OK for her to miss a detail or two; it's OK for her to ask questions about simple things she doesn't understand; it's OK for her to bare her heart, revealing her innermost thoughts and secrets.

47   Very little judgment is passed on her. In other words, it's OK for her to be in her **womanhood** because she's now around a man that resides in his **manhood**.

48   She can be vulnerable but still be looked at as more valuable, more desirable and more precious than other women (the plus 1). Why would she want to be anywhere else?

49   As I've previously stated, you must polarize yourself to the opposite of women; in thoughts and behavior. But this doesn't mean that you don't accept their *nature*.

50   You don't tolerate any disrespectful behavior towards you. But you do accept their very nature. And this is what she cares about most anyway.

51   Once again to make sure this point gets through – when you check (correct) a woman, check her behavior *not* her nature.

52   By working with a woman's nature, you'll earn her soul because you're allowing her to express her womanhood.

53   Don't forget, women don't need to be earned. As a male they are here on this planet to be with you; it's the natural order of things.

54   But you do have to earn a woman's submission to you. A real woman will not completely submit to anything less than what she feels is a real man.

55   Part of this submission involves you working with her nature and part of her nature is the desire to union.

56   But union with what? Just you? This may work for a little while but a Mack isn't about just short-term, he's about the long-term.

57   A Mack knows that good conversation will not hold a woman; good sex will not hold a woman; buying her expensive things will not hold a woman; bowing down to her every whim and desire will definitely not hold a woman – in fact it will make her lose interest.

58   This might sound like another contradiction, but you want a woman to want more than just you. You also want her to desire to be about what you're about.

59   She needs to know that her man is guided by something greater than himself. What is a real man guided by? He's guided by his Standards, Principles, a philosophy and a Program. These are the first and second steps in showcasing your manhood.

60   So what exactly *is* a Program? I'll explain it in a couple of different ways before breaking it down bit-by-bit so you can design your own.

61   A Program is made up of systems. As a king (or company owner) you have positions open beneath you and as a Mack these positions will be filled by women – temporarily or permanently.

62   These women are not necessarily your "workers" or "subjects" (depending on your Program), but they'll help support your power structure, meaning your realm. Up to this point I've been referring to your **realm** as your **little world**.

63   Your realm is everything your kingdom (company) touches – from your little world to the outside world. It's the power structure, the rules and regulations of your Game.

64   Always keep in mind, a king has very little power outside of their kingdom. You cannot "topple" Social Conditioning. But you can limit the effects of Social Conditioning in your personal realm (little world).

65   Your realm (kingdom/company) is your seat of power. All roads your women travel on must lead to it and from it.

66   Kingdoms don't run themselves. If they did, no management would be needed. A Mack is always striving to be in a constant state of peak efficiency. This state is called being Game Tight.

67   As a leader it's your Responsibility to stay on top of everything in your realm as much as humanly possible. This of course includes staying on top of what you think and what you feel.

68   But you're human. One person can only do so much because one person only has so much time and energy to spend per day.

69   Let's break this down by looking at it from a business Perspective.

70   A small to medium-sized company is based around the vision of the owner (just one owner in this example for simplicity).

71   Almost everything about the company came from the mind of the owner – The Company's name, the mission statement, the

logo, the brand, etc. And within all of that, the employees that work there are taught to handle things a certain way.

72   They're supposed to dress a certain way, greet customers a certain way, they have paperwork they're responsible for and there are many other rules and regulations that must be followed if they're to remain employed there.

73   Each and every activity or procedure an employee must perform has a *reason* to be there. It should help the company run smoothly, avoid legal issues and remain profitable.

74   Every responsibility that an employee has is an *activity* or *procedure*. These activities and procedures are **systems** – the way the business owner wants work completed and company matters handled.

75   **Your Program is made up of systems**. Systems coordinate activities and procedures. These activities and procedures must be in place for a *reason*. That reason should be to keep your Program (plan) running effectively.

Effective Systems = An Effective Program

76   Knowing this helps you strengthen your overall Game as a Mack when you're dealing with women.

77   Things may still seem a little unclear so let me give you another analogy.

78   Let's look at education here in America. A Program would be the *entire* educational agenda (plan for advancement). Ignoring its power structure, what's the Purpose of the educational agenda? There are many answers but the most common is,

"To create responsible adults; valuable members of society with a lifetime curiosity to learn. Also, to prepare them to compete in the global environment."

79   These goals are set forth by the School Board (upper-level managers), which pass them along to the superintendent (mid-level manager), which then get passed along to school principals (low level managers/coaches) who then pass it along to the teachers (the upholders of the structure).

80   And none of this means anything without the students, the "consumers" of what this "Game" produces. Are you following me?

81   The teacher, principal and superintendent have *activities* to perform and *procedures* to follow; they have **systems**. These **systems** must run efficiently or the Program (plan of advancement) set down by the School Board may never come to fruition.

82   If the Program is not effective, the goals set forth by the school board will not be met. If the goals are not met, the Purpose of the educational agenda will never be achieved – it will fall apart.

83   Let's take all of this and bring it down into the real world of what you may experience as a Mack. I'll be using another educational analogy but it doesn't relate to the one above.

84   Let's say you're in a University and you're majoring in criminal law.

85   In order to graduate there's research to be done, papers to be written, assignments to be completed and you still have to take care of yourself; you still require food, clothing and shelter.

86   An average male might meet a young lady during this time and get stuck in love. The girl and him talk, have sex, go out on dates and may occasionally study together.

87   This is fine for an average male but not a Mack. A Mack would require more from a young lady (or ladies) than that.

88   You're only one person and only have so much time and energy, why not *design* something that will make everything more manageable? Let's break this down into smaller bits.

89   You have a goal. That goal is to graduate and become a criminal attorney. From this goal you should form a plan of advancement. How you can get from point A to point B and then point C and so forth? Having a successful career as a criminal attorney would be the end of your plan, point Z.

90   If you don't graduate then your reason to be in school would serve no benefit. It would be nothing but a waste of time, energy and money. If don't graduate, you'll never get to point Z.

91   Included in your plan would be a means to handle all of your Responsibilities of school, work and personal needs. You want them to be easy to handle and still efficient.

92   If you meet a girl, instead of just talking, dating and having sex, you would explain to her your ultimate goal in *school* and *life*. The ultimate goal in school is to graduate top of your class. Your ultimate goal in life is to have a successful career as a criminal attorney.

93   If you accept any woman into your life you have to make her understand that you need more than just a cute smile and what's in between her legs; you need all the help she can provide.

94   She could help you write those papers – or proof-read the ones you've written.

95   She can help you out with research, help you build cases, tighten up your litigation strategies and when the time comes, she can assist in making sure you'll blow through your State bar exam.

96   She could also help cook meals so you have more time to research and study. She could also be washing clothes and even help keep your apartment clean (if you had one).

97   Since a Mack doesn't *use* women (or anybody for that matter) you would Reciprocate (Principle number 3 of the 9 Principles) all her efforts by helping her in her classes as well and fulfilling her 5 basic needs. You would only provide the plus 1 if you planned to keep her long-term.

98   Each area of your life would be a system. You would have a schedule for when the apartment needs to be cleaned; the day clothes are washed; the times to study; the days for leisure activities and everything else.

99   Every area of your life runs at maximum efficiency so that the entire Program functions at maximum efficiency.

100   Like the gears, pistons and belts of a machine, each system needs to be maintained and constantly checked for wear and tear. When all the *parts* of the machine work properly (systems) the *entire* machine (Program) will perform at its optimum.

101   Weak males are terrified to even think of asking a woman for something. However women feel it's their right to ask males for things. They ask for things frequently in fact.

102   Again this goes back to Social Conditioning. A male is taught that he isn't supposed to look like he needs anything. Looking like they need something, especially from a woman, is not "manly".

103   Yet this same male will bend over backwards to do everything a woman asks for. How is that equality? How is that fair or right?

104   Peep this Game in case you missed it earlier: A woman doesn't mind helping out a man she cares about, as long as he's already helping himself.

105   When she sees a man in motion with goals and plans, by nature, she doesn't mind assisting. She wants to help out because that makes her feel included and important.

106   Your Program includes the goal (or goals) you're currently working on – the things you're trying to establish in *your* life. You create a plan to get there and any woman coming into your realm either accepts your Program or you ask her to leave.

107   Macks have no business carrying around dead weight. This includes from other males and especially from women.

108   If a woman is in your life in a romantic capacity, she should be helping you carry some weight. It's not her Responsibility to carry *all* the weight, that Responsibility is on you as a leader.

109   But she needs to be doing something to help you move forward. If she's with you, she'll also be helping herself. Her desire for union will be met because you'll want her around for the long-term. Plus you'll be helping her as well.

110   Any woman not working *with* you is actually working *against* you. She'll ask for your time, attention, help and sometimes money and trade those for sex. This is the hook she uses just to keep you pacified. And a weak male won't even get sex – just the possibility of it.

111   As a Mack you want more than just sex. On a scale from 1 to 10, with 1 being the highest priority, sex would fall somewhere near 5 or 6; maybe even 7.

112   Your goals for Advancement (Principle number 6 of the 9 Principles) should be the most important thing going on in your life. If you don't go after what you want, no one else is going to do it for you.

113   Your Program with its many systems is what you design to help you achieve those goals. You should be willing to lose out on

any woman who doesn't accept that your goals come first. That's right, they even come before her.

114   The reality is she might not be around in five years. If you slow down (or stop) going after your goals because of her then you're breaking your pace and delaying getting to where you're trying to go. You must learn to put yourself first more often.

115   A weak male will think that this will push a woman away when it's actually the opposite – it will actually pull women toward you.

116   The ambition and passion you show for your goals shows certainty in yourself. And certainty in yourself is a huge element in confidence. As we already discussed, it's a fact, confidence is very attractive to women.

117   This is the "secret ingredient" of why a well designed Program for your life is so effective at helping hold the women you bring into it.

118   A plan is nothing but a road map. If you lived in the State of New York and wanted to drive to California, you would want a map to get there.

119   You need to know when to turn left, turn right or go straight and for how many miles.

120   You have directions that will take you from point A to point B then point C, etc. all the way to point Z – arriving in the State of California.

121   As leader and king of your realm (owner of your company) you need to know when to turn left, turn right or continue straight with your plan to get to your end goal.

122   The woman should be in the passenger seat helping you find those turns and calling out directions to help keep both of you moving forward to the destination.

123   When you get tired, she should be the one driving and carefully following the directions and road map you've given her.

124   This is a team effort and you're not just the coach, but also the General Manager and owner.

125   Before we get into how to design your Program there's some more Game you need to know.

126   People perform best when they're doing things they feel they're good at. Not every woman you bring into your life is best qualified for a particular position.

127   A Mack creates positions in his kingdom (company) and each position is a role of Responsibility. He must be wise enough to fill these positions with women who are best suited for them.

128   Would you go rob a bank with someone who never stole a dime? I hope not. The chances of failure would increase exponentially.

129   There are basically four types of women. Each one is only worth what they're worth. Depending on your Program, some types may be more valuable than others. As a Mack you need to know what positions needs to be filled and who would function best in them.

130   These four types are not cut-and-dry, you'll find that some of the attributes that define a single type overlap and bleed into others. Also when you actually begin to bring women into your life, you'll find that they may fit into two categories; although they'll be strongest in only one. It's your Responsibility as Mack to determine which one that is.

131   You must know your woman (or women) backwards and forewords, inside and out.

132   The four types of women are defined as follows:

133   **(1) Domesticated** – These woman are naturally caring and nurturing. They're great with children and because of this they have strong maternal instincts. They're generally very family oriented and very supportive of a strong man.

She doesn't mind cooking and keeping the house clean because she wants her man and family to be comfortable. She takes pride in her home and the decisions concerning it are very important to her.

These women are great cheerleaders. They're generally positive with a positive Perspective on life. These are also the hardest women to bring into your life. They think about family and therefore if the SECURITY and PROVIDING isn't there, she may keep a distance.

Domestic minded-women are natural administrators. They excel at keeping up with important dates and anniversaries. They enjoy adding their own special and creative flair to gifts and working with their hands.

When it comes to their family and their man they'll generally push aside their own wants and make sacrifices. Because of this you want to give them some space now and then. This gives them a break and allows them to mentally and emotionally "re-fuel". If you don't PROVIDE this they can turn into a stressed-out ball of knots.

These women usually prefer more aggressive sex from their man. Not all the time though, sometimes they really need it to be slow and passionate. All in all they're very accommodating.

134 **(2) Creative** – These women are either very social or very shy (at least until they feel comfortable around a person). They're deep into creative aspects such as music, writing, poetry, art, design and other things along these lines. Sometimes they may be into spirituality or metaphysics also.

Despite not being their strongest suit, they're generally very business minded. This makes it easy to bounce business concepts and ideas off of them.

Because they relish in the creative, they dream a lot and easily lose focus. You'll constantly need to help keep these women focused by reminding them of the big picture – your Program and the goals you as a team should be going after.

These women need a lot of attention. They're big on COMMUNICATION and ENTERTAINMENT. Creative women are very turned on by intelligent well-rounded men they can learn from.

They're generally average in bed (because they spend a lot of time "in their heads") but are open-minded to exploring things within reason. However if this woman is more into "spiritual" matters, she'll usually be very good in bed and very passionate.

135 **(3) Educated** – These women love to learn. In fact they place a huge Value on education. They like structure and are generally organized. Don't confuse the word educated with just being "book-smart"; sometimes these women are just full of good common sense and insight.

They have a wild side that has to be pulled out of them but they're generally conservative. Surprisingly, these women love ENTERTAINMENT. They like to see and experience new things. A strong sense of humor will make these women melt.

They're generally not good "home-makers" and prefer to use their knowledge in a financial capacity. They're very business savvy and are usually good with managing money and finances – they understand the importance of a dollar. Even then, sometimes these women can have very expensive tastes. They won't spend carelessly though because they Value SECURITY.

These women are good planners and will fall in line with your Program without much convincing. They respect Advancement in life and usually base a large part of their daily routines around it.

In the bedroom they are usually how they are in life – conservative. Make no mistake though; with the right man they can be extremely "freaky".

136 **(4) Confidant** – These women are all about their man and their children – they're very sensitive to their wants and needs. For her man, she will cater to him with ease if they feel he's deserving.

These women have trouble focusing and will constantly need to be reminded of where you as a team need to be headed. She'll greatly respect a man who is leading because in general, she's not very good at managing certain aspects of her own life.

This woman needs a lot of direction. She'll frequently ask for her man's opinion because she's often undecided about even the simplest things. COMMUNICATION and SECURITY is the key with this woman.

Once this woman is with a man, she's with him. They're usually very loyal and can also be very territorial. If she even thinks another woman may pose a threat to her position, she'll keep women away from her man. On the positive note, you can talk to her about anything and she'll pass little judgment because she's not very opinionate about things. She's kind of, "go with the flow" most of the time.

The confidant woman is usually easy to please and makes few demands as long as she feels secure and stable in the relationship. But if her man does not lead properly, she can become lazy and unmotivated. However, if she discovers a strong personal goal, she'll begin to neglect her home life in favor of it. She can move to either extreme; she doesn't know how to balance.

These women are generally excellent in bed. They'll sometimes be submissive and other times very aggressive but they'll make sure their man is satisfied with them.

137   If it helps, you can think of each of these four types as positions on a sports team. Each one is best suited for a certain area on the field or court. They should be assigned to those areas accordingly.

138   With this knowledge and your Program in place, you'll be able to recognize the strongest personality traits of a woman and place her in the correct position; a position that she'll enjoy and will perform best in.

139   They'll keep particular systems running well and that makes it easier to manage your entire Program.

140   Let me give you the following Game because it's something extremely important to keep in mind:

"Everything you want out of life comes from your plans on how to get it."

Fundamentals of Program Design

141   A Program literally by definition is: A plan of action to accomplish a specific end.

The key word here is *plan*.

142   I hesitate to give a step-by-step guide on how to design a Program for yourself (although I'll give you something close); because there's no best way to do it. The only "right" way is what

makes it effective for you. I gave many examples and analogies so that you can visualize just what it is.

143   Just like there are differences in the organizational structures for companies around the World; there will be differences in the way a Program looks and functions from Mack to Mack.

144   Programs are progressive. They're based on life advancement and are road maps to get you toward a goal. To go from where you are now to finally obtaining what you're after.

145   Once a goal is achieved, you need to make a new goal. This new goal will require new systems. And with new systems you need an entirely new Program that uses those systems.

146   Unless you have a true definite life Purpose (Principle number 1 of the 9 Principles) that will take your entire life to accomplish, you'll never have just one Program.

147   When you accomplish a major goal, you need to make another goal and another Program based around it.

148   Depending on the grandness of the goal, you could have a Program in place for many, many years. If the goal is smaller, the Program for it might only be in place for a few months or a single year.

149   A Program is a plan for advancement, and this plan includes:

(1) A goal.
(2) What you need to do (strategy).
(3) How you need to do it (tactics).
(4) The systems (procedures/processes) that need to be followed repeatedly to maintain areas of your life and move you toward your goal.

150   Some people look down upon making goals and I can understand this because the way it's usually taught is far too complicated.

151   But keep in mind the quote I gave you earlier,

"Everything you want out of life comes from your plans on how to get it."

152   And let me give you another one to further expand your Perspective,

"When you're just *interested* in a goal, you'll do what's easiest and make excuses to put off doing what you need to do. When you're *committed* – you'll give up on excuses and find out how you can and will succeed."

153   A Program is a form of *commitment*. It's not just something you put in place to impress a woman and appear you have something going on in your life.

154   When she discovers that this isn't true, you'll lose her trust and respect. These can be earned back (sometimes), but why even place yourself in that situation to begin with? The way you start with a woman is the way you must continue.

155   You need to make the decision to commit to something in your life. When a woman can see, think and feel your commitment to your Standards, Principles, philosophy and goals, she'll recognize you as a man that has the capability to be committed to her.

156   A woman interprets many things a man does (or doesn't do) in relation to how it affects her; because her favorite subject is herself.

157   I like to keep things simple. So the best way I can think of to put all of these abstract ideas and concepts together is to lay them out in story form.

158   The name of the main character in this story is, Jay. And Jay has decided it's time to step-up and be a man and become a Mack.

159   Don't just read the story; analyze it so you can see how to put together a Program of your own. This is an extremely important aspect of becoming a man. A man that doesn't know where he's going can't lead anyone, anywhere. He'll usually end up being led by someone else.

CHAPTER THREE

Designing a Program – Jay's Story

1   Jay wants to be successful. He's single with no children and in his early twenties. It has finally struck him that he needs to stop procrastinating and decide on some firm goals for himself because if he doesn't do it, no one else will.

2   To add to that, having a goal and a Program (plan for advancement) are critical requirements to be both a man and a Mack.

3   Jay lives alone in a tiny 1-bedroom apartment on a fairly bad side of town. He has a regular 9-to-5 job which doesn't pay much, but he's able to pay his bills, eat everyday and go out to enjoy himself if he budgets well.

4   It's night time and the apartment is quiet. He sits down at his small table with a few sheets of paper and a pencil.

5   He understands that when you write things down, there's a strong psychological effect that happens in the mind. It's this psychological effect that speaks to both the logical side of the brain (left-side of the brain) and the creative side of the brain (right-side of the brain).

6   The mental "scales" are balanced which helps the goal seep into the sub-conscious mind.

7   The **FIRST STEP** Jay takes is to come up with a serious goal. Something slightly outside of his comfort-zone but something he will commit to. Jay understands that commitment is one of the keys to achieving anything.

8   A goal is a final destination. It's the motor of a boat that helps give it power and a definite direction. If you don't know where you're going, you can end up anywhere. Jay is fed-up with just floating along aimlessly.

9   After thinking for 30-minutes, Jay decides what his goal is. He writes it down.

10   **'Become an independent music artist.'**

11   Jay has always loved music and being creative. This is something that he can honestly commit to. Nothing else in his life has really been that important.

12   Jay's **SECOND STEP** is to define his terms. He needs to know *exactly* what this goal means to him. No one else matters in this decision. Not his family, relatives, friends or even his children if he had any.

13   As selfish as that may sound, Jay knows that to be a real Player he has to put himself first. Not taking it to the extreme where it's *all* about him, but if he doesn't guide himself, he's susceptible to be guided by someone else. Jay's been letting that happen most of his life and the time has come for that to stop.

14   Jay thinks this through for a few minutes and comes up with many terms. He writes down the most important one:

15   **'Being able to live only on my music without having a job.'**

16   Jay's **THIRD STEP** is to answer the age-old question of, "Why?" Why is the goal of becoming an independent music artist so important to him? Jay's "reason why" is the motivating factor that will help him push forward despite obstacles.

17   Again, Jay takes his time to think everything through. He jots down a few things but nothing really moves him. He continues

writing until something stands out to him that he just can't ignore. At first Jay thought being wealthy was a good enough motivation, but what really moved him and made him feel good was this:

18 **'I want to positively touch people and affect their lives with the messages in my music. It's about the art more than the money – the money will come.'**

19 Jay's **FORTH STEP** is to make a reality check. A goal of being the next multi-millionaire music mogul may sound good, but early goals should be more realistic and obtainable. Jay understands how the mind works. If a goal is too big, the mind will fight against it. If his mind is fighting against him, this will defeat his efforts.

20 Jay has to deal with reality, not all "dreams" can come true. He would like to develop the super-power to crawl up walls too; but that's just a fantasy.

21 Jay takes his time because there's no reason to rush. He gets up for a few minutes, makes himself a cup of noodles and sits back down. He reasons that his goal is not only realistic but very obtainable with enough effort and hard-work.

22 Jay grabs his pencil and paper and writes down *why his goal is possible*. This is what he comes up with:

23 **'Many others have done it before me. This alone makes it possible. And there's so much technology and outlets available that it's even easier to do than it was 5-10 years ago.'**

24 Jay is satisfied with the work he's mentally done so far. He has completed the **FIRST PHASE** of **SETTING A GOAL**.

25 After he finishes eating, he sits back down more determined than ever to "flesh-out" his goal and create a general plan. This

will be an outline where he can judge his progress as he works toward his goal.

26   Jay moves on to the **SECOND PHASE** of actually **MAKING A PLAN**.

27   He recalls a quote from the old successful Players, "Everything you want out of life comes from your plans on how to get it."

28   Jay already has a general goal. But now he needs to move on to the **FIFTH STEP**, brainstorming and getting more specific. He grabs a blank sheet of paper to freely write down some ideas and thoughts. He doesn't judge them he just writes down what comes to him.

29   He understands the key in this process is to fantasize about possibilities. Not to think about what he *can't* do, but what he *can* do.

30   Thinking in this way (pondering possibilities) generates ideas. Everything ever created by human beings began as nothing more than an idea. It's in the seed of ideas where great things can grow.

31   Once Jay can't think of anything else he takes the **SIXTH STEP** and corrects or crosses out anything vague. Jay knows that vagueness is useless – it leaves too much room for misinterpretation.

32   Women are often vague and indirect. A man should be more specific and direct, especially with where he's headed in his life.

33   Jay is left with a number of specifics. He puts them together and comes up with a short detailed paragraph which he writes down. The basics of what he writes look like this:

34   'Be able to write, produce and release my own music. I want all my music to be completely digital. I will make money through internet sales (mp3s) and physical CD's.'

35   For now this is specific enough for Jay. If he feels the need to make adjustments later he'll do it. But for the moment he feels confident in the specifics he's created.

36   Jay takes a short break before getting back to the matter at hand. As he sits back down he readies himself for the **SEVENTH STEP** – determining what he's going to need.

37   Jay writes down a long list of everything he can think of. He also scourers the internet to help him "fill-in-the-blanks" of what he might have missed. The list of what he's going to need looks like this:

Artist name
Record label name
Record label logo
Means to set up a legal entity for business purposes
Computer
Good internet connection
Music software
Instrument samples
Keyboard
Microphone
Headphones
A way to make a sound booth to record vocals
Good monitor speakers and larger speakers
Software to master and digitally compress music
Register domain name (will put up website once a decent sized catalogue of music is ready)
Graphic software
Hire a graphic designer
Find a web-site designer for the near future
Business cards
Accounts to internet music outlets to sell music

Means to copyright music
Place to manufacture CD's
Bank account to receive payments and track sales
Email address to be used strictly for label
Social media accounts for promotion and communicating
with other artists and fans
Create a bio

38   The list may not be totally complete but Jay reasons that it's a
damn good place to start. There's plenty to work with here.

39   It's now time to go back to reality for a moment and
realistically look at what obstacles and future problems he might
expect. This brings Jay to the **EIGHTH STEP** – identifying
obstacles.

40   After some more brainstorming and free-writing Jay comes up
with yet another list. He numbers the obstacles (just for reference)
and accepts that there may be more lurking in the wind
somewhere. But so what? He can only operate with what he
knows right NOW.

41   He's not a psychic and can't predict the future. There's no use
is wasting too much energy and time on it. Plus as a man, he holds
the Principle that he will solve all problems as they arise. It's what
a real man does every single day.

42   Jay's obstacle list looks like this:

**#1: No one is waiting for my music. If people are going to
become fans of my music, I must promote it! I must also do
live shows (gigs) and find a way to do it.**

**#2: I must represent quality in everything I do. From logo,
graphics, website to the music itself.**

#3: I need a quiet place to work on and record my music.

#4: I must make time to record music between work and my other responsibilities.

#5: I must find an effective way to market and promote my music with a small budget.

#6: I must find a way to do shows, starting off with at least one a month.

#7: I need to find a way to have enough money to invest in my music and still take care of the household and all the bills. I refuse to let my quality of life suffer too much. A roof over my head is more important.

43   It's been a long night for Jay. He has completed **PHASE TWO** but it's time for him to go to sleep and get ready for work in the morning.

44   He goes to bed with his mind still working and thinking about the future and all the possibilities that can open up for him. He's excited and feels strangely better about himself and his future in general. He knows that doing this work so far has been well worth the time.

45   Jay returns from work the next day and looks over everything he's written down. He's excited to take all his notes and form his Program.

46   He now knows where he's headed. He has put a motor to his boat and now has a direction to begin travelling He's still not sure exactly how he's going to get there but things are much, much clearer.

47   Jay is face-to-face with the **THIRD PHASE** and final part of designing a Program. He must now **DETERMINE SYSTEMS** (procedures).

48   Jay gets some more paper because it's time to write again. He moves on to the **NINTH STEP**, where he must make some firm decisions of where his *time* has to go from now on.

49   Jay understands that to accomplish anything above average, it requires a great deal of time and energy. With that he knows that he can't lose himself in the pursuit of his goal – a little "off" time is fine every once in a while.

50   There are many things Jay can do to help make this entire process easier and keep him focused. At the end of the day though, most goals are achieved by putting a lot of time and hard work into making them a reality.

51   Jay accepts reality. There's no way to get around putting in the work. Since he has made the commitment to his goal, he must do what it takes. Period.

52   Jay brainstorms, free-writes and comes up with a few areas that are going to take up his time from now on. His short-list looks like this:

53   **'Have to work. Eat. Sleep. Set up label and musician platform. Write music. Record music. Master music. Digitally format music. Market and promote music. Try to do shows. Need graphics and to get website ready.'**

54   With that out the way, Jay moves on to the **TENTH STEP** of turning these areas where time and energy is needed, into general routines. This is the discipline that Jay has chosen to keep his life in order.

55   Daily routines equal slow steady progress and focused effort. Doing something every day is what's going to help turn his goal into a reality. Jay writes down the schedule he comes up with:

'*Monday through Fridays:* Work from 9am to 5pm. Eat. Work on music (3 hours minimum). Prepare for next work day. Sleep for at least 6 hours.

Saturdays and Sundays: Wash clothes. Clean house. Wash car. Grocery shop and other shopping. Eat and prepare lunches for work. Do my music for a minimum of 6 hours over the weekend (try for 3 hours each day or all in one day). Study music marketing and create systems for it.

On some weekends will take a Saturday or Sunday off to spend time with family and friends. No more than three "off-days" a month.

I will approach at least 10 women a day just going through my normal daily routine. And I'll approach more on my "off-days". I'll only take women out on my "off-days" because my goal comes first.

A reminder to self – I should never slack on my Program for anyone, especially for a woman I've just met.'

56 Jay feels great now. Everything is so clear, organized and makes sense. It doesn't look easy but this is the life he's now chosen for himself.

57 No one gave it to him. No one told him what he should be doing and how he should be doing it. He has chosen his own direction and made plans to make it happen.

58 This process alone has taken him from behaving and thinking like an average male into the threshold of manhood. Strong, determined, advancing in life and autonomous (a person free from external control and constraints in action and judgment).

59 Jay is almost finished. He digs into a drawer and pulls out a blank notebook. It's with this notebook that he'll measure his progress from this point forward.

60   This notebook will become his journal. It will help keep him motivated and focused. It will also keep him accountable for sticking to his routines (systems) so that he's constantly working his Program. He will also be able to spot weaknesses in his systems. This allows him to find a means to correct them immediately. Jay knows this is important because if too many systems fall apart, his Program will weaken and eventually fall apart too.

61   Jay will write in his journal once a week for everything he has accomplished during that week. This includes accomplishments with work, music and women. He adds this to his Sunday routines. It's something he'll do before he goes to bed and begins his new week.

62   This will end Jay's story.

63   Now, let's chop up some Game about having a Program and adding women into it.

A Mack's Program and How it Relates to Women

64   The systems (procedures/routines) form solid daily routines that must continue to run until you reach your goal.

65   The systems will change slightly as things get accomplished and you get closer to your goal. The overall reason for the Program to be in place however does not change. The goal doesn't need to change until the goal is reached. So you have the same Program (plan) but the systems running it will change because new situations will come up that need attention.

66   This is another reason to keep a journal so you can track this. If you don't like writing you can find an app for your phone or tablet. Use whatever works for you.

67   The important thing is that you constantly measure your progress. Liken it to keeping your boat on course.

68   Measuring progress will assist you in *knowing* (not guessing) what systems are no longer needed and what system (or systems) to add based on hitting milestones. This is all part of you managing your kingdom (company). Don't forget, **effective systems** make for an **effective Program**.

69   Since you've been given Game on the four general personality types of women, you can examine your systems and assign women to assist you with them.

70   Do you see the point in all of this? By designing a solid Program you already have ways women can assist you with your life Advancement.

71   No guessing. No wondering. No uncertainty. No looking clueless or foolish. You'll be managing your kingdom (company) with complete confidence. You'll *already* be in a position of leadership because you'll be leading yourself. The woman just needs to recognize the Value of it.

72   Using Jay as an example, if he met an attractive **Domesticated** woman, he would assign her to help take care of his household systems on the weekends – washing his clothes, cleaning his house and cooking so he has lunches to take to work.

73   The system is *already* in place; all he needs to do is express to the woman *why* this is so important to him by sharing his vision and goal for his life.

74   He needs to express to her how much time this will save him; it will give him time for his other systems and free up more time to spend with her.

75   Once she understands all of this, it's his Responsibility (Principle number 7 of the 9 Principles) to be a man and simply ask her.

76   If she sees how dedicated he is to his goal, she probably won't mind. If she does have an issue with it, then he would either assign her to another system, or tell her to leave and enjoy her life. He doesn't have time for just another average "girlfriend".

77   Jay is now a man with a goal and the woman he chooses should want to be part of a team. When it's all said and done, she'll benefit as well. She gets more time with him and when he's successful she'll be right there alongside him for the ride.

78   If the woman has graphic design skills, possibly an **Educated** woman, she can help him with his website, logo and/or album covers.

79   If the woman is good at communicating she can assist him with researching where he can do shows then calling the venues and trying to book gigs for him.

80   If he meets a woman who is a Social Media fanatic, she can share his posts and song releases to her "friends" and groups – or even make videos of him creating music and share those.

81   If Jay finds a woman who is **Creative**, she can possibly help him write songs or put together press releases. She may even contribute to the website design. Maybe she can do some interior decorating around Jay's apartment; helping him acquire things that keep him inspired and focused.

82   All of this and more is available to the Mack that has a Program. Along with his Standards, Principles and life philosophy he's able to showcase his manhood at all times for everyone to see.

83   What do women get in return for kicking into (contributing to) Jay's Program? Not only do they get to assist Jay's goal, but they're provided with the 5 plus 1. Something they'll have a difficult time finding in an average male.

84   Some final notes that are extremely important for a true Mack.

85   A true Mack *does not* have sex with a woman that is not contributing to his Program. Read that again so it sinks in.

86   A Mack will date, flirt, tease and spend time with any woman that he finds attractive and interesting. But he **will not** do anything sexual with her if she's not doing at least **one** of two things:

(1) **Qualifying** to assist in his Program. Qualifying means a woman has both the ability and desire to contribute. She'll give her time, energy, access to personal resources and connections to help a Mack Advance. She'll help keep him motivated and focused and he'll do the same for her. Once a female has officially qualified (meets the Mack's Standards, Principles and fits into his Program) she usually becomes the Mack's woman. She is welcomed into the realm and treated with respect.

(2) **Campaigning** for him and his Program. Campaigning means that although a woman may not have the time, energy or personal resources to offer (or spare if she has a busy life); she still speaks about him highly to others. She passes on information about him to influential people; or even to other women who may qualify for his Program. A campaigning woman may also provide valuable information that will benefit a Mack. A woman who campaigns is a faithful cheerleader and the Mack shows her respect. However, she's usually not considered the Mack's woman.

An Important Note: A woman is only brought in to *help* – she isn't supposed to be doing *all* the work. A Mack does his own work; he just passes certain systems to his women. If she's doing all the work then the man isn't Macking, he's acting like a gigolo.

87   A woman who isn't qualified or campaigning gets "friend-zoned" by a real Mack (or forgotten about altogether). A woman who is placed into this friends-only role still has a use to a Mack, because Macks use everything they can to their benefit. I'll reveal the uses of "friend-zoned" females later.

88   A Mack only gets intimate with women who are truly *with* him. A woman is only really *with* you when she is helping you. And the best way a woman can help you is by assisting you to Advance/Grow (Principle number 6 of the 9 Principles). Advancement is measured by moving toward your goal on which your Program is based on.

89   A Mack must have extreme self control with his penis. He must Value it more than he Values a woman's vagina.

90   To a real Mack, a woman isn't even worthy enough to sleep with unless she's holds Value to him. A woman's Value to a Mack comes by way of her being **qualified** or **campaigning**. She shows this through her actions. Not what she *says* but by what she *does*. No support, no dick. Period.

91   A Mack makes time for women who are truly for him. He doesn't make much time for female friends. A Mack doesn't indulge in casual sex. To a Mack, the penis is golden – it should be treated with Value. When you treat it with Value, so will the woman.

92   This Perspective also plays on her psychology. When she sees and experiences that you stand firm on this, she'll also see you as trustworthy. She'll know that you're not out in the world having sex with any woman who's willing to open her legs. Any woman you encounter must *earn* your sex, just like she did.

93 She might not like it at first, but she will respect it. This will give her further SECURITY and confidence in your relationship.

94 And to a Mack a relationship is only what the word actually means. The root word of relationship is – *relate*. Relate basically means: *to bring into an established association or connection.* It also means: *To establish a sympathetic relationship with a person (or thing).*

95 When a Mack establishes a relationship with a woman who is qualified (she has both the ability and desire to contribute to his Program) the relationship is based on the rules they agree on.

96 You can establish any type of relationship you want as long as you're honest upfront. Be a man and be direct. Don't be sneaky, manipulative and conniving. Those are traits of weak males (and some women) who are scared.

97 Do you want a woman you just have sex with on occasion with no other ties? Tell her that's what you want (and also make sure she's campaigning for you at the very least).

98 Do you want the freedom to date many women at once? Tell them this is the reality of your dating life. You're not looking for anything serious. You're not looking to settle down – at least until you find an extraordinary woman. Explain to them that currently your top priority is your goal/s.

99 Do you want to hold two or three women in your life for a long period of time? Explain to them what you're trying to do in your life. Give them the grand vision. Break down your goal and everything involved within it. Explain to them why having more than one woman is crucial to your overall Program. It's not *their* Responsibility to figure it out – it's *your* Responsibility to tell them and show them.

100 If you can't be truly satisfied with just one woman, be honest and make clear the "reason why" you'll never be satisfied. Explain it logically and with confidence (be certain and sure).

101   Do these ideas frighten you? If so, then you're not ready to cross over into true Mackhood and that's OK. It will come with time and experience.

102   With your manhood developed and properly showcased, you'll be utterly shocked at what a woman will accept when she recognizes your Value.

103   Women are malleable (capable of being shaped). It's part of her very nature.

104   Male energy is outward and direct. This is represented by the penis, the male's sex organ. It's external and hangs outside his body.

105   Female energy is receptive and indirect. This is represented by the vagina, the female's sex organ. It's internal and rests inside her body.

106   One of the great mysteries of Macking lies in the ability to correctly utilize your masculine energy on anyone who is receptive to it. This includes women and weak males. No, you're not going to have sex with males; this is not what I'm saying. But weak males can also campaign for your Program. People who can't lead themselves usually seek a leader.

107   A Mack has the capability to manage both females and weaker males in his kingdom (company). This ability comes from wielding strong masculine energy. This is reflected by what's called your "Aura" in the Game.

108   This power of the Aura is generated by your confidence. In the next chapter we'll explore this subject in detail so you can begin to develop yours.

CHAPTER FOUR

Your Aura – Inner & Outer Radiance

1   Without trying to sound metaphysical, an Aura is an energy or "vibe" that a Mack gives off.

2   It's the, "ooh" and, "ahh" factor that will speak to a woman long before you open your mouth. She'll be intrigued by just your presence alone.

3   The radiance that your Aura gives off is primarily generated by your confidence. A woman can almost literally "feel" a confident man when she's around one.

4   Your Aura is the ultimate display of manhood. It has the ability to speak volumes. Having nice clothes, nice jewelry and a nice car are great tools to have at your disposal. But these things are inanimate objects. They don't talk, they don't speak. Only you can speak and it's your Aura that speaks first.

5   Your Aura is like a super-power. It will "open-up" a woman and put her into a natural mode of receptivity. She'll find herself slightly curious about you.

6   It's easiest to think of your Aura as your overall *presence*. It's the sum total of the way you carry yourself and behave. Behind this presence are your Standards, Principles, philosophy and your Program. All these together magnify your confidence and therefore give strength to your Aura.

7   When I first heard this concept, I'll admit it sounded a little far-fetched. But once I developed it, I couldn't deny its subtle power.

8   With a properly developed Aura, you'll walk into a room full of people and many heads will turn your direction.

9   People will respond to you more positively and give you almost immediate respect. People will smile more at you and be more attentive to what you have to say. Others will feel immediately comfortable around you; so much so that they may start telling you about their life even when you haven't asked.

10   Women will secretly comment about the way you carry yourself and that there's just, "something about you".

11   This may all sound fantastic, fabulous and grand but to understand your Aura you have to know what's actually taking place behind the scenes. You're now going to be made privy to a "secret" that has been kept hidden for a long time.

12   Before we dive in let me ask you a couple of questions. They may sound basic and ridiculous but follow along with me.

13   How does a dog know when it's hungry? How does it know when it's thirsty? How does a zebra know that it should run from a lion?

14   At what specific moment do you realize that you're attracted to a woman?

15   All these questions can simply be answered with the blanket statement, "It's in our nature," or more specifically, it's programmed into our DNA – the storage place of biological information.

16   Since our DNA stores biological information then it stands to reason that over generations there's a lot of information stored there. Many things remain in us from our ancestors.

17   You might be prone to developing diabetes if your parents and/or grand-parents had diabetes.

18   If your parents or grand-parents wore glasses, chances are you may end up wearing glasses as well.

19   Many of these things are outside of our immediate control because they're stored in our DNA and genetics. The information in our DNA are *instructions* to put it plainly.

20   Now let's look at a woman. When a woman begins to have sex, the instructions in her biology tell her body that her hips should spread slightly and prepare for child-rearing.

21   And when a woman gives birth to a child her body follows the instruction to produce breast milk for the baby.

22   What does all this have to do with an Aura? Well keep following along because this is some Advanced Game that many Mack's don't even know.

23   Women have biological instruction to respond to certain internal and external influences. Let me give you an example:

24   If you study the behavior of women (some of which is child-like as we previously covered) you'll notice that almost all women want a single thing from a mate. Whether they are hetero-sexual, bi-sexual or homo-sexual, the base desire remains the same.

25   Women desire to union. We talked about this before. But *why* is this need so prevalent and strong?

26   Because women desire to feel complete. It's the essence of their receptive nature represented by their sex organ, the vagina, which is internal – resting inside her body.

27   This desire for "wholeness" or "completeness" extends far beyond just having a mate. This desire bleeds into every area of their life. At work, with family, with friends, with their religion and with any project or hobby they may undertake.

28   If something isn't "whole", from their Perspective, they won't be content.

29   Women just want things to work. If there's something wrong with her car, she wants it fixed as soon as possible. If the lights don't come on when she flips the light-switch, she wants it fixed as fast as possible.

30   If she doesn't get along with her boss on her job she'll find a way to kiss his or her ass to "smooth" things over for as long as possible; even if she honestly dislikes her boss. To her it's something that might "break" so she puts a band-aid on it as a temporary fix to hold it together.

30   She doesn't care so much *how* things get fixed, as much as she cares that things *do* get fixed.

31   This is why she likes to feel secure and protected even though in reality you can never truly be 100% secure and protected.

32   Women are also (generally speaking) much more social than males. Social connections are important to her. It's an area of her life that brings union or completeness.

33   This is embedded in her biological instructions. Don't believe me? Have you ever had a heated argument with a woman you were in a romantic relationship with?

34   As a male, when you're extremely upset, you want distance. You want to be alone to "cool" down, compose yourself and think through the issue.

35   Most women on the other hand want to talk the issue out; right then and right there. She has to try to "fix" what appears to be "broken". She doesn't care so much how it gets fixed but it must be fixed as soon as possible.

36 Her willingness to talk about the issue (or yell about it) shows her receptive nature. A female tries to keep a male **pulled** to her while a male **pushes** her away because of his transmitting nature. He doesn't want to "receive" anything when he's upset.

37 Now let's look briefly at the nature of magnets. Yes, magnets. Follow me on this one, I promise it's important.

38 A magnet is any object that has a magnetic field. It attracts objects like iron, steel and nickel. In history, lodestone was found to attract iron pieces. According to history, the Olmecs in Central America used this to their advantage; and later the Greeks and Chinese.

39 In the modern day, magnets are artificially made with a magnetic field. A magnetic field is the space surrounding a magnet and where a magnet's force is exerted.

40 A magnetic field is produced by the motion of electrical charges. Magnets have both a North Pole and South Pole; emulating the natural North and South Poles of our planet.

41 The North Pole of one magnet will only attract the South Pole of another magnet. Two North Poles from two different magnets will repel each other. Likewise, two South Poles from two different magnets will also repel each other.

42 Un-alikes attract, and alikes repel. Or as the old saying goes, "Opposites attract."

43 So a man is a **transmitter** while a woman is a **receiver**. Like the North and South Poles of magnets, they naturally attract. They are drawn into union.

44 So let me repeat this here. You are already, by nature, what a woman wants (if she is attracted to males). What you **transmit**, a woman is ready and willing to **receive**.

45   When you showcase your Value as a man through Standards, Principles, a life philosophy, a Program and confidence you take on the exact polar opposite nature from that of a woman; she posses very few, if any of these things.

46   Since un-alikes attract, you become almost a literal magnet to women. Her biological desire for union will be met with your very presence (Aura). If she finds you attractive, she'll want what's broken (not having you) to be fixed (having you).

47   This is in her very nature. It's nothing you have to create, convince her of, or "trick" her into. She'll desire it just by you being an above average male; a real man.

48   The secret of the Aura lies primarily in your confidence. The energy you carry with you of high self-esteem (the way you *feel* about yourself) and high self-image (the way you *think* about yourself).

49   Hopefully the pieces of this puzzle are starting to be put together for you.

50   This is some of the Real Game that so many lack.

51   Your Aura is a magnetic force that acts upon anyone (female or weak male) that is in a state of **receptivity**. It comes off as charisma or natural charm.

52   To strengthen your Aura you must stand on all your Standards and Principles; you must work your Program and live your life philosophy. All this in turn will boost your confidence to an extremely high level.

53   You'll be completely comfortable with who and what you are. You'll represent, inwardly and outwardly, what almost every woman craves – a man.

54   Something she must have in her life and secretly doesn't want to control.

55   Don't forget. A woman doesn't care so much *how* something gets fixed just as long as it *gets* fixed.

56   **Translation**: A woman won't care so much how she has you in her life, just as long as you're in her life to some capacity; *if* she's honestly attracted to you. We'll explore attraction in detail later.

57   A man who is very confident (certain and sure) in himself and with everything he does is extremely Valued by a woman. This is because it's something she longs for in *herself*. A woman's favorite subject is herself and she interprets everything in relation to how it benefits her.

58   Because of her receptive nature, she can be very insecure with herself. She worries about how her body and face look, how she talks, walks, dresses, moves, and is viewed by others.

59   She is a ball of insecure knots and like everything else in her life, this is something broke that she wants fixed – but she usually doesn't know how. The union she desires includes a union within herself too.

60   The above description does not apply to *all* women but rest assured a woman is always insecure about something.

61   Your Aura, when properly developed, will catch the attention of women. You'll stand out in a crowd. When you add in the rest of the Inner Game I've given you, you'll blow her mind.

62   Of course there's more you need to know. Communication is extremely important because you must first capture a woman's mind. Then you capture her heart, then her body and finally she will give you her soul.

63 We'll talk about communication in the next Book. For now let's briefly discuss body-language and how to dress to further add to your radiance of power; to allow the outside of you to reflect the greatness inside of you.

Aura Extension – Clothes & Body Language

64 It's been said that how you dress isn't really that important. And to some degree this is true. You don't need the latest most expensive fashions. There's no need for them because you're not trying to impress a woman.

65 What's more important is that your clothes are clean and look "new". You have to be "suited and booted" or "crisp" as we say in the Game. Take care of all your clothes and take the time to iron them. A sloppy or wrinkled appearance doesn't properly reflect confidence and attention to detail.

66 Accept it or not, people *do* judge books by their cover. If you're going to be a Mack then dress in a way that reflects the greatness you've been developing within you.

66 If you don't have a freshly "new looking" wardrobe then you can start putting one together with these simple tips. This is not a book on fashion but I do want to point you in the right direction.

67 First, pick three main colors for yourself. These should be colors that you genuinely like. As you build up your wardrobe you will pick out shirts, pants, shoes, shorts, hats, etc. that have one of these three colors (or two of them).

68 This will give you a variety of outfits to put together with the least amount of actual clothes. All your clothes should be able to be mixed-and-matched to some degree.

69   If you're starting from scratch I suggest getting three pairs of nice pants. Jeans are universally acceptable; each pair in one of the three colors you've chosen.

70   Next I would recommend at least six shirts. Two shirts in each one of your three colors; you should end up with two shirts that match each pair of pants. Makes sure the shirts are different styles of course.

71   If you picked more neutral colors such as brown, blue and black you'll be able to stretch your outfits out a little more but do what you feel is best for you.

72   You'll need at least two pairs of new shoes. They should match with the colors of your pants and shirts. If you've chosen some more obscure colors such as lime-green for example, you'll have to spend a little more money in the shoes department to ensure that all your shoes match an outfit. Again, if you've chosen more neutral colors, you might be able to get away with a pair of all white shoes and a pair of all black shoes.

73   If you're into hats or caps then get two or three to match with your outfits accordingly.

74   If you have it in your budget, I suggest getting a one nice necklace. It doesn't have to be big or gaudy. Find a charm to hang from it; something that represents your philosophy is extremely effective; and makes for interesting conversation.

75   Your necklace could even be made of black or brown leather with a simple silver, gold or stainless steel charm hanging from it.

76   Also if you can, I suggest getting either one nice name-brand watch or a ring – both if you can afford it. Avoid fake "bling". That's old and tired looking. A simple band with an interesting design or engraving is perfectly acceptable for a ring.

77 For a watch I would avoid a leather band unless leather is part of your overall look. If you have a leather necklace then your watch's leather band should match its color.

78 These simple attentions to detail are what women will notice. Give them something to look at when they see you – a man who pays attention to detail with his appearance.

79 When a woman sees that in you, she'll relate this to herself as: "If he cares about his appearance, then he'll care about mine."

80 If you're a really sharp dresser, you can make a woman feel immediately self-conscious by just your appearance alone.

81 Next your body itself should be clean and your hair, beard and/or mustache nicely trimmed.

82 Also keep your fingernails and toenails clipped. Yes, women pay attention to those things too.

83 You're going for a total overall look. Having nice clothes but untrimmed nails and hair that haven't been cut in over a month doesn't match.

84 From head to toe you must be crisp. Everything on you should be in place; hair, facial hair, shirt, pants, shoes, jewelry and hat (if you wear one).

85 Invest in a small bottle of cologne; real cologne, not any cheap fragrance. A nice scent is also important to a woman and it helps to capture her mind because it speaks sub-consciously to her senses.

86 Don't have money for a good cologne? That's fine. It's better to wear no fragrance then to have on a cheap or bad smelling one. An acceptable alternative is to use a good quality scented lotion made for men.

87   If you're unsure about fashion then grab a female friend or family member to help you shop. They'll most likely love to help out. Or ask the clothing store's associate to help you. Don't be ashamed or embarrassed about this. Keep in mind what you're working toward.

88   And who knows, if the store's associate is a female, you'll get to practice your communication skills while you shop – killing two birds with one stone. You're becoming a Mack; learn to start using situations to your advantage.

89   The main point I want to make here is that the way you dress should be a direct reflection of you both as a man and a Mack. If it helps, think of Macking as a "job" and you need uniforms to go to "work". Let this Perspective help guide you in making smart fashion choices.

90   Let your outward appearance *add* to your showcase of manhood; not take away from it.

91   Now we'll touch briefly on confident body language. I recommend finding some solid information on the subject because it's very important. You also want to be able to read a woman's body language. Don't worry, we'll cover that later.

92   Your Aura, your clothing and your body language equal your **first impression**. It's very important to realize that the way you position yourself, walk, move your hands, make eye contact, stand, and even smile says a lot about you to a stranger; female or male.

93   A person must like you *first* in order to trust you *second*. The first impression is very important in this area.

94   A Mack has what's called *flair*. They have a way of moving that's all their own. There's no one way to have flair. It needs to be designed and come from you otherwise you'll look stiff and robotic. And we don't want that, right?

95   Confident people aren't stiff – they move smoothly, gracefully and deliberately.

96   Flair is picked up by people on a sub-conscious level. They're not focused directly on your movements but they do pick them up sub-consciously. Body language does influence their opinion of the person you might be.

97   This is particularly crucial with women because this helps reinforce the confidence that they'll pick up from your Aura. They will not only "feel" your confidence, they'll also literally see it.

98   **(1) Walking and Standing** – Macks stand and walk with authority. It's similar to how the police and military are trained. They take up space.

99   Stand up for a moment. Now put your feet about shoulder width apart. Look directly forward. Now bring your shoulders slightly back so that your chest moves forward while your arms naturally fall at your sides.

100   Let your weight settle into the mid-sections of your feet and heels. Bend your knees very slightly to help properly distribute the weight.

101   Now take a deep breath and exhale. When you take that breath in, your stomach will expand as well as your chest. Place one of your hands on your stomach to feel this as it happens.

102   This is proper posture. This posture radiates confidence and authority. In this position your spine will be perfectly aligned with your hips.

103   Slumped over shoulders and improper weight distribution usually indicates that person is tired or in a low (depressed) state of mind. It can also give the appearance of low self-esteem and low self-image.

104   Now while you're in the proper posture walk around a little. Walk at a normal pace and just see how it feels. Don't be stiff and robotic. Just let your arms swing naturally with each step and breathe normally as you walk.

105   Keep your head up and your back straight. By keeping your chest up and slightly poked-out, you'll find it easier to stay looking forward while also keeping your back and shoulders straight.

106   This is the walk of someone who is confident; it exudes authority. The walk seems "purposeful", like you know exactly where you're going. Remember, this speaks to people's sub-conscious mind.

107   If this feels odd or strange then this is something I suggest you practice. It must become natural and feel smooth.

108   Now, this is where the mental work comes in. You should be mentally checking your posture and the way you're walking constantly throughout the day. You can add this posture and walk into your "mental programming" that I taught you in the chapter called, *Bringing Out Your Confidence* (Book 2 – Chapter Three).

109   From this proper posture you can develop a more relaxed and laid back stance. The most important elements are that your head is up and that your shoulders always remain aligned with a straight spine.

110   For example, even when you're leaning on something, like having one elbow on a counter, your back is still straight, your chest is slightly poked out and your shoulders aren't slumped forward.

111   Practice, practice, practice. Let this become a new "file" in your mind. You'll feel uncomfortable or even silly at first but keep the image of royalty in the forefront of your mind.

112   Ask yourself, "How would a king walk?", "How would a king lean?", "How would a king sit?" Let your mind pull those files and allow them to benefit you.

113   You must represent the greatness in yourself through your walk and overall posture as much as possible.

114   **(2) Eye Contact** – You must learn to make eye contact with people you're talking to. This again signals confidence.

115   There's a big difference between staring at someone and making good solid eye contact.

116   When you look at someone, look into their eyes until you feel they're looking back into yours. Then refocus your eyes to the bridge of their nose – the space right between the eyes. This will prevent you from staring. This will also help prevent you from blinking too much (or not blinking at all).

117   Since most people watch a person's mouth as they speak, a large percentage of people won't realize that you're really focused on the bridge of their nose instead of their eyes.

118   During a conversation, occasionally bring your focus back to their eyes and look into them. Make this contact briefly, a split second, from time-to-time.

119   This is especially effective when you're making a strong point during a conversation, or saying something laced with sarcasm.

120   Again, don't be stiff. Raise your eyebrows when you're being expressive. Let your eyes occasionally scan a woman's body (don't stare at her breasts) or roam briefly to take in your surroundings.

121   **(3) Arms and Hands** – I'm personally very animated. When I'm really into what I'm talking about my hands and arms are

moving around a lot. I had to learn to be very aware of what I was doing.

122   Too much hand and arm movement is not necessarily a good thing when you're meeting someone for the first time. In fact it's best to make as few arms and hand movements as possible.

123   To help make good use of your hand and arm movements, keep everything below your neck-line. Try not to cross your arms in front of you – this indicates being "closed" or "stand-offish" to the person you're speaking with.

124   With hand motions, use your wrists to help cut down on wide arm movements. Also use your elbows with arm movements to cut down on jerky shoulder movements.

125   I suggest looking at a video of your favorite lecturer or motivational speaker. Pay close attention to their overall posture, hand and arm movements. If they're effective they use their bodies, hands and arms to help add emphasis to what they're saying. This is also how a Mack should be – not stiff, but not overly animated either.

126   All movements should be deliberate and smooth. From sitting down, standing up, walking, leaning, moving your hands and arms, and even looking around.

127   Slow down everything you do with your body – just a notch or two. It's these slow, deliberate and smooth body movements that show off your flair.

128   If you have a difficult time remembering all these body-language tips while you're in real-life situations, don't stress or obsess over it. Do yourself a favor and remember to just slow down *everything* you're doing. You can work on the details over time with enough practice.

129   These are the basics. Another technique to incorporate later as you get more comfortable, is to slightly lean in toward the person you're talking to. This sub-consciously shows that you're giving them your full attention. Women in particular appreciate attention.

130   My final body-language tip is to smile more. Not an over exaggerated wide-mouth grin; but just a sincere smile.

131   This is a powerful communication tool when opening a conversation with most women. It shows that you're interested in them, that you're comfortable with yourself and of course, that you possess confidence.

132   As your Aura develops, you drape yourself in the correct clothing and master your body language, in time you'll stand-out.

133   This is something that you must learn to accept as a Mack. You'll garner a lot of looks and stares. Not because you're walking around with expensive clothes and diamonds on your neck, wrist and fingers, but because you give off a strong sense of confidence and authority.

134   One thing to be cautious of is to never "push-out" your energy. You want to concentrate it. You want to imagine your Aura as a blanket wrapped around you. This is your magnetic energy field – electrified with the essence of your manhood.

135   You don't have to "force" your Aura on anyone, it will radiate on its own simply by being concentrated. It's this concentration that provides its intensity; not "throwing it off" to everyone around you.

136   We've covered a great deal of Inner Game. Your Outer Game is only as strong as your Inner Game. Nothing can rise higher than the source from which it came.

137   Weak Inner Game equals weak Outer Game. There's no other way it can be.

138   If you haven't done the necessary work in all the previous chapters and this one, I can say with no hesitation that you're going to stumble using the techniques covered in the next few chapters.

139   It's like a bread maker trying to bake a loaf of bread with only flour, water and a stove. He has *some* of the ingredients but he's missing the most important ones.

140   I've covered a ton of **what** to do and **why** to do it – now it's time to learn the **how**.

141   I'll continue to give you more Inner Game, although we'll be moving on to learning Outer Game. This is important because both these aspects must be working together – able to play together on the same playground.

142   If you've reached this point and done the necessary inner work, pat yourself on the back. Seriously! Because the Outer Game I'm going to lace you with will transform you into the ultimate hunter. Women will be your prey and they'll be at your mercy.

143   As a Mack, you want to first enter a woman's **mind**, then you'll capture her **heart**; you'll then have her **body** and she'll willingly offer you her **soul**.

144   Mind, heart, body and soul. This is the Mack's way. It always has been and will continue to be as long as this layer of The Game is respected.

145   To position yourself for entrance into a woman's mind you must have a strong Aura of confidence, Standards, Principles, a Program and a life philosophy. You must know and believe in yourself to an extremely high degree.

146　All of this is to be showcased and displayed "for sale" – The real Value that's placed on the table. As a hunter, this is the trap you lay down to tempt your prey.

147　But to actually catch your prey, you must learn to **transmit** all of these ideals to her so she can **receive** them.

148　And this all starts with knowing how to effectively communicate. This is the most direct route to open a woman's mind and enter it.

BOOK 4 – CONVERSATION, APPROACHING & ATTRACTION

CHAPTER ONE

The Chaos of Conversation

1   The female species are creatures of sound. The male species are creatures of sight. Just like you can get "caught-up" by the appearance of an attractive woman, females are easily "caught-up" through good conversation.

2   Women are natural receivers and communication is one of the strongest ways to receive ideas, concepts, information and feelings.

3   If you have ever really listened to two or more women hold a conversation you can see just how much communication means to them.

4   Women can talk on and on for hours about every subject under the sun. But if you listen close enough, you'll hear them reveal a truth about their nature.

5   It doesn't matter what they talk about, their favorite subject is really themselves.

6   Sure they'll talk about their job, the kids, their family and friends, but during almost every topic of discussion they find a way to relate it back to themselves.

7   They'll take a topic and turn it around to what they feel or think about it. Basically they have a strong urge to let their Perspectives be heard.

8   You can call this selfish or give it another name, or you can use this to your advantage.

9   Males are generally scared to speak to women because in the back of their mind they fear either saying the wrong things or running out of things to say.

10   As a Mack you'll have an extreme advantage over the average male. Why? Because (1) You know yourself very well (if you did the necessary inner work) and (2) You know women like to talk about themselves and relate subjects to how they feel and think.

11   Armed with this knowledge alone, there is no way you'll *ever* run out of conversation. So relax and erase that weak thinking from your mind. Remove that file from your file cabinet (file server) forever!

12   What you must do however, is get a woman comfortable with you. The more comfortable a woman is with you, the more she'll talk about her favorite subject – herself.

13   This is the measuring rod you'll use to gauge how well your conversation is going with a woman.

14   Good communication is like a dance: one-step, two-step, three-step, four-step – then repeat.

15   It's this back-and-forth that creates a connection between you and the person you're speaking with. Even if you have opposing views a conversation can still move forward and a connection can be made.

16   One thing that weak males do, because they lack Game, is to constantly agree with everything a woman says. This is pathetic. You're now a man, becoming a Mack. You've developed Standards, Principles and a philosophy on life.

17   If these are in opposition to what a woman says, then so be it. This shouldn't change your mind about the way you think at all.

18   Never play yourself down to please anyone. Never! Make this a Standard for yourself.

19   Be a man and stand firm on who and what you are; and also where you're going (your Program).

20   These are the true Value that must be placed on the table. If a woman can't see the Value in them (or at least learn and try to see them), that's not the woman for you. Don't waste your time, energy or money on her. Hunt elsewhere.

21   To become better at conversation, you need to know how conversations work and what they're composed of.

22   The core of the following conversation basics were taken from my book, *Holding Magnetic Conversations*. But I have altered these to fit the needs of the modern day Mack. Let's get to work.

23   Conversation is chaotic in nature. What do I mean by that? Within chaos lies the *potential* for something to develop.

24   Said another way, there is no order in chaos, there is only *potential energy* that can be captured and used.

25   Within a conversation anything can happen and anything is possible. You can make a connection with a person or turn them off from you completely.

26   You can solve a problem or make one. You can blend ideas and Perspectives into greater heights of understanding or you can tear apart ideas and drop into a heated argument.

27   The potential for all this to happen and more exists in the chaos of conversation. And as a Mack, it's your Responsibility (Principle number 7 or the 9 Principles) to bring as much order out of chaos as possible.

28   You must direct and control a conversation, since women are creatures of hearing (sound), they'll unknowingly help you in this process. Mainly because they don't want to break something that they'll feel pressured to fix later.

29   The first thing you must understand in communicating with anyone is to force a person's mind to give you more of its attention.

30   As we have already learned, the mind is like a vicious animal. It roams around wild and is difficult to catch. Did you know that a person only catches about 70% of what you actually say?

31   The reason behind this is because a person's mind is roaming and they're often thinking about what they want to say next instead of actually listening.

32   In relation to women, you must pull them from the "world" in their mind, into your "world". You must occupy as much of their mind as possible by making your conversation engaging.

33   To accomplish this, the energy within your voice must be higher than theirs.

34   It doesn't matter so much *what* you talk about but rather *how* you talk about it.

35   Your voice (and your conversation in general) must contain enthusiasm. You must Value what you're saying and be confident with it.

36   This enthusiasm is important because you want to affect a woman's mood. You want to communicate with her on both an emotional *and* logical level.

37   What you actually say may be logical, but when you say it with confidence and enthusiasm, it will become a thing of emotion.

38   Study great comedians and public speakers. They are masters of mixing the mundane and logical with enthusiasm, vocal thrust and tonality.

39   Since you're a man and natural transmitter, the stronger the signal is you give off, the easier it is for a woman to receive it.

40   This doesn't mean you have to be loud, brash or over exaggerate your words. But it does mean that you have to actually care about what you're saying and how you're saying it. You must pay attention to what and how you're transmitting.

41   Another way to look at this is to imagine that when you're communicating with a woman, you're on a stage. And you must command your audience.

42   There is an old saying in the Game, "Water seeks its own level."

43   In science this simply means that without any outside forces acting on water, the top level of water will even out. Think of a large empty bowl. Even if you pour water in from a single side, all the water will level out evenly once the pouring stops.

44   This simply means that the lower (energy level is this case) will attempt to compensate to balance out with the higher. Nature seeks balance, and as a part of nature, so do human beings.

46   When your energy with your conversation is high, a woman will in turn seek to match your level. This is psychological. Not only will this give a woman's mind a focal point, but it will also affect her mood.

Conversational Control

47   Let's cover the basics first. In the next chapter we'll use these basics so you can learn to effectively approach women.

48   You can start a conversation with anyone by making a comment or asking a question about one of three main subjects:

(1) The person you're talking to
(2) Yourself
(3) The situation

49   Asking a question is usually best. Why? Because it's the person who asks questions who actually controls a conversation. As a Mack, conversational control is important.

50   What do a group of Macks talk about when they get together? No one knows because they're all talking at the same time.

51   Conversational control reflects leadership and confidence. You're literally leading a conversation by determining the subject matter and you have the balls enough to ask questions.

52   Think about it. The person asking the questions determines the next topic to talk about. You can literally go from talking about something boring like the weather (like weak males do) straight into what a woman does for fun.

53   No "transitioning", no "framing", no tricks or anything else. You can steer a conversation in any direction you choose simply by asking a question.

54   The best way to ask questions is to use an *open-ended* question. An open-ended question is a question that cannot be answered with just a yes or no. You want to avoid questions that women can give one-word answers to.

55   Open-ended questions force women to give you information. And knowing how and when to use this information is the beating heart of good conversation. A few examples:

What did you do today?

What's the best place to eat around here?
How do think this shirt looks on me?
How can we form a bond that will last forever?

56   If you noticed, all these questions began with the words "what" or "how". There are eight basic ways to begin open-ended questions:

(1) Who
(2) What
(3) When
(4) Where
(5) Why
(6) How
(7) So
(8) Are (And Are)

56   If you're a beginner to communication I strongly suggest you stick with "what" and "how" until you become more skilled and confident.

57   The extraction of information can only be done when the question is structured correctly.

58   So now you've asked a woman an open-ended question. They have given you a response. Now it's your job to take what's in that response and do one of two things:

(1) Run with the "ball" (do the talking yourself) or;
(2) Put the "ball" back in their court (return their answer and ask a new question)

59   A simple example:

You: What are you going to eat today?

Them: I've been craving a hamburger from, _Snackers_. I love their burgers!

60   For this first example, you're going to run with the ball (do some talking yourself) so your response may be something like this:

You: A burger. Wow, I haven't had a good burger in a long time. I think the last time I had a *Snackers* burger was like three or four months ago.

61   In this example we built a response by pulling out a "key-word". A key-word is one single word that is taken from the person's response to our open-ended question. This helps us stay on topic if we choose to do some talking by "running with the ball".

62   The key-word we pulled was, "burger", and we formed our entire response around it.

63   Now let's look at your possible response if you decided to "put the ball back in their court" – return their answer and ask a new question.

You: A burger doesn't sound too bad right now. Hey, what are you doing tomorrow?

64   In this example, instead of talking about yourself from the information they gave you, you just took what they gave and asked them another question.

65   You completely changed the subject and this forces them to continue to opening up and give even more information. And when you get this new information, you can either run with it, or put in back in their court.

66   And the conversation continues back and forth like this. This is the basics of the dance and bringing order to the chaos of conversation.

67   You may be thinking, which option should I use? Should I "run with the ball" or "put the ball back in their court"? The simplest way to answer is that you want to "run with the ball" when you want to:

(1) Make a point (or give your Perspective)
(2) Tell a story
(3) Or relate to what they're saying

You "put the ball back in their court" when you want to:

(1) Continue to dig for specific information
(2) Want them to tell a story
(3) Want them to reveal information about themselves or the topic (give their Perspective)

68   If you feel a little lost please stop and reread it until you understand it. Almost all the conversation techniques I'll teach you are based off of these basics.

69   Remember when you ask a question you must listen to their response. Out of their response you want to pull out a key-word. This key-word gives you a basis for what to say next.

70   If you're running with the ball (doing the talking yourself), use the key-word to form your response and remain on topic.

71   If you put the ball back in their court (return the answer) you use the key-word in your response to let them know that you heard what they said, and then you ask a new question.

72   There is no right or wrong way to grab key-words. Don't get hung-up on finding the right "magical" key-word because it doesn't exist. If you're really paying attention to the answers you're being given, you can easily find a key-word; sometimes two or three.

73   This does take some practice. But when you become proficient, you can literally create entire conversations out of thin air.

74   Now you be saying to yourself, "If I just ask question after question after question, won't this conversation start to feel like an interrogation or job interview?" and you would be right.

75   So now that you understand how to begin to bring order out of chaos I'll share with you a few basics that will add spice to any conversation; keeping them interesting and engaging. Look at these as tools. And you have a toolbox full of them that you can pull out to do a specific job.

Conversation Tool 1: Being the Playful Observer

76   Asking open-ended questions are great, but you have to involve more of yourself and your personality to keep a conversation interesting, engaging and flowing.

77   If you're speaking to a woman you just met and she tells you that she's originally from New York, you can make an observation about it. But it should be done in a teasing way.

78   This teasing adds "spice" to the conversation. When done correctly, this playful and light-heartedness turns a simple conversation into a challenge.

79   Not only does teasing speak to the child-like side of women, but it also holds their attention (keeps their mind focused on you) and affects their mood. This is a lot of what you want in a conversation.

80   Here's what I mean:

You: You know, I came all the way over just to meet you. You're gorgeous! What's your name?

Woman: Tracy.

You: Tracy? That's it? You're parents just gave up being creative right there huh? *(tease)*

Woman: What? What's wrong with Tracy?

You: Don't worry about it. Tracy is a good name for you I guess. Where are you from Tracy? *(open-ended question)*

Woman: I'm originally from The Bronx in New York.

You: The Bronx? Really? How many car-jackers do you know? *(open-ended question)*

81   You may look at this conversation and think to yourself this is bordering on rude, but to some women (not all) a conversation like this is something new, fresh and different.

82   It presents them with a challenge and tickles their child-like side. And if worse came to worse the woman would just do what most women do, give off a bad attitude. If that happened you could just save precious time, wish her a happy life and go hunt somewhere else.

83   An observation lets the person know you're listening to them and that you have an interest in the topic. This subtle difference plays right back into what we've just talked about – the back-and-forth dance between a woman and yourself.

84   You ask them to reveal some information and they do. You make an observation about what they say and then "run with the ball" or "put the ball back in their court" to get even more information.

85   Not all observations should be playful and teasing. But if you can work a couple into the conversation, then do it with confidence.

86   Another example with using more of a "running with the ball" style:

You: You know, I came all the way over just to meet you. You're gorgeous! What's your name?

Woman: Tracy.

You: Tracy. I have a cousin named Tracy. She's pretty cool. I practically grew up with her. She was good in school; I used to copy off her homework all the time. You probably don't care about any of that. Anyway, where are from Tracy? *(open-ended question)*

Woman: I'm originally from The Bronx in New York.

You: The Bronx? Really? I never been there. I guess I watch too many crime movies. How bad is it up there, really? (open-ended question)

Woman: It depends on where you go I suppose. Doesn't every city have its bad parts?

You: Sure they do. Wait, though! Are you some kind of trouble maker? I can recognize a trouble maker when I see one. *(tease)*

87   By mixing observations in with your question techniques you'll find that it's not very difficult to keep a woman engaged.

88   In the above example we took The Bronx and made it our key-word. Then when took a stereotype of New York being a crime infested city and used that to tease her through observation.

89   Observations don't have to be right, factual or even logical. Make no mistake, sometimes they can be and sometimes its best that they are. But they can also be ridiculous and stereo-typical.

90   In the second example, you should also note that we revealed some information about ourselves before we even asked the woman to reveal information about her.

91   Being this forward exudes confidence. And **transmitting** this comfortableness with being yourself will be **received** by the woman allowing her to be more comfortable with you.

92   You take on the Responsibility to be the conversation's controlling factor and you should because most women won't. And you shouldn't expect them to.

93   You're the hunter and you must stalk your prey.

94   When making more serious (less playful and teasing) observations it's fine to give your Perspectives, but if you can bring in facts about the topic as well, this can be even more powerful.

95   If a woman drops some facts your way that you can't deny are true, then pay them a compliment on their knowledge and/or expertise.

96   People in general love being thought of as intelligent and insightful; women are no exception. There's nothing wrong with giving a woman acknowledgement (not praise) for being intelligent. A truly confident man wouldn't be frightened by a woman's intelligence and he also wouldn't be scared to tell her he thinks so.

Conversation Tool 2: Thinking Out-Loud

97   Males are so afraid of not looking cool and being impressive to women that they get lost in their head trying to figure out the "right" thing to say.

98   There is no "right" thing to say. You must be yourself and you must learn to remove the filter you have put on your conversation.

99   As a Mack, you are the consummate transmitter. The entire pace, direction and tempo of a conversation is solely directed by you. Especially when you first approach a woman.

100   A male will think in his head about how good a woman looks in her heels, but he won't say it to the woman who is actually standing right in front of him.

101   A male will think in his head that something he just said sounded corny (dull or foolish). But he won't be confident enough to admit this to the woman and laugh at himself.

102   A male will wait and wait and wait for a woman to give him some sign that she's interested, instead of just telling a woman that he's interesting and that he's worth getting to know.

103   A male will keep a conversation going and wait on just the right magical moment to ask for a woman's phone number. Instead of doing it when the thought first crosses his mind.

104   A male will agree with everything a woman says because he's afraid to tell her he disagrees. In his weak way of thinking he figures he might "lose" her (or turn her off). When in reality he doesn't even have her yet so what's to lose? Why not just be a man and tell her he disagrees and *why* he disagrees? Then use this to his benefit to spark a deeper more meaningful dialogue.

105   A male will force his way with trying to hold the attention of a woman although she shuns him and shows she's not interested. He should just accept his loss; tell her have a good day and go hunt elsewhere. This saves time that should be Valuable to anyone with a Program for their life.

106   A male will think of countless ways to explain why a woman should choose him instead of asking a woman specific questions to see if she's even qualified to hold a place in his life and Program.

107   A male will buy a woman drinks at a bar before he even knows if he would honestly enjoy talking to her.

108   A male will look at a woman across a room repeatedly because he thinks she's attractive, but he'll never approach her and tell her so.

109   A male will see a younger woman and feel ashamed that he finds her attractive even though spread all across television, the internet and magazines everyone pushes the idea that youth equals beauty.

110   A woman can smile at a male or even make extended eye contact and a male will pretend like he doesn't see it because he doesn't think he'll impress her when he opens his mouth.

111   A male will approach a woman with tired pick-up lines; use props and ridiculous excuses like asking her what time it is, instead of just saying what he really wants; and that's to meet her.

112   A male will wait and wait for the right moment to speak to a woman because he doesn't want to "interrupt" her. And he'll wait so long that he loses his opportunity. He'll justify to himself that she was "busy" anyway.

113   A male will see an attractive woman with another one of her girlfriends and tell himself every excuse in the book as to why he can't make his move and introduce himself.

114   A male will walk right past an attractive woman, find a position to stand, turn around then look at her as she walks away. All that weak behavior when he could have stopped her in her tracks and told her how beautiful she looks.

115   A male will hesitate asking a woman he enjoys talking to for a date in hopes that she'll eventually "get the hint" and give him a sign. Instead of just telling her that he enjoys her conversation and would like to take her out to get to know her better.

116   A male will ask just to "hang out" as friends instead of directly telling a woman that he's attracted to her, he enjoys her company and he doesn't want to be just friends.

117   A male will go out on a first date with a woman and sit there idiotically while she flaunts unacceptable behavior instead of telling her that she has completely turned him off and he wants to take her back home.

118   A male will take a woman on a date and avoid talking about his past sexual experiences even if the woman brings the subject up first.

119   A male will talk openly with a woman he's known for a while but when an attractive woman joins the conversation, he'll suddenly limit the topics of discussion.

120   All of the above behavior is weak, childish and ridiculous. Get rid of these limiting files.

121   Stop being a male! Remove the filter from your conversation and think out-loud more. Say more of what's on your mind. Speak up. A closed mouth doesn't get fed.

122   Become a man and transform into a real Mack. Become the hunter and go after your prey.

123   Stop hesitating to bring up subjects or say the wrong thing. Speak with confidence and with enthusiasm. Be confident; more sure and certain in yourself.

124   Stop waiting and start creating. Make things happen. This is what a man is supposed to do. And a woman will respect him for it.

125   Stop being timid. Stop being scared. Stop trying to be impressive. How far have those lines of thinking gotten you?

126   Speak to women almost like you would a long-time male friend. It doesn't matter if they're single, have a boyfriend or are married.

127   Be yourself and let them tell you what they will or won't accept from you as far as "acceptable conversation". Be yourself and give them the option. And respect their boundaries if they choose to give it.

128   It's not about being an arrogant asshole. A Mack is always the ultimate gentleman.

129   But you should put yourself first more. Being who you are at all times is important. But you should respect that women have the right to be themselves too. And they may also have Standards of what's acceptable in a conversation.

130   Let them tell you. Don't assume or make up their mind for them. If they have different ideas, they'll let you know. They do it more often than you think and they're very proficient at it. Tell them you meant no disrespect and leave it at that.

Conversation Tool 3: The Master of Implication

131   Human beings since recorded time have always learned best in pictures, images and stories. The biggest reason being is that we naturally think in terms of images. Not words.

132   Quick example. If I say the word, *woman* what comes to mind?

133   The actual word woman? Spelled out with every single letter, w-o-m-a-n? No! An image of an actual female pops into your head.

134   How about the word, *fire*? Or the word, *house*? Or the word, *car*? These words all make your mind respond with images, correct?

135   Even abstract concepts are visualized in the mind as images. How about the word, *love*? What symbol represents that? A heart.

136   Here's an interesting one. How about the word, *hate*? You probably either see multiple images or even a short scene play out in your mind to represent that abstract word.

137   All these images are associated with words based on the files you have in your mind.

138   When you hear the word, *sex*, what images immediately come to your mind? The images that arise are based on what sex means to you and the files you placed (or accepted) that represent that to you.

139   If a woman said during casual conversation something like, "I feel sweaty. I can't wait to go home and take a bath."

140   You can grab the key-word, *home* and imply an idea without actually saying it word-for-word. It could come out something like this, "There's nothing wrong with being at home getting all wet."

141   What idea has been implied? Sex has been implied – her vagina being wet and she's at home while this happens.

142   Now you could have been very direct and just said, "I would love to watch you take a bath and then have sex."

143   There's nothing really wrong with the above statement, but to a woman who is socially conditioned not to look "slutty", this might turn her off or even make her hesitate as the conversation continues.

144   By implying an idea, using the correct words that form the correct mental images, you can be forward without sounding crass.

145   When you imply ideas you're not only keeping a woman mentally engaged because you're feeding images to her which forces her to pull files, but you're also building a connection. You know what you mean and she knows what you mean and it's something that you both share – the same images inside both your minds.

146   It's subtle but powerful. The following examples are light-hearted and imply sex.

147   First example:

Her: I like riding motorcycles.

You: I can tell you like riding (key-word) on big things between your legs.

148   And another example:

Her: I think you're cute, but I have a boyfriend.

You: That's cool with me; I didn't plan on letting your boyfriend (key-word) watch anyway.

149   And another example:

Her: I can't go out with you. I don't even know you.

You: You can't know (key-word) what's under the covers until you pull them back.

150   And yet another example:

Her: I can't get this nail into the damn hole!

You: You can't always just force things into holes (key-word). Sometimes you have to take your time.

151   Not all implications need to be sexual. They could be used to make her see your Standards or Principles too. In the following examples strength and urgency are implied.

152   First example:

Her: My boss is so rude. She pisses me off!

You: If you don't like someone pissing (key-word) on you then maybe you should stop being a toilet.

153   Another example:

Her: Oh my god! I really need to clean-up my kitchen, it's a mess.

You: Cleanliness (key-word) is next to godliness and god (key-word) makes things happen.

154   And another example:

Her: I just don't have time to date right now.

You: Over time (key-word) even the sharpest knife goes dull.

155   Implications aren't easy to weave into a conversation. This is fine because they should be used sparingly. They take practice and sometimes even planning. But they are extremely powerful.

156   You use implication when you want to imply a desire, poke fun at something (behaviors or statements) or showcase your Standards, Principles or philosophy.

157   I was once walking down a steep flight of stairs with a woman wearing heels. She looked ridiculous trying to maintain her balance and not trip. She was bumbling around and couldn't have looked any less graceful.

158   I could have laughed but instead I made an observation and phrased it as an implication. I said, "Being sexy is a hard job baby. I see it keeps you on your toes."

159   I implied that despite how funny she looked, and how hard she was "working" at moving cautiously, she was still attractive. This lightened the mood, reminded her that I saw her as sexy and made her laugh.

160   Another side-effect of using well-timed implications is that they show the woman you're socially aware. Being socially aware means that you understand life and people and how things play out.

161   And since almost all women are social creatures, they'll appreciate a man who can look at life and people from a unique Perspective. His own personal Perspective.

Conversation Tool 4: Your World Through Your Stories

162   As you're speaking with women, asking questions and making observations, it's important every now and then to relate fully to something that the person is saying.

163   The best way to do this is by telling a story. If you're not a good story teller it doesn't matter. All you have to remember is that a story is composed of three simple things:

(1) What the regular routine is
(2) What comes along to break that routine
(3) What happens after that routine was broken

164   Don't just say, "I went to the store yesterday to pick-up some things. When I got back home I realized I should have bought some bread."

165   Turn this into a story. Go through what you did, what you thought and how you felt. And don't forget to add in enthusiasm. Something like this:

166   **"I looked in my refrigerator getting ready to fix me a sandwich (regular routine) and when I opened it I saw I was out of cold-cuts and I was out of mayonnaise. I slammed the refrigerator closed, threw on some clothes, got in the car and went to the store (broken routine),"**

"So I'm in the store and I hate stores because I can never find the right aisle. I mean I only went there for like seven or eight things and I was in there for like 30-minutes,"

"So I find everything, pay for it and head back to the house. And you know what? I laid out everything to make my sandwich, opened my cupboard and realized my bread was stale (broken routine). There was no way I was going all the way back to the store. So I just made a breadless sandwich (what happened after the routine was broken)."

167 I'll give you another example. Don't just say, "I can't believe my son got suspended for fighting yesterday. I had to leave work just to go pick him up!" Turn it into a story, add in the details.

168 "I'm at work, I didn't feel like being there as usual (regular routine). Then my cell phone rings and it's my son's school. I'm listening to the Assistant Principal tell me that my son was in some physical altercation with another boy. I thought this was odd because my son doesn't fight. So I'm asking the man if he's positive it was my son that was involved,"

"He tells me he's sure and says that I have to pick him up from school. Now I'm pissed but at the same time I'm happy because I get to leave work (broken routine),"

"I drive to the school and go into the Principal's waiting area, or whatever they call it. There's my son sitting there with his shirt all torn up and scratches all over his face. He's looking pitiful,"

"I sign some form and make an appointment to meet with the Principal because my dumbass son can't go back to school until we all have a little sit-down. So I'm in the car with Mr. Fisticuffs and ask him what happened,"

"He goes on and on about how this boy kept making fun of his shoes, all the little girls were laughing and he just lost it. I was mad at first but then I realized that he was just standing up for himself. Just like I taught him,"

"We had the regular conversation about talking to a teacher first and all that jazz but I kind of felt proud in a strange way. My son isn't a punk,"

"Before I took him home we went to go get his favorite ice-cream. And I made him vow not to tell him mother. He's a

good kid so I just gave him a light punishment. Problem is, he's going to be in the house by himself over the next three or four days. I don't know if that's good thing or bad thing (what happened after the routine was broken)."

169   The power of the story (properly told) is powerful. Do you realize that almost everything is a story? Books, movies and television shows. Even commercials (the good ones) tell a 10 to 30 second story.

170   Use stories to "run with the ball" when a woman brings up a point that you can expound on with a relevant experience.

171   Stories can also be used to literally put files about you into a woman's mind. So that she'll see you the way *you* want, not the way she assumes.

172   Stories are also great to train a woman about how you want to be treated. We'll cover this in more detail later.

173   Stories don't need to be dramatic or over-the-top. The most important thing you want out of telling a story is to reveal *how* you think. You'll be indirectly (or directly) giving a woman your Standards, Principles and philosophy in a way where she won't even realize what's happening.

174   Stories make a woman more comfortable with sharing how she thinks as well. And when a woman is comfortable, she'll talk a lot about herself.

175   This is a very effective way to learn your woman in and out; backwards and forwards.

176   You may think you don't have any stories to tell but that's simply untrue. If you're 22 years old for example, you have almost 20 years of stories to tell. Nearly 7,000 stories in fact – at least one story for every day of your life.

177   These stories include things you've done, places you've visited, things you thought about doing and experiences you've had; whether good or bad.

178   It's a game of, "I share, you share". You're the transmitter. Take the lead and reveal yourself first and she'll follow.

Conversation Tool 5: When Things Fall Apart

179   Sometimes no matter how many questions you ask, how many observations you make or how many stories you tell, a woman is not going to give out a lot of information about herself.

180   This can be scary for the average male. He will think that he's "bombing" with her. Sometimes this is true. She may genuinely not be interested. But most of the time it's not.

181   What's usually happening is that a woman is trying to define you. She's trying to figure out where she can put herself within a conversation with you.

182   When this happens don't tense up and don't stop being your enthusiastic self (unless she's just overly negative, then my advice is just get away from her and go hunt elsewhere).

183   What you do in these situations is simply reverse roles.

184   This simply means that instead of leading the conversation (with questions); flip it around so they lead the conversation. How do you do this? Simply get them to start asking questions. Put them in a position that they must ask you questions if they want the conversation to advance.

185   It's as simple as saying something like this, "You know, I feel like I'm taking up the whole conversation. Tell me what's on your mind. I'm just curious."

186   This question, or something similar to it, puts complete control of the conversation in her hands. A woman will usually respond with a mundane topic that doesn't really mean anything.

187   It's at this moment you take back control. How? By going back to making observations, teasing her quietness with implications or telling a story if you have one that's relevant to the topic.

188   However you do it, make sure you keep them involved by ending with yet another open-ended question. Usually asking them what they think about what you just said.

189   Be careful here, getting women to open up who are shy, or simply don't want to, requires you to slow down the pace of the conversation. Always keep in mind that you want a woman to feel comfortable.

190   Another way to do this is when they respond with what's on their mind you just say, "Interesting, go on."

191   This allows them open up at their own pace and find a way into the conversation.

192   The worst thing that can happen here is that they say nothing is on their mind. Or they just shrug and close up. So this is when you pull the big guns out.

193   You simply shut-up and sit there in silence. That's right, silence. This applies a very uncomfortable pressure to the situation.

194   Pressure bursts pipes. If you can remain in silence long enough, they'll eventually "burst" and attempt to start some type of conversation. This is a game. Games involve strategy and tactics.

195   If a woman isn't receptive in the beginning just giving them the opportunity to have some conversational control will usually get them to open up; especially if they're attracted to you.

196   It's amazing how long five or 10 seconds in silence can be. Especially when sitting next to or across from each other.

197   If a woman shows no interest to start a conversation back up then make your exit and go hunt elsewhere. You're a Mack, not a therapist. It's not your job to pull conversations out of lame women.

198   Don't look at this as a failure; just simply understand that you can't win them all. Forcing conversation is a lot more embarrassing then staying silent for a moment or two.

199   Sometimes, regardless of what you do, things between you and the woman just won't "click".

200   When this happens, don't worry and don't start to play yourself down to please or impress them. Don't drop to their level.

201   Being completely comfortable, even in silence (or at the risk of failure) exudes strength and confidence.

202   Don't be an ass-kisser. Sometimes you'll just have to accept that this woman is boring (or not interested) and be satisfied that you didn't compromise your manhood.

Conversation Tool 6: Contrast for Difference

203   Imagine your favorite movie for a moment. Think about the character you most identify with. Next think about your favorite scene in that movie.

204   Now imagine having to watch that same exact scene over and over again. I'm talking back-to-back. Same dialogue or action, same setting and the same situation happening repeatedly for hours on end.

205   Wouldn't that just bore you to tears? After a few hours I'm quite sure you'll just lose interest. Unfortunately many of us do the same thing in a conversation – repeat ourselves.

206   We tell the same stories, make the same observations and talk about the same topics.

207   If I repeated the word, *run* over and over again, how long do you think I would hold your interest?

Run, Run, Run, Run, Run, Run, Run, Run, Run, Run, Run, Run, Run, Run, Run, Run, Run, Run, Run, Run, Run, Run, Run, Run, Run, Run, Run, Run, Run, Run, Run, Run, Run, Run…

208   That's just boring enough to read let alone say to someone, am I right? Now if I repeated the word, *fast* over and over again, eventually the same thing would happen. Boredom and a loss of interest.

209   But if we put the words, *run* and *fast* together and give them contrast we slightly increase the attention span of the mind.

Run fast, Fast run, Run fast, Fast run, Run fast, Run fast, Fast run, Run fast, Fast run, Run fast, Run fast, Fast run, Run fast, Fast run, Run fast, Run fast, Fast run, Run fast, Fast run, Run fast…

210   Is this great? No. But the contrast of it makes it slightly more interesting; both to read and say out-loud.

211   It's this idea of contrast in the way words and sentences are grouped together that can help if you find yourself in a position where you have to repeat yourself.

212   For example, let's say you told a story to a woman you're interested in. She thought it was funny or interesting and she asks you to tell the same story to another person.

213   Use the tool of contrast to tell the same story but introduce different elements.

214   Maybe you'll dig more into how you felt at a particular moment in the story. Or perhaps you'll be more descriptive of a particular person. You could even end the story and roll into another short story that relates to it; and this new short story is something that your woman hasn't heard before.

215   Keep things as fresh and new as possible. Add contrast to turn the "same old same" into the "same new same".

216   This tool is very effective because when you choose the lifestyle of a Mack, you'll be holding women for a long-time. They'll learn a lot about you and you'll learn a lot about them.

217   You want to have something new to say to your woman (or women) almost every day. How is that accomplished? How could you possibly have something new to say so often?

218   By having the ability to say the same thing in 20 different ways. With a little thought and creativity this is very easy to achieve.

Conversation Tool 7: The Illusion of Choice

219   This is a very simple and easy tool to use. What follows is a very simple persuasion tactic that requires very little forethought and can be used in many ways and situations with women.

220   As a Mack, conversational control is important. And control comes through asking questions.

221   I'll teach you a questions technique that's designed to do one thing – allow you to move forward in the direction you have pre-determined.

222   The way this question is structured gives the illusion that the woman has a choice. And you should always give a woman a choice (within reason anyway).

223   But the reality of this technique is that whatever she chooses will still get you moving in the direction you've *already* decided.

224   The key here is prior planning and careful sentence structure. In other words, you need to have a direction in mind and a strategy.

225   Here is a regular structured question: "Where are we going out to eat tonight?"

226   Yes, this is an open-ended question. But if we have decided in advance that the woman *is* going out with us regardless, then we need to structure our question in a way that gives her the illusion of a choice.

227   Here is an illusion structured question: "When we go out to eat, are we having Italian or seafood?"

228   Here's the Game on how this all works.

229   First we present the woman with an option. Or better said, the illusion of an option. In this case it's whether to eat Italian cuisine or seafood.

230   But guess what? We wouldn't mind eating either one. And we have already decided that she's going out with us.

231   We made the choice first. Then we give the woman an illusion of a choice. Whatever she chooses, we win! We'll not only get to eat something we want but we also get her company.

232   You get what you want as long as she chooses one of the options you provide in other words.

233   Imagine: The woman and you have never even agreed to go on a date. And instead of wondering or hoping if a date is even a possibility, you make the decision first. Next you properly structure a question so that however it's answered, you get what you want.

234   With the above question we never asked, "Do you want to go out to eat?" We *assumed* agreement and then gave an illusion of choice.

235   Again I'll repeat, as long as they choose an option, we win.

236   The game was won before it even started. I told you this was easy, didn't I?

237   Here are some more examples of illusion based questions:

After we finish eating or we going to my place or yours?
Am I coming to pick you up at noon or after three?
Am I going to get on top or are you?
Are you going to text me or call me?
Do you want to watch, *Killer Sam* or *Summer Heat* at the movies?
You're still getting dressed? Are you going to wear the black skirt or the red one? *(on the phone with her while driving to pick her up)*
It's loud in here. I want to talk to you. Do you want to go outside or go sit over there in the corner? *(at a packed nightclub)*

238   You might be asking yourself, why ask questions at all? Shouldn't I just lead at all times? Well Player, don't forget that a Mack is always the ultimate gentleman. Give the lady a "choice" every once in a while.

Conversation Tool 8: The Secret Sauce

239   As we've already covered, the majority of communication with women has very little to do with *what* you say. *How* you say things is more important.

240   Say the word, "Hello" out loud in your normal speaking voice. Notice the plainness of your tone.

241   Now say the word again but drop your tone at the end of the word. Make the last two letters, "l-o" very low.

242   You'll probably feel a little strange doing this but look at the effect. You said the same word but the "feeling" of it was different.

243   Say the word, "Hello" again but this time raise your voice slightly on the last two letters, the "l" and the "o". Don't raise the volume of your voice, just the tone.

244   The word should feel warmer and more inviting. If not, try it again and pay attention to your voice's inflection and tone.

245   Now say the word, "Stop" in your plain speaking voice. Then say it again forcibly, as if you were trying to prevent a child from touching a hot stove.

246   Notice the authority of that tone. This word became not just a word, but a command just by changing the tone. Same word, but the "feeling" of it was different.

247   What changes the tones of the words you use is simply the intention behind them.

248   Say the following sentence out loud in a normal speaking voice.

"I think you look gorgeous."

249   Plain and boring. There was no strong intention behind it so it lacked energy and enthusiasm.

250   Now say the same sentence out loud again, but this time as you say the word, "you" raise the tone. The intention behind the word should be directness and intensity. If you were actually saying this to a woman, you want her to hear the emphasis and feel it.

251   You want to convey the message that she really has caught your eye and that you're serious with what you're saying to her.

252   The sentence alone is simple. But by adding in tonality and emphasis you breathe life into it. Tonality is the "secret sauce" that will turn even the most basic sentences into mind-grabbing *hooks*.

253   Quick changes in tone are very effective when forcing women to zone-in and listen to you. Say the following sentence in your plain speaking voice:

"Hello, Jennifer. Do you mind coming over here a moment? I have a secret to tell you."

254   We have three sentences and now we will give each its own tone.

255   First we say, "Hello" and will raise our tone on the letters "l-o" like we did before. This commands attention and piques interest.

256   With our second sentence we will hold the *intention* of urgency. Say this sentence as if what you have to say is the most important thing Jennifer can hear at this moment.

257 Practice this second sentence a few times. If you listen carefully you can hear the correct tone when you finally hit it. The emphasis in this sentence should be on the words, "mind" and "coming".

258 If you're having trouble squint your eyes as you say it. This physical action will provide a psychological trigger in your mind. This squinting will help your words flow with urgency.

259 In our last sentence, we will drop our tone. Dropping it nearly to a whisper, but low enough to make it feel as there is really a secret to be said.

260 The word *secret* itself implies something that is to be shared quietly. Not yelled or even said in a normal speaking volume.

261 Whenever you say anything with the intention of secrecy or mystery behind it, the tone and volume of your voice will naturally drop. Remember; think about the *intention* behind what you're saying to help bring out the tone of voice you're trying to achieve.

262 Try this third sentence a few times. Once again, you'll feel when you get it right.

263 Practice each sentence separately. One after another while taking a brief pause in-between each.

264 When you feel comfortable, put all three sentences together into one smooth flow.

265 Pique interest by raising your tone in the first sentence. Create urgency by conveying seriousness in the second sentence and finally draw Jennifer to you by creating mystery and secrecy in the final sentence.

266 You just used three different vocal tonalities to convey three different emotions.

267   As you grow more skilled with communicating, begin to pay attention to the tonalities you use. Proper tonality can command attention, demand compliance, captivate, empower and influence.

268   As an aid, you can study your favorite actor or comedian. Instead of watching them, close your eyes and just listen to their tonality as they deliver their lines (or jokes).

269   Once you fully develop this skill it will become second nature. You won't even have to think about it.

270   These are some important tools for your conversation toolbox. Don't worry about learning them all at once, just work on the ones that stand out to you at first; add the others after you get more proficient.

271   In the next chapter I'll show you how to put these tools to use for approaching *any* woman you want. In the Mack Game this is a part of what's called your, "catch hand".

CHAPTER TWO

Designed Responses
The Fundamentals of Approaching Women

1   With a basic understanding of conversational control and some tools in your toolbox. It's now time to make a new file cabinet (file server) in your mind.

2   This new cabinet (server) will hold files for quick responses to pieces of conversation that you'll use when approaching and dating women.

3   This will not only help in the area of confidence, but it will also train your mind to think more quickly overall. This is a great at preventing you from getting "stuck". You'll have on-the-fly responses prepared for common things that will come up over and over again as you're getting to know women.

4   Legendary ex-Pimp John Dickson, formally known as *Rosebudd Bitterdose*, calls this concept "having an arsenal". And this description is a solid one.

5   Having pre-planned responses is like having a different gun loaded and ready to fire for different occasions. When fully developed, you'll rarely be caught off guard with how women respond to the things you say.

6   You're creating short-cuts to keep a conversation moving in the direction you want.

7   When I discovered this concept I didn't have a specific name for it. I just did it because it was a natural evolution as I gained more experience.

8   As a Mack, you'll be playing a game versus a very skilled opponent. To win you have to have a planned strategy and tactics going in.

9   There's no hoping and wishing that things will go in the direction you want. A Player doesn't hope and wish. He does his best to *make* things happen; to create a way out of no way based on how he thinks and his Perspectives.

10   Let me explain what I mean by the term skilled opponent.

11   Let's take a slightly above average looking woman. On a scale of 1 to 10 (10 being the highest) this woman in our example is a 7.

12   She's attractive but not drop-dead gorgeous. Not quite model material but she would be worth seeing laid out naked on your bed.

13   On average this woman will be approached and "hit-on" at least five times a week; especially if she dresses well and keeps up her appearance. If she works in a service industry where she encounters a lot of males, she'll probably be "hit-on" no less than 10 times a week.

14   If this same woman goes to a club or bar on the weekends, she'll be "hit-on" no less than five times within the few hours she's there.

15   Being "hit on" is defined as receiving prolonged stares, being given generous compliments, hearing pick-up lines, being engaged in flirtatious conversations, being offered help, and getting free drinks.

16   Some women find this attention flattering because they *know* they're attractive. They don't have to guess or wonder if they are. That fact is reinforced continuously many, many times.

17   Other women find all this attention offensive and even intrusive. They appreciate knowing that they're attractive, but sometimes too much of something can be a bad thing.

18   This is the kind of attention a 7 gets. Imagine an 8 or 9. The rate at which these women get "hit-on" increases significantly. Usually the more attractive a woman is the more stares and compliments she receives but less actual conversation.

19   This is because the more attractive the woman, the more intimidated weaker males are around her.

20   Now, as a male or man how often do you get "hit-on" by women? How many stares, compliments, pick-up lines and being approached out-of-blue do you receive in a week?

21   Even the most attractive males may only get this type of attention once or twice a week. And he may only be "cold-approached" (approached out-of-blue) maybe a couple times a year.

22   Why is this? Much of this has to do with Social Conditioning. It's just not "lady-like" for a woman to approach a man. Plus many women (not all) are just as afraid of being rejected as weak males are.

23   But for the above average attractive woman, (7 and up on the attraction scale) she usually develops a filtering process. She'll only respond positively to being hit-on under three main conditions. These three conditions aren't rules, they're just written here as a general reference to expand your Perspective.

(1) She's in a good mood. Even if this good mood is artificial – meaning they come from outer stimuli. Examples: She may be feeling great because she just got a promotion on her job; she may have just hit the lottery; or she may be drunk. These artificial good moods are fleeting and are not an indication of her normal everyday mood.

(2) She thinks the male or man hitting-on her is attractive in some way. This can be his physical looks or through his Aura which radiates confidence, strength and manhood.

(3) She's feeling lonely because she had yet to find a man (or male) she thinks is worthy of her time and attention. She's open to meeting more men/males and giving them a chance.

24   If a man or male can't get past these filters then she'll reject him. She has become very good at it because she does it repeatedly multiple times a week.

25   It has become a file in her mental file cabinet (file server) and a response she gives without too much thought. It's like becoming proficient in a sport. The more you practice the better you'll get. In the realm of rejecting males, an attractive woman gets plenty of practice.

26   By the time an attractive woman reaches the age of 21 she has entered the big-leagues and has become a professional rejecter; a skilled opponent.

27   She will have developed her own style of rejecting men/males based on her personality and what she picked up from other females in her social circle.

28   I have personally seen women be nice about it – letting the male speak and then excuse herself and get away before he can ask for her phone number.

29   I've seen women smile politely at a male's compliment and just continue walking as if that's all he had to say.

30   I've seen females lie and say they had a boyfriend. I've also seen them be more direct and just tell the male that he isn't her type.

31   This is the reality you have to face as a man and as a Mack. You're willingly placing yourself into a Game where she has an advantage.

32   I mention all of this not to scare you but to help you understand how important the information I'm about to share is.

33   The average attractive woman has plenty of practice rejecting males/men. But the average man doesn't have enough practice getting past her rejections and still pushing his agenda.

34   Both the good and the bad sit at the same table at all times. In order to get the good you have to also accept the bad and be confident enough to still approach women regardless.

35   Don't be scared about being rejected. A real man or a Mack doesn't fear a possibility of the unknown. Sometimes it doesn't matter how confident, wealthy or good looking you are. You'll be rejected more often than you'll be accepted.

36   Many times being rejected has nothing to do with you personally. A woman is just playing out the files she has in her mind out of sheer habit.

37   Like I mentioned earlier, she does it so often that she doesn't even really think about it. These files of rejection become the normal response to men or males that don't make it through her filters (if she has them).

38   Women, your prey, take pride in outsmarting, rejecting and trying to control males (a woman shouldn't be able to control a man).

39   Just listen to any female music artist sing about a bad relationship. Watch sitcoms where men are weak, the butt of jokes and are manipulated by the women on the show.

40   Some of this behavior stems from them naturally wanting to test a male to see if he's worthy of her submission. Like a child, she needs to be shown where her boundaries are.

41   If we look at this as percentages, for every 20 women a Mack with average Game approaches, he may only get one phone number.

42   A Mack with average Game will get around five phone numbers for every 100 women he approaches; an average success rate of about 5%.

43   Sometimes he may get five phone numbers in the first 20 women he approaches and no phone numbers for the next 100 women he approaches.

44   Sometimes a Mack with average Game will not get a single phone number for the first 100 women he approaches and will suddenly get six or seven phone numbers back-to-back. When everything averages out, he's looking at about a 5% success rate.

45   In the street Game of Pimping, what do you think a Pimp does most of his day? Other than managing his ho or hoes, he spends a large part of his day trying to catch a new ho.

46   And what do you think the success rate is for a man whose life literally revolves around catching women? It will never be close to even 50%. That's an unrealistic fantasy.

47   The percentages increase or decrease depending on the environment you're in and the culture of the women. But getting one phone number for every 20 women you approach is a realistic number to start with.

48   If you find this discouraging then there is some work you have to do with your Inner Game. This reality shouldn't bother you one bit. Because in truth, if you had the time, you could easily approach 100 women in a week.

49 And out of five phone numbers you would probably end up on about two or three "dates". Out of those two or three dates only one of those women would be worth seeing if she's qualified enough for your Program.

50 Let me mention this here because it's an odd fact: It's easier to find a woman to have sex with than it is to find a woman qualified (or willing to campaign) for a Mack's Program.

51 If you had five phone numbers and went on three dates, you could probably sleep with two of those women with a tight Game. But a Mack isn't looking for just sex; he demands more from a woman.

52 A Mack with above-average Game can increase his average percentage of getting a phone number past 30%.

53 Now with all that said, getting a phone number is **not** a measuring rod of success. Getting a qualified woman into your Program is. Achieving a means of further contact with a woman is only the beginning.

54 But you must learn to crawl before you walk and learn to walk before you run. Let's focus on crawling by developing "designed responses" for yourself. These will help you face your skilled opponent and level the playing field. She'll be skilled at rejecting and you'll be skilled at moving around her rejections.

55 This is necessary because it will force a woman to really *hear* you and pay attention, breaking up whatever files her mind is pulling to reject you. Once her pattern is broken, she'll be dis-armed and therefore nearly defenseless.

Designing Planned Responses

56   There is no right way to develop planned responses. They should be based on you as a man and as a Mack and directly reflect your personality. You are who you are at all times.

57   To give you an idea of what they are and how they work let's look at the following scenario.

58   Rich, our new Mack, is going through his daily weekend routine. He's at the grocery store buying food and other items for his apartment. He has just paid for his items and is headed toward his car with a cart filled with a few bags.

59   He sees an attractive woman walking near him and in true Mack fashion, he approaches right then and there. Why? Because he wants to and that's the only reason a Mack needs. A Mack puts himself first.

60   Rich takes a deep breath and repeats his COMMAND WORD to himself, 'Manhood!' to settle his nerves and force his mind to pull the files he's created for approaching women:

Rich: Excuse me Lady. Excuse me *(the woman stops and looks at him)*. **I know you're probably busy but I just had to stop you because you caught my attention. You are gorgeous. My name is Rich and what's your name?**

Woman: Oh, thank you. I'm Dee.

Rich: Nice to meet you Dee. What's Dee short for? (Rich could have asked what she was doing but it's already obvious she's going into the grocery store)

Dee: It's short for Deborah.

Rich: *(walks in closer, holds out his hand and gives Dee's hand a very gentle shake)* Well then Deborah I'm about to get your number so we can talk later.

Dee: Um, no.

Rich: Yep. That's what's about to happen *(set-up for a designed response Rich has planned)*.

Dee: *(rolls her eyes)* I'm not interested.

Rich: *(Rich's designed response)* But that's the thing Dee, I'm going to probably be the most interesting (key-word) person you've met in a long time.

Dee: Really?

Rich: *(another designed response)* Without a doubt. You see, life is a grand adventure. So many people just go through life day-by-day doing the same boring routine. People are so scared to get out of their comfort zone and try new things. Sometimes living life should be like spinning a roulette wheel; taking a few chances every now and then *(Rich gives a piece of his life philosophy)*. Be bold and adventurous. Let's exchange numbers.

(Rich pulls out his cell phone)

Dee: What? I don't know even you.

Rich: That's what I'm saying. Let's get to know (key-word) each other. Are you an adventurous person *(close-ended question to set-up for another designed response)*?

Dee: Sometimes. I guess.

Rich: *(gives a designed response)* Well let that sometime (key-word) be this time. It'll be worth it. Trust me.

Dee: I'm dating someone right now though.

Rich: That's cool. I didn't plan on letting him watch anyway *(a playful sexual observation)*.

Dee: *(smirks)* Really? You can't say that!

Rich: I can and I did. What do you do for fun Dee *(open-ended question)*?

Dee: I like being outdoors. I run and hike sometimes.

(Dee is giving information about herself – this means she is getting more comfortable)

Rich: Well I don't run (key-word) or hike (key-word) but I do think people should be more active. Being healthy is important. Maybe we could go jog together sometimes?

Dee: I doubt you could keep up.

Rich: I wouldn't keep up (key-words) on purpose just so I can watch you running in front of me *(playful sexual observation)*.

Dee: *(laughs)* That is so not what I meant.

Rich: So what's your next move going to be (open-ended question)?

Dee: I don't know what you mean. What move? My move with you?

Rich: Are you going to be adventurous and make a new friend? Or are you going to stay in your comfort zone?

Dee: Well, like I said. I'm kind of in a relationship.

Rich: I don't mind. But a relationship (key-word) is only based on how two people relate to each other. *(follow up with a designed response)* Take a chance, spin the wheel and be more adventurous. Life's boring without it. So, are you giving me your number or are we exchanging numbers *(illusion of choice)*?

(Rich hands her his phone)

61   As you can see in this example Rich had some clever responses to obvious rejections that Dee had in mind. But because he was prepared, he dis-armed her.

62   Rich remained the hunter and continued to stalk his prey until he was able to trap her. Let's look behind-the-scenes and see how you can develop something like this for yourself.

63   There is no such thing as a magical opening-line. The best line is simply to introduce yourself and tell the woman directly *why* you're approaching her.

64   From the very beginning you want a woman to respond to your lead. When you ask her name, she gives you her name. When you hold out your hand to shake it, she shakes it. When you ask her a question, you want her to answer it.

65   If a woman is so stuck-up or in a bad mood and not doing any of these things, accept the loss, tell her to have a good day and go hunt elsewhere. Don't waste your time or energy.

66   A woman must be **receptive** – she needs to be in her natural mode of receptivity. This allows you to **transmit** as a man. None of this works if the woman isn't receptive. She may be in her habitual rejection mode, but if you can get her to stop, shake your hand and respond to your questions, that's all you need to keep moving forward.

67   Your initial approach is designed to do one of two things. You want her phone number, or you give her yours. Or you want to take her somewhere right then and right there – a casual "social outing" like going to get coffee or a sitting somewhere private to talk more in depth.

68   That's it. That's all you're trying to do. The actually verbal Macking (telling her about yourself and seeing if she's qualified for your Program) comes later.

69   Now you should know that if you say something like, "What's about to happen is that you're going to give me your phone number," there are only a few possible responses a woman can say:

(1) No I'm not.
(2) Fuck-off! (or something along this line)
(3) I don't know you.
(4) Why should I give you my number?

70   The initial question is only a set-up. It's used to keep the conversation moving forward. You want her to respond and you'll have your own response already planned based off hers.

71   Let's look at what you could have designed to counter each of the four responses mentioned above:

(1) No I'm not. – You could respond with, "Yep, that's what's about to happen."

(2) Fuck-off! – You could respond, "Very eloquent for a lady. Is fuck-off (key-word) your best rejection line?"

(3) I don't know you. – You could respond, "Well I'm trying to get to know (key-word) you. How is that going to happen if we don't converse?"

(4) Why should I give you my number? – You could respond, "Because I'm probably the most interesting person you're going to meet in a long time."

72   You would think all this through before hand and practice it. Yes, write these down, get yourself in front of a mirror and practice them.

73   By doing this, you're putting new files into your file cabinet (file server) that will allow you to have responses already set-up for many situations.

74   Remember, your designed responses should reflect your personality. These examples are only in place to stimulate your creativity in this important area. There's no reason to be fake. Be bold but also authentic.

75   Let's look at another example. Let's say you say something like this: "Excuse me. I see you're busy but I want to flirt with you for a few minutes."

76   You would sit and think of what a woman could possibly say to something like this. Then design your responses. What you write down and practice could look like this:

(1) I really am busy. – You could respond with, "Like I said. I just need a few minutes then I'll let you get back being busy (key-word) when I'm done."

(2) I have a boyfriend. – You could respond, "I'm just flirting. I'm sure your boyfriend (key-word) won't mind just as long as you don't enjoy it."

(3) I don't flirt with strange men. – You could respond, "Well I flirt with strange (key-word) women. Especially with women as attractive as yourself."

(4) Is this what you do? Flirt with women all day? – You could respond, "Yeah. I flirt (key-word) with thousands. According to my last count you're number seven-thousand and forty-eight."

77   Be challenging. Always challenge her. Invite her rejections. Invite her drama. Don't run from them. Open the door and let them in your house.

78   Running is the behavior of weak males and that's what she's used to; she has plenty of practice in that area and takes pride in it. But she has little practice rejecting someone prepared for whatever she can dish out.

79   Can you prepare for all the possible responses a woman can give to what you say? Realistically, no you can't. But by going through this process you'll train your mind to come up with on-the-fly responses as you gain more experience.

80   And that's what's required to excel in approaching women. Experience. There's no way around it and there's no short-cut. Be a man and face this reality.

81   Go in practiced and prepared. Just like a batter in baseball practices hitting the many pitches that can come his way. How effective would a batter be if he didn't practice and prepare?

82   How do you think you're going to have solid Game without practicing and preparing? You must give what's necessary to get what you want. This is Reciprocation (Principle number 3 of the 9 Principles).

83   I suggest you study the approach example with Rich I gave above. See how open-ended questions, playful observations and even his philosophy were woven in.

84   Most of this would be prepared and practiced. The Game was almost over before it even begun. From the first line to the last,

Rich kept moving forward to what he wanted; an exchange of phone numbers.

85   Over time, Rich would have pages and pages of designed responses as he became more experienced. He would tighten his Game up to a point that there would be very few things he wouldn't be prepared for.

86   With all that practice and taking this serious, even the occasional odd curve-ball wouldn't throw off his swing. His mind would pull files and he would formulate a suitable response.

87   When you make a mistake, acknowledge it and make a mental note of it. Later when you're at home and have time, use the technique I gave to you for "installing mental files" in Book 2 – Chapter Three.

88   Use this technique. Play-out the scene in your mind and then re-play it. Imagine you saying and doing the right things and getting the results you want.

89   Don't let a mistake fester and take root. Don't beat yourself up over it or dwell on it. Give your mind a better file to work with. This will help to keep your confidence up for future approaches.

90   Approaching women is an art. Not a science. There are no hard and fast rules. Remember, conversation itself is chaotic. And within that chaos lays *potential energy* that must be directed and controlled.

91   Its through conversation that you'll establish attraction. Since women are creatures of sound, the best way to enter her mind is by way of your words.

92   To do this effectively however, means that you should know what attraction is and how it develops.

CHAPTER THREE

Attraction – The "Secret" Within

1   Stripping all the nice and fluffy terminology away, initial attraction is a human biological function predicated on nothing but sex and procreation.

2   A male sees an attractive female and being the creature of sight that he is; he's mesmerized by her curves. The shape of her face, breasts, hips, thighs and buttocks.

3   His first instinct is to see her naked and he imagines what it's like to feel on those curves and to have sex with her. Biologically he sees her as fit to bear his children.

4   On the opposite side of the coin; a female sees an attractive male and she also becomes mesmerized. Not by his curves, but by his overall look. The shape of his face, shoulder to hip ratio (broad shoulders), height and muscles (if he has them).

5   Her first instinct is not necessarily to see him naked, but a flash of what it would be like to have sex with him does go through her mind on occasion. Biologically she sees him fit to protect her and her children.

6   Curves, smooth skin and "softness" (youthful appearance) is both *physically* and *sexually* attractive to males.

7   For the average male, his mind doesn't travel too far out of the zone of sexual gratification. In fact, most males will bend over backwards to have sex with a woman. Then eventually have sex with her, and lose interest shortly after. The thrill is gone, as they say.

8 While physical stature and the appearance of vigor (strength and health) are *physically* attractive to females, they're not necessarily *sexually* attractive. With a female, what follows after the initial biological physical attraction? Sexual attraction in women develops from a male's behavior.

9 It doesn't matter her age, race or culture; a male's behavior is constantly scrutinized. What he *says* must match what he *thinks* and both of these must match his *actions*.

10 For a female, even the most physically attractive man can turn her off based on his behavior. She still may sleep with him based on her physical attraction but will lose interest shortly after if she doesn't like his overall behavior.

11 Males can be content with the surface – physical attraction and sex; while a woman generally looks beneath the surface. A Mack also looks beneath the surface. But his motivations are very different.

12 A Mack would rather deal with a 5 (an all-around average looking woman) that is into him and his Program, than deal with a 9 (extremely beautiful woman) that acts like a spoiled bitch.

13 In fact, a true Mack will elevate a woman. He'll take a 5 and make her into a 7 or 8 in appearance and behavior. He will empower her. This mentality of "building-up" excels him in the sphere of attraction. A woman will see Value for herself.

14 A male is often so insecure that he tries to dis-empower a woman so that he feels he has leverage (advantages) in the relationship. Similarly, an insecure woman will try to control and tear down her male so that she feels she has leverage on him.

15 Many more refined women are the opposite – they'll try to build a male up; help him dress better and try to boost his confidence.

16   The problem with this however is the simple truth: **A woman can be many things, but she can't be a man**. A woman cannot define a man, but she'll know when she comes across one.

17   Because of this, it's very important to never take dating advice from women. It doesn't matter if it's your mother or your sister. They can only give what they have; and that's usually based on what's socially acceptable.

18   Never allow a woman to define what being a man is. She honestly doesn't know. She just has pre-conceived notions based on her upbringing and social programming.

19   Relationship advice from women usually leads to you becoming the "nice-guy". Often times, this is the exact opposite of the type of men that she's attracted to.

20   What's the "secret" behind attraction? Look the word up in a dictionary. What you'll see is that attraction is only based off of what another person can do for *you*.

21   We are attracted to things that thrill us; entice us; may be able to give us pleasure; and even offer us entertainment.

22   Attraction is a selfish thing – it's completely internal. It starts with the physical (biological), becomes mental and then emotional. This is why a Mack enters a woman's mind *first*! He creates attraction instead of relying on external factors that may or may not play out to his benefit.

23   How is attraction created? By placing who he is as Value on the table. The following **man** behaviors (plus those listed in Book 1, Chapter Three) are extremely important for developing attraction in women:

(1) He must be consistent in what he says, how he thinks and how he acts.

(2) He must show resourcefulness – be able to handle difficult situations.

(3) He must be assertive – be confident with aggressive self-assurance.

(4) He must be fearless but not foolish

(5) He should take care of his body, mind and material possessions (home, car, etc.)

(6) He should have a Program – a desire and plan to Advance in life.

24   As a Mack, he should also keep his penis off the table until a woman submits to his Program. To re-emphasize, a Mack *does not* have sex of any kind with a woman who is not kicking into his Program or campaigning for it.

25   He cuts off the physical and forces a woman to deal with him mentally, first. And this works because women (generally speaking) are very similar in their dating approach.

26   If a woman is honestly attracted to a male she'll place on the table what she feels is the best thing she has to offer. It will either be (1) her mind, or (2) her body.

27   A Mack will deal with a woman's mind, first. Even if she's offering her body up front.

28   This goes against the grain. Especially in the new world of modern seduction techniques and instruction; where a male is taught to sleep with women as fast as possible.

29   A Mack must develop extreme sexual self-control. This is not easy because it requires a male to go against his natural sexual animal instincts.

30   The pay-off of this though is worth it. A woman will develop an extreme trust in you and give you respect. Why? Because you're unlike most of the males she has come across in her life.

31 When sex is removed as Value on the table, this dis-arms the average woman because she's used to dealing with (and rejecting) males that think that way.

32 This is intriguing to most women and can also be a turn on. Being dis-armed in this way leaves an open door of mystery that she has seldom walked through. It's new, different, challenging and adventurous. It plays directly on 1 of her 5 basic needs; the need of SECURITY.

33 A Mack that behaves in this capacity (and is consistent in this behavior), makes a woman feel more secure when dealing with him. Dating, having conversations and "hanging-out" are extremely comfortable; and stable.

34 **A Word Of Caution Here**: This does not mean that you don't flirt, make the occasional sexual comment or playful observation. There should be no confusion. You absolutely should let the woman know you're sexually attracted to her. Again, it's not about being fake.

35 What you're doing is just not placing sex as Value on the table. Sex comes later, when *you* feel she has earned it. When you know that she's about your Program and what you have to offer.

36 Feel free to flirt and make all the sexual comments you want. Compliment her breasts, play in her hair, tell her how much the skirt she's wearing is making you think naughty things, even squeeze her ass on occasion (when that level of comfort is reached). But sex is off the table until she submits to your Program in some form or fashion.

37 This removes some sexual pressure from her. But another pressure is applied in its place. She'll wonder if she's worthy enough to get more of your attention.

38   Look at things from her Perspective. She meets a great guy; he's confident, takes care of himself, has a direction for his life and has great conversation.

39   He also flirts, teases and does the occasional touching so he's probably attracted, but he hasn't made a move to have sex. So, what gives?

40   Her mind will begin to ramble – Is he maybe not *really* that sexually attracted? Does he have another agenda? Is he a virgin? Am I doing something to turn him off? Is he gay? Does he have other women? Is he not confident with his sexual prowess? Or maybe he's too confident – will I be enough to satisfy him?

41   Don't take all these literally. The bottom line is the woman will be totally dis-armed, confused, but yet intrigued at the same time.

42   This is attractive. You may be wondering why? Because attraction is a selfish thing. She wants to know if she's woman enough for you and if she can conquer you. This is where the Mack Game truly begins.

43   Her mind has been captured and now it's time to go for her heart. Remember the Mack's order of mind, heart, body and soul.

44   Baby steps first though. Let's just deal with building basic attraction for now.

45   You must realize that no matter how expensive your clothes, the jewelry you wear, the car you drive or the house you live in, these are only tools.

46   A Mack uses these things (like he uses most things) to his benefit. These physical accoutrements aren't necessary to have a woman. But they do get her attention. And that's all these tools are for.

47   A Mack knows that if he's looking good and smelling good this helps break down a woman's guard. Leaving her a little more open to being approached. But these nice expensive things don't speak – they don't talk – only the Mack does.

48   This is why you could have little money, dress within your means (as long as your clothing looks crisp – newish), have no car, no home of your own and still find attractive women who will submit to your Program.

49   This may sound unbelievable to some of you reading this, but I speak from personal experience. I know it's possible because I've personally done it many, many times. And I know many other men who have done it.

50   At one time I lived in a hotel efficiency – a hotel room you pay by the week to live in. I was street Hustling and struggling financially.

51   I had little money and no car. But guess what? Even with all those disadvantages, I still had no shortage of attractive women to sleep with (I wasn't even fully Macking at this time).

52   How did I accomplish this? By building attraction through sheer conversation and being a man with Standards and Principles.

53   As my Hustle Game developed and I began to make real money, I developed a Program for myself and started Macking. Still to this day, I'm friends with a few of the women I was with back then.

54   Some of them still campaign for me now that I'm an author. Mind, heart, body and soul. How strong do you want *your* Game to be?

55   Mental Attraction is built through deep, meaningful conversation. Let me say that again with more detail. **After**

biological attraction, *mental* attraction is built through deep, above average conversation.

56   This depth of conversation creates a *mental* connection. The woman begins to reason she may find some forms of pleasure in being with you. It's becomes about her.

57   If you can effectively enter a woman's mind, you can make your way into her heart. She'll go from *thinking* into actually *feeling* that what you can PROVIDE what she wants. She'll care about you and have affection towards you.

58   She will be comfortable telling you her problems and life stories. She'll want to spend more time with you. She'll ask you for hugs, want to introduce you to her friends and get uncomfortable when you mention other women. A powerful Mack can go from a woman's mind into her heart in a single "date".

59   You must become socially aware and powerful. This doesn't mean you have a lot of friends. Honestly a Mack doesn't have many friends; kings only hang with other kings.

60   What it does mean is that you're never hesitant to speak and interact with anyone; male, female or child regardless of their social status.

61   You live in your own little world where you're pleased with yourself. You could be completely alone and still be just as happy and content as the average person. You don't seek company but you don't shy away from it either.

62   Some women are socially awkward. Like children, they're shy at meeting new people and they're slow to reveal too much of themselves.

63   A Mack however, isn't. He is confident and at peace with being himself at all times. Remember, as a man your behavior must be polarized in direct opposition to a woman's.

64   Where she's shy, you're outgoing. Where she shuns Responsibility, you take it on. When she hesitates to make a firm decision, you have enough belief in yourself to make a firm choice and let the chips fall where they may.

65   Your conversation must be developed to a high degree. The best way to do this is to simply practice.

66   If you're currently shy around women, come up with a way to introduce yourself and give a compliment. Then go out there and only do that.

67   It could be as simple as this: "Excuse me. I stopped you because I just wanted to tell you that you have beautiful eyes. You have a wonderful day." And then just walk away.

68   When you get comfortable with that, then start introducing yourself and asking for their name. Give them a compliment then ask them what they're doing or where they're going. If they have a unique accent, you could even ask where they're from.

69   Design some responses to their possible answers, and then design some closing lines where you bid them a nice day. Then you go on your way.

70   Once you get comfortable with that, try starting and holding conversations with new women. Not to get their number, although don't stop yourself if the conversation goes well. You just want to get a feel of the back-and-forth "dance" – bringing conversational order from chaos.

71   Implement some of the conversational tools from the previous chapter, and prepare to bypass their rejections by designing responses.

72   Then keep going and going and going. Be the scientist – experiment. Try different things, practice saying lines with various

tonalities. Learn to work in playful observations and illusions of choice.

73   Get yourself to the point where you're completely comfortable having a regular conversation with a woman. Where you can talk to her like a male friend that you've known for years. You do want to add in a little flirting of course.

74   Learn to work in your stories and your Perspectives on yourself and life (your Standards, Principles and philosophy).

75   Become the man she's comfortable talking to and who she comes to for advice. Keep a limit on giving advice though – you're not a psychologist (at least to women not kicking into your Program), a Mack must have boundaries.

76   Be encouraging to her and uplifting. Place yourself in the position of a good companion. And when you can achieve this level of communication expertise, you'll have all the necessary experience you need to transition into real Macking.

77   All of the above practice is just to "flesh-out" your Mack style. You're not a Mack yet. At this stage you're just a good, respectable, friendly man. But you're well on your way.

78   Despite the modern "seduction doctrine", some males should learn to be friends with a few new women before they transition into Mackhood.

79   Some males need this practice. They need to perfect their style and learn how to be more social with women. All the while developing their confidence, Aura and working on their behaviors.

80   If you feel you don't need these practice steps then you can skip them. You should know yourself well enough to know what you need to develop and what you don't.

81   After you reach this point. It's time to bring out the Macking; to weave a spell with conversation to enter a woman's mind and make your way into her heart.

Conversational Macking – Getting From Mind to Heart

82   A Mack's conversation is aggressive. Not in a pushy obnoxious way, but in a way where a Mack has an agenda and he's constantly finding a way to reach it.

83   When a Mack approaches a woman, he's only trying to get her to a certain level of comfort; just enough to get a phone number (or give her his business card). And the majority of his conversation is based around this agenda.

84   With the first phone conversation (or text conversation), his agenda is to get face-to-face with a woman. And his conversation is based around this agenda.

85   And when he finally gets face-to-face with a woman (first social outing – not an official date) he then unravels his pedigree. He reveals a lot about himself. He shares his Standards, Principles and philosophy.

86   He may also mention his Program; a very important area of his life. His agenda here is to get the woman very comfortable. And you know a woman is comfortable when she begins talking a lot about herself.

87   It's at this first "social outing" when a Mack determines if he enjoys the company and conversation of the woman enough to officially go on a first date.

88   But we're getting a little ahead of ourselves. Let's track-back to aggression in conversation.

89 Conversational control is always having a reason to speak. You should *always* be Playing. Always.

90 Almost everything you say and every story you tell serves a purpose. And that's to advance your current agenda. And your current agenda is what you choose. Although I gave some general examples above, you must become your own man and decide your agendas.

91 If you've practiced having regular "idle" conversations with women, to transition into having Mack conversations, you need to add in the element of having an agenda. Trust me when I say, often times when a woman talks to you she *has* an agenda.

92 Regardless of the agenda you choose, in the back of your mind you must never forget that you should be gently pushing toward deeper more meaningful conversations – you want to establish a strong mental connection.

93 Talking about the weather or her family or her job are fine at first. But you want to go deeper. You want to explore her who, what, when, where, whys and hows.

94 **Why** did she choose her job? **Why** did she move to the city? **Where** did she move from? **Why** did she dump her last boyfriend? **What** did she see in her last boyfriend? **What** does she *feel* about love? **Who** was her first love? **Where** was he from? **What** happened to that relationship? **Why** does she like the music she likes? **When** did she first hear her favorite band?

95 These may sound like interview questions and they are. You're trying to qualify a woman for your Program. You're seeing if she's the right fit for your company (kingdom).

96 You must divide these questions up between regular conversation and your own stories that relate to what she's saying. You don't want to ask questions back-to-back-to-back.

97   A constant stream of nothing but questions makes the average woman uncomfortable because it applies a lot of pressure. That's not what we want (usually). We want a woman to feel comfortable answering questions and revealing herself.

98   So it's your Responsibility to take the lead and start by revealing yourself. Tell her the story of your first love. Talk to her about your job and what you hate about it. Tell her about your Program and what your current goal in life is.

99   Explain to her some of your Standards and why they're so important to you. Tell her where these Standards came from.

100   Relay to her what you did on your last vacation and how you felt doing and seeing new things. Paint the picture so her mind will literally pull up images.

101   I hope you get the idea. Open up first and as the woman gets more comfortable, she'll open up.

102   All of this gets you into her mind and builds mental attraction. It's a natural side-effect of getting to know someone on a deeper and intimate level. It's nothing that needs to be forced.

103   If you can keep her engaged, opening up, laughing at your jokes, fascinated by your stories and reinforcing the fact that you find her attractive, she'll mentally begin to think of you differently.

104   You'll no longer be, "just another male". You'll turn into someone who she wants to get to know better. She'll be intrigued and her child-like curiosity will be piqued.

105   An important note here. You often (not always) want to ask a woman how she *feels* about something instead of asking her how she *thinks*. Explaining how you feel requires more introspection (contemplation). It forces a woman to give a more honest explanation.

106   When a woman can openly explain how she feels about something (especially experiences that have deeply affected her), and she's not judged for it, this will lead to deeper more meaningful conversations.

107   Don't believe me? Go somewhere in public where you can over-hear women having a conversation. They'll explain how they feel about things quite often.

108   It's no secret that the way a woman talks to another woman is not the same way she talks to a male (or man). Just like most males never speak to women like they do their "boys".

109   Never fear running out of conversation. You should know *you* very well, and I've taught you that a woman's favorite subject is herself. All you have to do is make a "marriage" of these two.

110   You share, and then ask her something so she shares. You relate to something she just shared and ask her something else so she shares more.

111   Ask for details (who, what, when, where, why and how) and push in deeper. Add in flirting and the occasional light touch and get her so comfortable that you don't even have to ask too many questions.

112   She'll start to take over the conversation (unless she has extremely low self-esteem). Just make sure you're actually listening! You want to learn her.

113   When you perfect this, you'll be one of the most charming (if not the most charming) man she has ever met. And all you're doing is building mental attraction through conversation and finding a way into her heart.

114   When you *really* listen she'll reveal to you exactly *how* you can get into her heart. That's right! Read that first sentence again.

115   A woman who is extremely comfortable with you will tell you *exactly* how to seduce her! How to get to her heart (emotional attraction) and from there to her body (sexual attraction).

116   Abracadabra! It's like magic, isn't it? This used to be one of a Mack's "secrets". No guessing, no wondering, no hoping or wishing. Just opening her up, sharing with her, asking the right kind of questions and *really* listening.

116   She will tell you (not necessarily directly), what she likes, what she thinks is romantic, what behavior she doesn't like in males, what she likes to do or not do in bed, how she treats a man she really cares about, what her goals are, what she think about her family and friends, etc.

117   So as she's revealing herself, take mental notes. If you can provide some of what she likes, make plans to do it. If, and I stress *if*, you feel she's qualified enough to be in your life and hold a place in your Program; and *if* you feel they're reasonable.

118   Never place yourself in a position to be her personal ass-kisser. That's not Playing her, that's Playing yourself down to please her. If her "requirements" don't resonate with you, then "friend-zone" her (or cut her off completely) and hunt elsewhere.

119   At this point it starts becoming a matter of training a woman as to what *you* like and your "requirements", which we'll cover how to do later.

120   Once you have the biological attraction checked off the list and mental attraction checked off the list, then it's time to develop emotional attraction by going into her heart and creating it.

Biological Attraction + Mental Attraction + Emotional Attraction =
Sexual Attraction

121   Mind, heart and body (a woman must offer you her soul). To be honest, physical attraction isn't that important but it can help. Your overall behavior is far more important though.

122   *Biological attraction* gets her attention and opens her up to conversation. Deep and meaningful conversation produces *mental attraction*. Through conversation and carful listening you'll learn how to produce an *emotional attraction*. And she'll naturally become *sexually attracted* –ready to give you her body.

123   Once you take her body she'll be positioned to offer you her soul – the deepest level of respect, devotion and love she's capable of.

124   All of this is backed by what you represent as a man through your behavior. Standing firm on your Standards, Principles, philosophy, Program, confidence, plus all the Game you're learning from this book.

125   The Mack's way is meticulous but powerful. This is how you hold a woman for the long-term. In return you fulfill her 5 plus 1 basic needs and become her social conditioned fantasy of what a man is "supposed" to be – at least from her Perspective.

126   I have laid out the basics you need to approach women and pique their interest. I have also explained that the first approach is only to get a phone number.

127   And with that number you want to arrange to get her face-to-face for a social outing. But when you get to that point, what do you do? And how do you do it?

128   In our next book we'll be covering social outings, what to do on the first date and even ways to train a woman how to treat you.

BOOK 5 –
QUALIFYING,
DATING & TRAINING

CHAPTER ONE

The Mack's First Agenda – Qualifying the Woman

1   A Mack's Perspective (Principle Number 4 of the 9 Principles) is quite different than what is considered socially acceptable.

2   While most people advocate taking your time and really getting to know someone, they usually mean doing this with one person at a time.

3   A Mack takes his time too. Just not with one woman at a time.

4   Attractive women usually have many men that serve different roles in their life. She has the male friend that all she does is talk to. Then she may have another that she occasionally goes out with.

5   Some women have at least one person they're having sex with. And some women may also keep a male who she can run to for money and to help her with other problems.

6   When she finds a serious boyfriend, depending on the quality of woman she is, she'll limit interactions or completely cut off contact with these males and focus on her man. Some women don't however – it is what it is, learn to accept this possible reality. Both the good and the bad sit at the same table at all times.

7   The average male on the other hand usually has female friends and maybe one woman he has sex with. For weaker males, he may only have female friends; or none at all.

8   These female friends are usually women he's sexually attracted to. But due to his lack of Game, he got "friend-zoned" by them and then just settled for any type of relationship he could get.

9   This weak male hopes that one day this female friend will "see the light". That he really is a great guy and start dating him, give him sex and eventually end up in a relationship.

10   This fantasy torments weaker males and the chances of something like that actually happening are so immeasurably small that he mind as well just start over; find a new woman and try again. But he doesn't because he's intimidated by women.

11   As you practice and gain experience on your journey to Mackhood, you may find yourself getting "friend-zoned" as well. But if you can detach yourself from the fantasy that one day she'll magically change her mind (because she usually won't), then you can use these female friends to your advantage.

12   Let me give you some important Game right now. Something that once again flies in the face of modern so-called "dating game". This is something real Macks and Pimps have always known.

13   One of the best ways to keep your woman in check is to have *other* women around you.

14   You don't have to be having sex with these other women. Just the fact that you still communicate and occasional go out with them is enough to keep a woman attracted to you, in check.

15   She'll be more willing to cater towards you and be more patient with your requirements because she sees your Value and doesn't want another woman to see it and possibly take you from her.

16   A woman in check is a woman who allows her man to place certain levels of restraint on her. Not her nature, but on her behavior. A women will only allow a man to check her if she accepts his Value and respects him as a real man.

17   Keeping other women around affects a woman on a psychological level. She'll check herself because she doesn't want to leave any "gaps" where another woman can weasel her way in.

18   Be careful to *never* throw your females friends in your woman's face! This will spike her jealousy and she may retaliate and act out in a childish way; in a way that will make problems that you didn't need to create to begin with.

19   Just the mere fact that these women are around "somewhere" and that a woman knows that, is enough. She doesn't need to know what they look like, their names or what you and these other women talk about (although the woman will ask). Only explain these things to *your* woman – not to any female you're casually dating.

20   So even when you "fail" with your Macking and end up in the friend-zone, you can still use that situation to your advantage when you finally do find a woman who might be qualified.

21   Again I stress, this only works if you can honestly accept that this female friend is only going to be your friend. You must remove *all* desire to form a romantic relationship and to have sex with her.

22   Be real with yourself; be brutally honest. If you can't do this, it's best to cut that female friend off because you'll set yourself up to violate your Macking due to the way you think about her.

23   As your Game tightens you'll actually end up "friend-zoning" women who don't live up to your standards or who aren't qualified for your Program.

24   You still may enjoy the company and conversation of these women, but that's all. Keeping these woman around are even more effective in keeping a new female in check because these friends may be genuinely attracted to you.

25 Keep it real with these women and yourself; you are only ever going to be friends. If they can't accept that, cut them off. They will cause problems and may undermine your efforts when you find a qualified woman.

26 Be a man and a Mack and take Responsibility. Set the terms. Then leave the decision up to them.

27 If the situation ever arises where you must choose between spending time with (or helping) a female friend over doing something with (or for) your woman, your woman *always* comes first. Period! She's earned a place in your Program, give her that respect. Violate this at your own risk.

28 A Mack would never even consider doing something for a woman who's *not* doing for him (female friend) over doing something for a woman who *is* doing for him (female in his Program). I hope that's clear. A Mack must always have integrity.

The "Menu Mentality"

29 You should date many women. Most males usually settle for the first woman that accepts him. Other males might date two women around the same time and make the choice to settle on one.

30 What I suggest you do (especially if you're age 25 or younger) is date many women to discover what traits you really enjoy in females.

31 Settling for just the first (or second) woman to come along is what I call the "Menu Mentality". Let me explain because this behavioral thinking is quite common.

32 Imagine you go to a new restaurant for the first time. You look over the menu and choose something that sounds interesting. You get your meal, eat it and find it delicious. And what happens

now? The next time you go to that restaurant, 9 times out of 10 you'll look over the menu but still order the same dish you had the first time.

33   And you can continue to return to that restaurant another three or four times that year and still order the same exact dish (or a slight variation of it).

34   The restaurant has an entire menu of food to try but you never try them. How do you know that there might be another dish on the menu that you like even more? You'll never find out because you never consider other alternatives.

35   This thinking is the Menu Mentality - settling on the first (or second) thing you try and never exploring other options.

36   Consider for a moment how limiting this mentality is. Just like the restaurant menu, there's a whole world full of women to choose from. Why settle on the first woman you think you like, when there may be another woman out there better suited for you?

37   By doing a lot of dating you'll begin to see what qualities you really Value in a woman. And you'll also uncover what qualities you could live without.

38   There is no other way to learn this other than through experience.

The Social Outing

39   After a Mack gets a woman's phone number his agenda is usually to meet with her face-to-face. This is not a date. Just a social outing.

40   A Mack prefers to do his Macking face-to-face as much as possible. As you develop your Macking, you'll be extremely effective over any medium – phone, text, email, video-calls, etc.

41   Crawl before you walk. Get face-to-face with a woman as soon as possible. Keep phone and/or text conversations short and use them only to hold a woman's interest enough for her to agree to a social outing.

42   So what is a social outing? It's going to a public place where you can take a woman, spend very little money and have enough privacy to talk. It takes place during the day – this makes a woman feel more comfortable when being alone with a strange man.

43   This can be at a coffee shop; an ice cream shop; a park; walking downtown; a free art exhibit; a walk on the beach; window shopping; visiting a free or low cost historical attraction; having a picnic; get creative or just scourer the internet for more ideas.

44   Avoid places where there is too much noise and you can't hold a conversation. These would be places like free concerts, clubs, bars, the movies, etc.

45   The whole agenda for the social outing is to see if you and the woman are compatible. You also want to make her more comfortable with you during this time. This feeling of ease will help her "open up". As she does open up you'll discover how to get into her heart (if she proves to be worth more time).

46   While I would recommend not stretching this outing out for the entire day and eventually making it a date, if the conversation is great and the mood is right don't limit yourself and advance to the date stage.

47   A social outing should only last for two to three hours. Let her know this upfront. Tell her you want to meet her in person, in

a public place during the day and just talk and get to know each other better.

48   Reiterate that this isn't a date; you're just hanging out together. You'll be enjoying each other's company and seeing if you have a connection. And this isn't a lie; this is what you'll actually be doing.

49   The word, *date* implies many things to a woman – like getting dressed up, playing the "I'm a good catch" role or the "impress me" role. A date also implies that a man should spend money and it can even imply that the night should end with sex. As a Mack, sex isn't even on the menu at this point.

50   Make things easy for yourself and her and just "hang-out", talk and enjoy each other's company.

51   If you find that you don't get along too well, or that she's boring, or has a bitchy attitude, it's really not much of a loss. You didn't spend much money (if any) and the outing was only supposed to last a couple of hours anyway. Accept the situation and continue hunting elsewhere.

52   I suggest meeting the woman at the location. But if you need to pick her up, make sure your car is clean inside and out. Keep the music low – let yourself be the center of attention – not the music. Follow your agenda and engage her in conversation.

53   What you're doing at this stage, like I previously explained, is seeing if you're compatible. And to do that successfully you have to make her comfortable enough to talk about herself.

54   You encourage this by talking a lot about what you know best; you and what you're about – your Standards, Principles, philosophy, Program and your life stories.

55   Make sure your hair and facial hair are trimmed nicely. Also make sure your clothes and jewelry are clean, neat, look new and

cared for. Don't overdo the cologne and make sure your breath smells fresh. Also keep the physical touching to a minimum during a social outing.

56   It's OK to gently grab her hand or place your hand just above her elbow to guide her. Avoid trying to guide a woman by touching her lower waist area. Women can be insecure about this part of their body; especially if they had children – they may have "love-handles" there.

57   Make no mistake, you do want to touch her; you do want to add flirts and playful observations into your conversation. But you don't want anything more aggressive than that at this stage.

58   The flirting and playful observations, as well as the occasional compliment, are to keep in the forefront of her mind that you're attracted to her and this get together isn't completely innocent.

59   If you judge that the woman is worth more time, during an actual date is where you'll be more physically aggressive. For now, keep it cool. You may even want to gently place your hand on her thigh (or shoulder) when making a point or flirtatious statement.

60   Keep eye contact as much as possible; especially when you're speaking. Make her engage you and transmit your confidence. Keep compliments to a minimum but, when you make them, make sure they're honest and sincere – think out-loud.

61   If you don't think she looks good in her outfit. Don't tell her she does. You could tease her about her choice of clothes, but do it in a playful way and with a smile.

62   If you don't think she looks good with a ton of make-up on her face. Don't tell her she does. Keep your compliments sincere. Women are creatures of sound. The love compliments, but they can also "hear" when they're insincere or forced.

63   Women give fake compliments to other woman quite often. And most women can pick that up immediately. Don't think for a moment that she won't be able to pick up on yours. Don't play yourself.

64   Be the gentleman. Be enthused, lead, showcase your confidence and monitor your behavior. This does take practice if this is fairly new to you.

65   Once you master this stage, you'll be able to build strong mental attraction during this outing. If you're Game is extremely tight, you could even begin making your way into her heart.

66   Don't put too much pressure on yourself. Just do the best you can do. You're going to make mistakes. You're going to say the wrong thing. You're going to see that everything is going well and then you let out some childish behavior and feel her pull-back.

67   All this is OK. Some of these things happen to even the most experienced Macks from time-to-time (well, maybe not the childish behavior).

68   Make a mental note of it, learn your lesson and get back on purpose. Don't dwell on a mistake and let it affect your mood. That's feminine behavior.

69   You can even admit when a mistake was made. For example: If you said something offensive and you see she's offended there's nothing wrong with admitting you went too far. You don't have to apologize, just be man enough to acknowledge it.

70   Later that night when you're at home and have time, use the technique I gave to you for "installing mental files" in Book 2 – Chapter Three.

71   Play out your mistake in your mind and then re-play it so that you imagine a smoother scene that's mistake-free. Don't let a mistake fester and take root. Don't beat yourself up over it. Give

your mind a better file to work with to help you out in future situations.

72   Be yourself. Don't be fake; don't present a false image. But also make sure you're being the *best* you possible. If the woman is even slightly attracted to you, she'll be doing something similar. The Game is on, so always be Playing.

73   With everything that you already need to be aware of and concentrate on, I need to give you two more. Fear not! These are easy things to keep in mind.

74   First thing to remember is, Value. Showcase your manhood. You want to present it so that you give her the choice to "buy" it. When Value is on the table, what seems impossible can become possible.

75   This doesn't mean kiss her ass. This doesn't mean you have to brag and boast. This doesn't mean you act "so cool" that you come off like an egotistical prick.

76   Let who you are speak about you just as much as your words. When you develop your Aura, this is something you won't even have to think about anymore.

77   The Second thing to keep in mind is that when entertaining a woman, which is a smaller piece of the social outing (the larger piece being to qualify the woman), it's a lot of work to change a woman's *mind* but it's less work to change a woman's *mood*.

78   Use your enthusiastic conversation, behavior and Aura to elevate her mood. Or to keep it elevated if she's already in a good mood. And do your best to end the social outing with her in a good mood. Always be the transmitter. Always lead. Enter with your mood elevated and she will be receptive to it.

79   Depending on the quality and maturity of the woman, this won't always be possible. But don't let her sour mood affect yours.

You're a Mack – *you* control how you think and feel, not her – not her attitude and not her behavior.

80 If the woman is in a bad mood and chooses to stay there, oh well – amuse and entertain yourself. Don't get stuck on how she's feeling and acting. Definitely don't waste too much energy trying to figure it out either.

81 If it get's ridiculously bad end the social outing like a gentleman. Tell her you do not like her attitude; wish her a good day and leave.

82 If you picked her up, give her taxi money to get home. You're paying her to get out of your life. This is a great investment because you're saving yourself a lot of headaches later. A Mack is always the gentleman.

83 Extremes like that are very rare but they aren't outside the realm of possibility. Never play yourself down to please (or impress) a woman – especially one you barely even know!

84 Toward the end of the two to three hour social outing, you have a decision to make. You need to honestly ask yourself if you would like to talk to and see this woman again.

85 If you don't want to see the woman again, then end the social outing and don't lie. Don't say, "You'll call her later," or, "You hope to see her again," just thank her for hanging out with you.

86 If she asks if you're going to call, be honest. No need to be rude. Just tell her the truth. Something like, "No. I have to be honest. I don't really feel a connection between us."

87 This is going to sting when she hears that, but most women will understand because they've had to say this to another male at some point during their dating life. They'll get over it and when they do, they'll respect your honesty. They may even text you days

or weeks later. If that happens realize the truth, she got over the rejection and has gained respect for you.

88   If you do decide you want to see the woman again, tell her so. And be honest with *why* you want to see her again. Are you curious to learn more about her? Did she impress you with her conversation? Did you really have fun and enjoy her company? Think out-loud. Tell her. And then end it with giving her the option if she wants to see you again.

89   If she doesn't, then so be it. Accept the loss, thank her for her time, wish her a great life and then exit gracefully.

90   If she verbally agrees that she wants to see you again, then schedule the next stage of the qualification process right then and there – an actual real date.

91   Agree on a day and time. Ideally you want this date to be late evening – like 6pm or 7pm (I suggest no later than 9pm to make the idea comfortable to her). This gives her time to do what she needs to do early in the day and still get ready for you.

92   In the next chapter we'll cover what to do on the first official date, and also what your agenda is there.

93   Last thing. Sometimes you'll find that you genuinely enjoy a woman's company but you really don't feel she's right for you and your Program. This is the type of woman that you want to "friend-zone".

94   Again I need to stress do this only *if* you can keep the friendship just a friendship. No trying to get between her legs, no trying to see if she will eventually fit into your Program, no trying to be slick and slowly wear her down.

95   Once you get the ball rolling with social outings and actual dates, you won't have time to reach backwards. You'll be spending

a lot of time and energy moving forward to find a woman that's best suited for you and your Program.

96   Save yourself the headache. If you choose to "friend-zone" a woman you must stand by this decision. So make this decision wisely. A Mack must stand by his word and have integrity.

97   Are there exceptions to this "rule"? Yes. But part of my personal life philosophy is to keep things simple. Confusion only breeds more confusion. Within confusion are the seeds of unnecessary problems that will eventually grow.

98   Sending mixed-signals to a woman causes unnecessary problems. Alleviate those problems by not even starting them.

99   Before we dive into real dating, let's take a brief detour and learn basic female body language. This is important information to know when you're physically around any woman you're Macking to.

The Language of the Female Body

100   Since women have been socially conditioned to act more passive, the restraints they place on themselves are often communicated through their body language.

101   This is something she can't help. She may want to say something (or do something) but thinks it's not "right", but her body language will often indicate what's really going through her mind.

102   As a Mack, make it your Responsibility to learn a woman's body language. It will help you know when you need to back off; when you need to advance; when she's very comfortable; when she wants to be touched, hugged, held or kissed and even when she's horny.

103 I suggest getting a good book on body language if you want to study this is greater detail, but what follows is enough knowledge for a Mack to make powerful use of.

104 **(1) Language with the Head and Face:**

Hair toss –
A way of saying, "Look at me," or, "I'm happy (or confident)."

Ear tugging –
This often (not all the time) means lying.

Stroking or twirling her fingers through the hair –
She's flirting.

Rubs neck or moves hair to expose the neck –
She's attracted. The neck symbolizes vulnerability and "openness".

Raised eyebrows –
Shows interest.

Raised eyebrows with nodding while you're talking –
She is agreeing with what you're saying.

Raised eyebrows with wide eyes –
Submissive behavior. Her expression is made to look more helpless and innocent.

"Batting" of eye-lashes –
She is flirting.

Repeated eye contact and even a smile from a distance –
She's saying, "Approach me." or, "I'm intrigued by you."

Repeated eye contact while you're talking, also raised eyebrows and squinted eyes while you're talking –
She's completely into what you're saying and analyzing it.

Repeatedly broken eye contact while you're talking to her –
She's lost interest in what you're saying.

Looks quickly away or down and smiles when you try to make eye contact from a distance –
Usually (not always) means the woman is interested.

Slight nostril flaring –
She is very interested and/or aroused.

Lip nibbling –
She is flirting or anxious is a good way.

Repeated smiling and/or laughing –
She is flirting and letting you know that you interest her.

Repeated licking of the lips –
She is very interest and/or aroused. She is open to being kissed.

Side-ways glances –
She is flirting.

Head slightly leaning to one side while you're looking and/or talking to her –
She is flirting.

105   **(2) Language with the arms and hands:**

Slow rubbing of a finger across the lips –
She is open to being kissed.

Fast or "jerky" rubbing of finger across the lips –
Doesn't mean anything. Ignore it.

Slow stroking of an object such as a wine glass stem, the edge of a table, her glasses, her arms or thighs –
She is flirting and/or aroused.

Touches you on her own – Such as a playful shove, light stroke on the arm or shoulder, leaving the hand for many seconds on any part of your body or gently patting you on any part of your body –
She is letting you know that she is very interested and is flirting.

Many hand gestures and/or pointing while talking or telling a story –
She is very engaged in the conversation you're both having.

Plays with necklace, rings or bracelets while still making regular eye contact –
She is interested in you.

Plays with jewelry, rings or bracelets while NOT making regular eye contact –
She is anxious to get away or have more distance from you.

Constantly taps fingers or constantly looks at phone –
Usually shows that she's not interested and anxious to get away.

Minimal arm crossing –
Shows she is comfortable with you; open towards you.

Arms stay crossed for long periods of time –
She is showing she's not interested. Sometimes (very rarely) this may show she is very insecure.

Exposes wrists or has "limp" wrists –
She is comfortable around you. Exposed and/or relaxed wrists show she is "open" towards you.

Fingernail biting –
Shows she is nervous or insecure.

Faces you with open arms –
Indicates she is approachable.

Open hand touching upper chest –
Signals honesty.

106 (3) Language with the rest of the body:

Slumped posture –
Indicates she is bored or has low self-esteem.

Knees pointing toward you while sitting down –
She is focused on you.

Knees pointing away from you while sitting down –
She is showing that she is not interested in you.

Legs open towards you while sitting down –
She is very comfortable with you.

Leans in towards you often –
She is flirting.

Leans away –
She is not interested or wants distance.

Mirrors your movements: You turn towards her, she turn towards you. You take a drink, she takes a drink. You lean back, she leans back; etc. –
She is really attracted to you.

Places thigh against yours –
She is very interested and/or aroused.

Places arm around your arm while moving in closer –
She is flirting and wants more physical contact and touching.

Let's you leave your hand on any part of the body without flinching or moving away –
She is attracted to you and very comfortable.

Presses body against yours and looks into your eyes –
She is ready to be kissed and is aroused.

Intentionally moves so you can see down her shirt or up her skirt. Holds that position while looking or smiling at you –
She is flirting and is open toward playful touching and stroking.

Bends over directly in front of you, holds that position and looks back at you –
She is flirting and is open toward playful touching and stroking.

Places her head in your lap while you are sitting down –
Wants her hair, neck, shoulders and/or arms to be stroked.

While walking in front of you, stops suddenly and leans back slightly so you press up against her –
She is flirting and is open toward playful touching and stroking.

Intentionally rubs her breasts or buttocks against you while gazing at you –
She is flirting and wants you to get her in the mood for sex.

Gyrating of hips while sitting or lying down –
She is open towards possibly having sex. She wants you to get her in the mood.

Small side-to-side movement of the buttocks while lying on stomach –
She is open towards possibly having sex. She wants you to get her in the mood.

Throws one leg or both legs across yours while you're both sitting down –
She is open towards possibly having sex. She wants you to get her in the mood.

Sits in your lap or straddles you while kissing you and looking intensely into your eyes –
She is ready for sex.

107   Do you have to remember all of these? No. But make sure you get familiar enough with these lists so that you don't miss the more obvious body language cues.

108   So you've come to the point where the woman has your interest and you have hers. Now it's time to understand what to do, and what *not* to do, on the first official date.

CHAPTER TWO

The Dating Agenda

1   You've approached her and then took her on a social outing to get an idea of her personality. Next, you've gotten her comfortable around you and have seen if she agrees with many of your Standards and Principles.

2   Through conversation you've made your way into her mind. You've done this just enough to build sufficient mental attraction; and there's a possibility you've slightly touched her heart too.

3   She's possibly qualified enough to add to your Program but in reality, you still don't know very much about her, and she doesn't know much about you.

4   And although this is true, it's during the first date that you'll advance straight for her heart to build *emotional* attraction. This will put a "hook" in her that will help keep her around longer. Like a fish grabbing the bait at the end of the line.

5   Building emotional attraction will cause the average woman to become "wide-open" so you can really learn what you need to know.

6   This is the most effective way to see if she will be a valuable asset to your team (kingdom/company) and function in your Program. This is a Mack's agenda with the first date.

7   You should have already scheduled the date during your social outing with her.

8   The same preparation applies: Clean car (if you're picking her up), clean and "newish" (crisp) clothes; hair and facial hair tidy; clean jewelry, the right amount of cologne and fresh breath.

9 This time around you also want to make sure your house is in order. Clean up, straighten up and make sure it smells nice.

10 Although the objective is to *not* bring her back to your house, if it does happen you'll be prepared; one less thing to think about and stress over.

11 A true Mack should always keep his home clean anyway. His home should reflect his state of mind – clean, organized and orderly.

12 Just a few quick pointers concerning your household since we're on the topic.

13 Take pride in what you have. Even the simplest things women will notice. Make sure you have matching plates. You should have a set of matching cups and glasses. Your pots and pans should be a complete matching set and also invest in matching silverware. It's not the cost of the items, it's the fact that they match.

14 You should have a color theme for your bedroom and another one for your bathroom. Make sure everything you put in these rooms matches their color theme. This isn't an interior design book so seek out information about this subject – it's important.

15 If you don't have the money for fancy bedroom furniture, once again, just ensure whatever you have matches the color theme you set.

16 Can't get a fancy bed frame and headboard? Just find a huge picture with a nice frame that matches the color theme and hang it right above the head of the bed.

17 Sheets, pillowcases and bedspread should look new and match as well.

18   Get yourself some scented candles. You can also use incense or even wall plug-ins to keep every room in your home smelling pleasant.

19   Don't leave dirty clothes all over the place, not even on the floor of your bedroom. Make sure you dust and vacuum. In fact, every floor in your house should be clean no matter what they're made of – carpet, linoleum, wood, etc.

20   You're becoming a king, don't live like a peasant. Think of your home as what it is – your castle. Treat it with respect.

21   When you come up on a woman to add to your Program, she'll notice that you take care of your home and will automatically follow suit; she'll help keep your home clean and organized too.

22   If she doesn't, then you need to check her. Explain to her the "reason why" keeping a clean and orderly home is important to you.

23   The way you start with a woman is the way you must continue. Put your best foot forward and keep moving that way. Transmit it and she'll receive it.

24   Anyway, let's get back to dating…

25   It's your Responsibility to have the entire date laid out from start to finish. You should have in mind what time you're picking her up and what time you're dropping her back home (or what time she needs to be back home).

26   You should know how to get from her house to the first location and how to get from the first location to the second location; and from the second location back to her house.

27   There's nothing to be embarrassed about if you need to use navigation or a GPS; but you should at least have a general idea of where everything is and the routes to get there.

28   The woman will follow your lead and if she has other ideas, she'll say something to let you know.

29   Some women will test you by simply saying that whatever you come up with is fine with her. Why is this a test? Because this is her way of seeing what kind of man you are. Will you stand up and take Responsibility for ENTERTAINING her?

30   Macks don't take this personally; in fact this is what a Mack wants. By having the power to plan out a date, you can place her into specific environments that are best conducive to your Macking.

31   Just like the social outing, the first date (and possibly the second) should be somewhere you can actually talk to her. The locations need to be more private though. You want to avoid openly public places this time around. A nice restaurant is probably your best bet.

32   The restaurant doesn't have to be expensive but use a little creativity. If you have a favorite restaurant that she's never been to, this is a great option.

33   She'll have a first time experience with you and something like this can be very effective with your agenda of building emotional attraction.

34   Also keep in mind if the woman may be allergic to certain kinds of foods. This will make a big impact on her because it shows you remembered and you care (you did find that out when you were talking to her, didn't you?).

35   Avoid fast food restaurants. I shouldn't have to mention this but I did just in case. If you honestly can't afford to take a woman out on a date, then wait until you can – or get creative.

36 Just keep up the phone and/or text conversations. You could even invite her on a second daytime social outing just to let her know that you're still interested.

37 If she asks why you're not taking her out on an official "date", be honest. Tell her you want to do something nice with her but your money is "tight" at the moment.

38 If a woman is honestly attracted to you, she may even offer to pay for the first date or go "dutch" (she pays for herself and you pay for yourself).

39 If she does make offers like these, it should be obvious that money isn't the issue; she just wants to spend time with you. That's a good thing – you have inched your way into her heart in most cases.

40 As a Mack, do you accept her offer? Yes you do unless you personally have a Principle against it. It hurts more for you to turn her down than to accept it. Your dating agenda is your main priority here.

41 Usually a woman will only make offers like these if she's very attracted to you and respects you. She may also make them if she's desperate and/or very lonely. Either reason is acceptable. Again, unless you personally have a Principle against it.

42 What's important is, if there is a second date, you better "man-up" and do it right – pay for the entire date. You're a Mack, not a childish male that uses women for their money. Don't give her this impression. She'll lose respect for you.

43 If you don't have a car and the woman does, this is fine. Have her pick you up but be a gentleman and at least offer her some money for gas. She'll usually decline, but just by making this gesture she'll respect it because it shows Responsibility.

44   Be prepared. Have enough money set aside so that if she does accept the gas money, you'll still have enough money left for the entire date.

45   For this first date you're only taking her to one or two locations. So I would recommend a restaurant first and then something fun like miniature golf, bowling, going to a free concert, a movie (pick two or three movies *you* want to see and give her the option of which one she wants to watch), etc.

46   Whenever possible, you want to go to the restaurant first. This will give you the time and space to really talk to the woman. And if things go badly, you can just take her straight home from there (or tell her to drop you off – or take a taxi home).

47   Another reason to eat first is because you want to reestablish the mental attraction she should already have for you. Think of it like picking back up where you left off with the social outing.

48   This is important: Never accept a double-date as your first date. Your first date with the woman needs to be just you and her. Even if she invites you to a party or other social gathering, just politely decline.

49   Explain to her how you want your first date together to be just you and her – you really want to connect on a deeper level (or say something along those lines).

50   Your energy level should be high. You should be enthusiastic and be prepared to be playful. You want to tease her and be flirtatious. What you bring into a date sets the tone of a date. Transmit and she'll receive – the lower will rise to match the higher.

51   Also, remember to be a gentleman; open the door, pull out her chair, gently guide her while you walk side-by-side and so on.

52   What's the topic of discussion during the first date? Again, just pick up where you left off during the social outing or whatever you both have been talking about over the phone or through text.

53   Tell her more about yourself and ask her a lot of questions about herself.

54   Since your agenda is to make your way into her heart to establish an emotional attraction, you want to steer the conversation away from regular topics into more personal topics.

55   Great topics include: Goals, family, bad past relationships, dating, sex, personal beliefs (religion, spirituality, etc.), current events that are dramatic (women like dramatic), dream jobs, dream vacations, fitness (if you or her are into fitness), both your ideas about love and romance.

56   If done correctly, these topics alone could easily fill-up a two to three hour conversation.

57   Don't forget, reveal a lot about yourself. Explain what you think and why you think the way you do. This will establish comfort and she'll open-up and reveal herself.

58   Pay close attention to her body language to gauge how well the date is going.

59   If you feel the conversation slowing up just say something like this, "We must be really comfortable around each other to just sit here and enjoy silence together," while looking directly into her eyes.

60   She will take it as a criticism that she's boring and attempt to start the conversation back up. Or she will take it as a flirt and just smile shyly. This puts pressure on her and most women aren't good at handling social pressure.

61   Once this settles in, just start talking about yourself. You may want to have a few pre-designed stories or topics ready just in case something like this happens.

62   This is nothing to be alarmed about, just be prepared and you'll be confident enough to handle something like this before it ever happens.

63   After eating if you don't have anything else planned you'll have to escalate with her physically before she gets out of the car and goes into the house (or before you go in your house if she's driving).

64   So it's best to keep the conversation going on the ride home and then just keep talking while you're parked outside of her place (or outside of yours if she's driving).

65   If there is a second part to the date, this is the time to begin escalating physically. And truthfully this is much more effective because you have more time to work with.

66   Escalating physically means more touching and being physically closer. Depending on how comfortable the woman is, you can start this before you even get to the restaurant, or during the meal.

67   Some ways to do this include: Placing one of her hands in yours; rubbing gently on her arm; lightly touching her shoulder; briefly placing your hand on her thigh; leaning in close to smell her perfume and asking if she likes your cologne; moving in closer when she's standing in front of you (not too close though).

68   If the mood is more playful and her body language says that she's enjoying herself, you could use more playful methods to escalate physically.

69   For more playful physical escalating you could: Poke her in her side with your finger; tickle her; pinch her gently on her thigh

or upper arm; grab both her shoulders and then turn her so her back is facing you, then tell her playfully to leave; briefly grab her hand and then push it away telling her she's being "too aggressive".

Emotional "Poking"

70 Women are emotional creatures. Emotions affect a person's mood. Even if you have very little experience with women you have witnessed this before. It's no big secret.

71 What you may not know is *how* to use this to your advantage. Once again, a Mack uses everything he can to his advantage.

72 You want to work some of those physical escalations in; at least three.

73 This creates spikes of emotion within your interactions on the date. Emotionally "poking" her is a means by which you excite her. You become exciting because she becomes totally lost in your world and this hooks her interest.

74 It's like watching an action movie. There are a few moments of dialogue and then an action sequence; then a few more minutes of dialogue, then some more action.

75 So the way you lay down your Macking is like this: You talk for a while and then tease her. Then some more talking, then a physical escalation for just a moment then pull back; then some more talking, then you give her a compliment; then some more talking and then you tell her something you *don't* like about her (playfully); then some more talking and another brief physical escalation and then pull back; and repeat the cycle.

76 This is not a set formula and there's no correct way to do this. I only give an example of how you poke at her emotionally so you

can generate your own ideas. The means of emotional poking should be authentic and come from your personality.

77   You want to keep the overall mood of the date light – not serious. Also depending on your personality and hers, you can add in more playful elements.

78   It's like looking at a sound wave – it arches up and then drops down, then arches up again and drops down – like an ocean wave. This is the general idea you want to keep in mind when emotionally poking at a woman.

79   Take her out of her world and bring her into yours; a world where she is completely disarmed. She has no weapons to fight with because she doesn't know what to expect. She can only follow your lead – both mentally and emotionally.

80   Also in the back of your mind remember a woman has child-like qualities. Children like to have fun, so make the date fun. Elevate her mood as high as possible to appeal to her child-like side.

81   She may even exhibit child-like behavior like making funny or frowning faces when you tease her. She might poke out her lips when you tell her a sad story. Or she might jump away from you and laugh when she thinks you're going to tickle her.

82   When you start seeing things like this, know that you're doing extremely well on the date.

83   This isn't a measuring rod of success because you can still be successful even though she shows none of this behavior.

84   As you do this emotional poking, she will begin to become emotionally attracted. She will become engulfed in your confidence and your overall behavior. This will lead her to *feel* something for you. And this is what you want – to enter her heart.

85 For some of you reading this, you're probably thinking to yourself, 'What, that's all I have to do?' and the answer is, "Not entirely."

86 This emotional poking must be backed up by your manhood. What's happening to a woman is mainly taking place in her mind. And what she's thinking pulls at her emotions.

87 She sees your strength of manhood and confidence. Next she discovers that she enjoys your conversation – you're interesting. And added to all that is you're actually "fun" to be around. Not childish, but charming.

88 When she adds this equation up she'll reason that you're almost the complete package. How does she come to that conclusion? Because you're beginning to fit into her idea of a man – what she was socially conditioned to want *and* what she biological wants.

89 You're affecting her on many different levels at the same time – biologically, mentally and emotionally.

90 **Biologically**, you appeal to her ingrained feminine instincts. You're a real man. You exhibit very little childish or feminine behavior.

91 You also have a goal (or goals) you're working toward. You're confident and have a strong sense of yourself (Standards and Principles). You also have a view on the world and how you fit in it (your philosophy).

92 **Mentally** you're engaging. You know how to hold a conversation and you're not scared to say how you feel. She knows you're attracted to her and not afraid that she may not see you the same way.

93   You're still pursuing her because *you* want to. You're not overly concerned about what she thinks. Since she likes being hunted this strangely makes her feel very comfortable around you.

94   **Emotionally** you elevate her mood. You're confident enough to tease her and be playful with her but at the same time, you're still strong. Your "controlled playfulness" doesn't come across as childish.

95   Are you starting to see how everything you've learned in this book so far is coming together? Do you understand why each single piece is important?

96   By you affecting her on so many levels at once, this is what disarms her. She's not going to know how to respond to everything you represent. The icing on the cake is you haven't even tried to have sex with her yet. If you've been Macking accordingly that is.

98   Her strongest weapon against males is her sex, and she can't use that against you because you haven't shown much interest in that area. Her next strongest weapon is her skill at rejecting, but you've shown that you don't care about that either. You're still moving forward because *you* choose to – an unstoppable train that's going to run her over.

99   What else can she do? She's powerless and at your mercy. Yet, she's enjoying every minute of it.

Ending the First Date

99   As the first date draws to a close only give her a hug. A long and very affectionate hug and that's all. No kissing, no long hand holding, no running your fingers through her hair. Just a simple hug and tell her good night.

100   If you want to see her again say something similar to this while looking directly into her eyes:

"I really enjoyed our date. And I really want to see you again. I need to let you know that I don't just want another girlfriend or someone I have casual sex with. I want a woman who is really going to be down on my team."

101   Remember, be honest and let what you have to say reflect your personality. What you're doing here is reminding her that the woman you choose has to commit to you *and* your Program.

102   She should understand this if you've been explaining your Program and how important it is to you.

103   If she tries to kiss you, pull back and tell her that you want to take things a little slower. If she asks if she can come in your house, tell her maybe next time if she's a "good girl".

104   You can choose to set up the second date now, or later. And it's during the second date that you finally ask her directly, is she going to be involved with your Program, or not?

105   If things went extremely well, you could even ask her later that night over the phone or the next day – skipping the second "set-up" date entirely.

106   Only you can judge how much pressure you think you can get away with. The general rule is, the more a woman wants to give you her body the easier it is for her to strongly consider your Program.

107   Just as long as you have her mind and heart at this stage in the Game, that's what you really want.

108   Sometimes getting fully into a woman's heart will involve multiple dates. If you can't be successful after the third date then

you may want to consider just "friend-zoning" the woman and hunting elsewhere. You're wasting a lot of time and money.

109   How do you know when you're deep into a woman's heart? You'll know because she'll want more of your time and attention.

110   She'll respond to most of your calls and texts and look forward to them. She'll want to talk to you more about what's going on in her life. She'll also want to see you more and even introduce you to her friends and family.

111   She may cook for you or bring lunch up to your job. She'll send you cute little text messages about how she's thinking about you or how she misses you or how she's looking forward to seeing you again.

112   She'll make sacrifices like taking an extra off-day just to have more time with you. She might even invite you to go out of town with her for a weekend.

113   All these things can possibly happen and you haven't even had sex with this woman yet. This is the power of real Macking.

114   A Mack doesn't hold a woman with sex, he holds her with the overall strength of his manhood.

115   If a woman is ready to offer you her body (especially after only the first date), this doesn't necessarily mean you've made it into her heart. She could just be attracted and horny.

116   Look for signs beyond her sexual advances and flirting. If you don't see them, then keep pushing toward them. You want her heart *before* you take her body. You want her commitment to your Program first, sex can wait. That's just responsible Macking.

CHAPTER THREE

Managing Dating Difficulties

1   There are essentially four stages of dating, at least from a Mack's Perspective. At each stage, there is often a decision to move forward to the next stage or end the relationship.

2   **First Stage:** Mental attraction after the initial meeting. We've covered this in detail. This encompasses both the initial meeting and the social outing. There may be minor conflicts at this stage, but the time invested is so minor that ending the "relationship" here is no loss.

3   **Second Stage:** Emotional attraction. This develops between the social outing and the first date or during the first date entirely. You're peeking a woman's curiosity, her interest and making her feel a level of infatuation.

There's little conflict during this stage and if you've properly captured a woman's mind, then this is often the stage where they'll be trying to impress you by putting on their best behavior. She'll be asking herself, "What can I do to make him show me that he likes me?"

Usually somewhere early in this stage you'll discover if a woman is going to truly commit to your Program. If she is, this is where you begin training her how to treat you. We'll explore how to train a woman in the next chapter.

Toward the middle of this stage is probably when you'll also begin to have sex with a woman who has proven that she's qualified.

4   **Third Stage:** This is the deeper connection phase. Reality sets in around this time. The woman will be considering, where the

relationship is going. The time between the second stage and this stage can last as long as four months.

Around this time a woman's "best face" will begin to drop and her true personality will become more apparent.

It's also during this stage a woman will start asking herself, "Is this really the right man for me?" She'll begin to notice differences between you two that she either ignored or overlooked before. Little things that were "cute" may become irritating.

This is the stage where many problems and difficulties start coming to surface.

If she's accepted the man and feels the relationship needs to advance toward a firm commitment, it's at this stage where she'll really push for this. Somewhere during this stage is where loving you turns into being "in-love" with you.

This can happen faster or slower depending on the woman. The faster it happens the more you have to be on guard of *not* accepting a woman's soul. You must be really sure you want her around for a long time.

If you don't think you want her around long-term, turn her soul down and continue the relationship as is; or end the relationship at that point.

5 **Forth Stage:** The commitment stage. This is where both you and your woman have grown to understand each other on deeper levels. You'll fully understand each other's habits and Values. By this time you will have also shared many experiences. If they aren't pulling you apart, they usually help strengthen what you already have.

At this stage you'll probably have met many of the most important people in her life.

A woman will usually offer you her soul before this stage, but if she's been holding back, she'll usually offer it now because she has invested so much into you and your relationship.

If she was planning on leaving you, this also would have happened before this stage (generally speaking). She's fully committed now. Regular relationships usually transition from this stage into engagement and then marriage. This stage can literally last for years.

A Mack's relationship is definitely not regular but if marriage is something you want, then this is the make-it or break-it point for some women. You may want to consider making a firm decision.

6   I mention these dating stages so you'll have a better understanding of why a Mack changes the way he Plays depending on the relationship stage he's in.

7   This will also help you manage multiple women because you'll understand what dating stage they're mentally and emotionally in so you can deal with each woman accordingly.

8   Before we go further let's talk about problems that may arise before, during and/or after the first dating stage.

9   The one issue that trips males up the most is women not keeping their word.

10   You meet them, get their number, call them up and get them to say yes to a social outing. The day you're supposed to go out, they either don't pick up their phone or respond to texts. They may also give you an excuse of why they suddenly can't go.

11   This is going to happen. Its part of the Game, just accept it. Half the time it has nothing to do with you, but the other half of the time, it does.

12   Women break their word for many reasons, none of which should really matter that much to you. Don't waste too much mental energy trying to figure it out. It's all in the percentages.

13   Yes, it's true that you may have done something to turn them off. Or perhaps you didn't make a strong enough impression on them to decide to give you their time, but so what?

14   Work with the files in your mind and put in images of success and keep hunting. Mentally and emotionally regroup and step right back up to the plate.

15   Trying to figure out where or how you "failed" can be beneficial but only if you *know* where and how you failed. If you can't quite figure it out then don't feed too much mental energy into it. Just keep moving forward; keep hunting.

16   If you do find a few mistakes, you know what to do. Work with those files and visualize yourself saying and/or doing the right thing in its place.

17   A woman not returning text and phone calls or giving thin excuses happens to even the best Macks. No one, no matter how skilled and slick they are, has a 100% success rate. Don't beat yourself up over it. Remain confident and know that as long as you keep at it, you will be successful.

18   If you keep hammering a nail, eventually it's going into the wall. You might miss hitting the nail entirely sometimes if you're not used to using a hammer. But when you do hit that nail enough times, it's going in.

19   Just the fact that you approached the woman and got her phone number *is* a victory. Consider how many males don't even get that far. It's progress.

20   To ignore that small victory is like ordering a burger from a fast food restaurant and getting upset because it doesn't look

exactly like the picture on the menu. Is that really something to whine about?

21 You can eat. And sometimes that's enough.

22 If the woman has an excuse, it may be a legitimate excuse. You don't *know* so stay confident and tell her you'll contact her tomorrow and set up another day and time.

23 If she doesn't respond to you then. Just accept the loss and keep hunting.

24 If she comes up with more excuses, take the hint, accept the loss and keep hunting.

25 If you manage to set up another social outing or date and she cancels or doesn't come though this second time, just "friend zone" her or cut her off completely and keep hunting.

26 You don't want to waste your time with an unresponsive woman. You're more important. If she doesn't see your Value, so what? There are plenty of more women to go after. Don't get stuck on one or two.

27 One reason to not waste too much time is because once you really start approaching a lot of women (which I suggest you do), you're social outing and dating schedule is going to get hectic.

28 You're going to have a woman you just met that you're trying to get on a social outing. You're going to have another woman you just finished a social outing with and you think she's interesting enough to set up a first date.

29 You'll have another woman who passed the first date and wants to see you again. You'll have a woman who you "friend-zoned" or who "friend-zoned" you who regularly calls you for advice.

30   Once the ball gets rolling, you're going to have to come up with a system to decide who gets your time and when.

31   The way to manage this is to keep in mind what dating stage you're in with each woman.

32   A woman that's in the second dating stage should have priority over a woman you just met. A woman that's in the third dating stage should have priority over women who are in the first or second dating stage.

33   A very important rule of the Mack Game: **Do not Mack past your current woman (or women), trying to catch a new woman**.

34   Weak males get caught up in the "newness" of being around an attractive woman they just met. And they may already have a woman around that really likes him. But he will put this woman off and spend his time trying to impress the new woman.

35   Where's the logic in that? Don't forget your whole reason for meeting women and dating. It's not the sex you're after, it's finding women who will be dedicated to you, respect you and assist with your Program for a long period of time.

36   If you have a woman that you think can really be an asset to you, she deserves more of your time and attention. Why lose her for another woman who may not even be qualified?

37   Always keep in mind *what* you're doing and *why* you're doing it. You must manage your kingdom (company) efficiently.

38   Sometimes after the social outing or even the first date, the woman will try to "friend-zone" you. She may feel, for whatever reason, that you two didn't really connect.

39   You'll be able to pick up on this because she will ignore your flirts, be difficult to take out on a second date or may be hard to reach by phone or text. Suddenly she might get "very busy".

40   She may have legitimately gotten busy. You don't know so don't assume. Just pull back a little from her but still call or text her every once in a while just to "check up on her". She may come around, she might not. But like I explained before, even a woman like this is good at helping keep your other women in check. Regardless you should still be hunting so you won't have much time to waste on her anyway.

41   Depending on how much time you have. You may want to slow down hunting (just a little) when you have three or four women at the second dating stage.

42   These women are going to be inviting you places, wanting you to spend their birthdays with them; they'll want to take you around their friends and families and spend the holidays together.

43   They'll get a job promotion and want to celebrate. They'll all want to spend your birthday with you. And all this of course, eats up your time and requires careful navigation.

44   What helps here is that you've been honest upfront. These women should know that you date other women. And you date other women because you're looking for a woman who is really about advancing in life and into you.

45   Unless you're just completely heartless, you're not going to want to hurt any of these women's feelings. And you may be afraid to lose one of them.

46   Sorry, but this part of the Game. Accept it. And as such, it's your Responsibility to give the majority of your time to the woman (or women) who are really kicking into your Program.

47   Be a man, be honest and tell them sorry but you have other plans. Women aren't stupid so they'll naturally assume you have plans with another woman. If they ask, be honest.

48   Yes, this will upset them but they'll respect it. And you give them the option of either stepping up to earn more of your time or leaving.

49   Sometimes women will get frustrated with competing with your other women and tell you that she's just going to "back off" in one way or another.

50   It's at this time that you want to really talk to her and explain to her the truth. You make time for the woman that's really helping you and into you. You're looking for a deep, meaningful and undeniable connection.

51   It's also during the second dating stage that you'll "blow" a lot of women.

52   To "blow" a woman simply means that she leaves you and stops dealing with you intimately. Or she'll want to keep the intimacy intact and cut-off everything else.

53   As a Mack, since you don't have sex with women who aren't involved in your Program, just having a casual sex partner is unacceptable. You'll have to "friend-zone" this woman. Explain to her that maybe it's better that you're both just friends.

54   Be careful here. If you think you won't be able to control yourself around her sexually, then don't do it. Just cut her off gently. Avoid sending mixed signals to a woman. A friend should be just that, a friend.

55   This might sound harsh reading this, but when you're dealing with a lot of women you'll always have options available. Again, you won't really have time to try convincing women to stick

around. They should be convincing you that they're worth having around.

56   They should be dealing with you. You shouldn't be dealing with them. Don't you hold the most Value?

57   Occasionally you'll run into interesting women who already have boyfriends or are married. I would suggest you build a mental attraction with these women and then "friend-zone" them.

58   Males, like women, get very jealous and you'll be creating problems that don't need to be there. This is easier said than done because sometimes just trying to get a woman that has a boyfriend or that's married is very tempting.

59   You need to be the man though. You dictate what the relationship is and stand firm on it. Is the woman worth the baggage and problems that come along with her? Only you can decide that so think long and hard about it.

60   You'll also run across situations where a woman's friend or even a female family member will begin flirting with you. Usually she's curious because the woman you're dating has spoken so highly about you.

61   Being that women translate things into what's in it for them, they'll want to figure out for themselves what's so great about you. They don't have anyone like you so this is a part of their life that's broken, and they'll want to fix it.

62   Again, situations like this are tempting. But a Mack must exhibit extreme self-control here. If the woman you're dating is really qualified, why risk messing that up by going after someone who's just curious?

63   It's not worth it. Even if the woman you're dating eventually leaves or it just doesn't work out, don't go after her friend or family member. Don't create unnecessary problems unless you

know you can deal with them. These situations are extremely difficult to navigate successfully – I speak from personal experience.

64   I've personally been in a situation where I was dating an older woman and her own daughter flirted with me. Things like this are part of the Game. You have to Mack accordingly and stay down with the woman who's staying down with you.

65   You can check the behavior of a curious female by simply saying something along these lines, "I see what you're doing but I'm down with your friend (or sister or cousin or aunt or mother). Nothing can ever happen between us. We can be friends though."

66   I've also had a woman test me by having her own female cousin call me over the phone and flirt with me. I talked to her in a friendly way and kept mentioning the girl I was dating throughout the conversation.

67   I passed this test with flying colors. And it wasn't so much about the woman I was dating; it was about me standing on my Standards and Principles. I refuse to compromise my manhood for anyone.

68   This is all a part of being a Mack. These are situation that you must expect and accept. Deal with them properly to prevent future confusion and problems. This is being Responsible with handling the power you'll eventually possess.

69   As you continue to hunt, going on social outings and dates, you'll eventually find a woman who will impress you. She'll kick into your Program and completely accept what you represent as a man.

70   She will have "bought" what you've been showcasing and place the proper Value on you.

71   You'll be somewhere in the second dating stage when this happens. When you come across a woman like this, it's extremely important to train her on how to treat you because she may be around for the long-term.

72   By setting things up now (instead of later) you'll have less to worry about as the relationship grows. She'll learn what you accept and what you don't accept.

CHAPTER FOUR

How to Train Your Woman About Who You Are

1   Once a woman verbally agrees to your Program and lifestyle and actually participates by *doing* something (actions speak louder than words), that's it! You now need to make her your woman.

2   A woman becomes yours when you have her heart *completely*. This doesn't necessarily mean she loves you, but you're well on your way there. At this time she only needs to be completely infatuated with you.

3   First however, your relationship must be established. Remember, the word relationship comes from the root word, *relate*. How you and she agree to relate to one another *is* your relationship.

4   You're the man, you define the terms. Most of this is done by spending a lot of time with her (without breaking your Program and systems) and training her.

5   Training a woman is all about one thing – making her realize what you *will* accept, and what you *won't* accept.

6   Keep this quote in mind, "You train people how to treat you." This is meant to be taken literally because it's the simple truth.

7   When anyone, male or female, feels they can get away with certain behavior around you, they'll do it. A Mack is a real man. He must command (not demand) that he be shown a certain level of respect at all times; especially when it comes to his women.

8   People will only treat you the way you allow them to. A Mack stops this at the door. You must *check* (keep within limits) behavior constantly in the beginning and also throughout the entire

relationship; repeatedly over and over again. This just goes with the Game, accept it. This is a crucial part of managing women.

9   When checking a woman's behavior, be prepared in advance to explain the "reason why" you think and feel that way.

10   You must always have a "reason why". Always.

11   You must be able to explain in simple English why you don't like certain behavior and why you do like certain behavior. This comes from really knowing yourself.

12   The most effective way to train a woman is by using stories to illustrate your points. These stories will create images in her mind. These images will get filed in the file server (file cabinet) in her mind; the one with your name on it.

13   She should know and understand her boundaries with you. But just because she knows them it's still your Responsibility to keep them in place. Don't leave this up to her; you're the man so you have to do it.

14   Let me give you an example of how women use this very same tactic.

15   Say you just met an attractive woman. You get her number, text her a few times and you finally go out on your social outing. She starts talking about herself so you know she's comfortable.

16   So here she is telling you about all the men she dates and what they do for her. She tells you the story of the guy who bought her a new cell phone.

17   She tells you a story about another guy who used to take her on exotic vacations.

18   She tells you another story about a weak male who used to take her shopping almost every weekend.

19 As a Mack you should be listening very closely. But what is this woman doing by telling you these stories? She's trying to train you. She's telling you these stories to get you to think that you must "earn" her with money because that's what she's accustomed to.

20 Now is she doing this intentionally? Some women don't, but very conniving women do. In their own way, they're explaining the Standards they expect from a male. Weak males fall right into this trap.

21 Weak males are so focused on wanting to be around this attractive woman and trying to have sex with her that they suddenly end up in her Program. And next thing you know, they're trying to impress her by buying her things and taking her out on expensive dates they probably can't afford.

SIDE NOTE: How would a Mack handle a woman like this? He wouldn't flinch. He would continue with his agenda. If she submits then that's great. If she doesn't, he'll cut her off. A Mack doesn't run from the drama, he invites it in his house – even if it's just to test the level of his Game. Sometimes women like this will love the challenge a Mack represents and when he recognizes this, he'll completely disarm her of every weapon she has.

22 A Mack uses a similar process. He will tell the story about a time when a woman made him breakfast in bed and how much it impressed him.

23 A Mack will tell the story of when a woman acted an ass in public and how it turned him off so much; he just walked away and left the woman looking foolish.

24 A Mack would talk about the time he fell head over heels for a woman and all she did was complain. He suddenly realized that he deserves better in a woman and he learned from experience that he doesn't like women who complain all the time.

25   All these stories feed files into a woman's mind. So every time she thinks about him, her mind pulls up what he will and will not accept; and also what he expects from a woman.

26   Properly used stories are extremely powerful. In the beginning of the relationship all the way the way to as long as the relationship lasts.

27   If you have little experience with women you can still use stories. Just use whatever you can to develop a story to use for training.

28   You can use songs that contain a message you want to make a point about. You can use movies, articles, social media posts, pictures, even other people's stories.

29   Use whatever you can to make sure the woman understands how to treat you.

30   The reason behind all these stories and points you what to emphasize are to set boundaries of behavior. You want a woman to think twice about doing or not doing certain things around you, with you or to you.

31   You want a woman to respect that you don't have a lot of money? Tell her about a movie you watched where the woman fell so madly in love with the male that they conquered everything together. No matter how many situations and problems came their way, their commitment to what they wanted pulled them through.

32   You want a woman to consider allowing you to see other women? Tell her about a song where the female artist cared so much about her man that although he had other women, she knew he would always come back to her.

33   You want a woman to make more time for you? Tell her about your friend who tried so hard to be faithful to his woman

but he felt so underappreciated that another woman came along and gave him what he really needed.

34   If you're using personal stories or other people's stories these need to be true stories. Don't lie and make things up, it's not necessary.

35   If you're ever caught in that lie, she'll begin to question other things you've told her (and will tell her in the future). You're creating future problems that don't need to exist.

36   All these stories and points about your Standards, Principles, Program and philosophy are used to create a file server (file cabinet) in a woman's mind.

37   This file server has your name on it and it contains all the information the woman has about you. So when she thinks about you, her mind will pull these files. And these are the files you intentionally placed in there.

38   You must train your woman to only think about you the way you decide. When your behavior matches up with the stories and the rest of you manhood "showcase" (Standards, Principles, Program and philosophy), all she can do at that point is accept it or reject it.

39   If that's clear then we can go a level deeper. Women also have a file server (file cabinet) already in their mind about romance and love. And where did this information come from?

40   We already learned that. This information came from parents, family, friends, teachers, movies, books, music, etc.

41   Women are big on romance and love because this is a part of their nature – they desire union. And union to them includes romance and love because they want to feel more valuable, desirable and precious than other women (the plus 1).

42 So you can fight this Social Conditioning or you can use it to your advantage.

43 Use what's already in her mind about romance and love. Become a man who gives these things to a woman he thinks has earned it. Use stories (or anything else you can use) to reinforce this.

44 When you hear a song about, "unbreakable love"; tell her this is the kind of love you're looking for. If this is true for you (don't lie, keep it real).

45 When you and your woman are watching a movie that has a female really down for her man, tell her that's a real woman and ask her if she'll be down for you like that. That's real commitment to you.

46 let's say you come across a post on social media about how a man risked his life to save his wife because he couldn't imagine living without her. Use it. Show it to your woman. Tell her that she must be a hell of a woman to make her husband feel that way. That's the kind of love you want to find.

47 A Mack uses everything to his advantage. This is called a Game for a reason. Both your strategy and tactics dictate your next move. Just remember to be honest.

48 When you're talking about romance and love, what is this doing? She will sub-consciously link these files already stored in her mind to how she starts thinking about you.

49 In other words, when she thinks about you, she'll also think about romance and love too. All you have to do is be honest and make sure your *behavior* matches with what you've said. To make it even clearer – everything you think, say and do must match; you must be consistent.

50 Always be Playing!

51 Train your woman by putting the files in her mind that you want in there. Over time she'll make her own based on your overall character, but when you're genuine from the start, you'll have nothing to reap but benefits.

52 The way you start with a woman must be the way you continue with a woman. And training her how to treat you and how to think about you is part of that process.

53 Let me reiterate – make sure everything you think, say and do is consistent because this builds the feelings of SECURITY she needs.

54 At this point the moral question usually comes up, "Isn't all this a little manipulative?" And I'll answer that question with a few questions of my own.

55 Is being trained for a job manipulative? Is being trained to perform better at a sport manipulative? How about training your child to obey you as a parent?

56 People accept all this training as "normal" and necessary because they chose to do it. But, when it comes to training people (males and females) how to treat you, that's considered manipulative. Why?

57 Expand your Perspective. If you don't train someone how to treat you, then who is? Only you know, *you*. Only you know what you want, what you like and dislike. You should also know what you will and won't accept from other people.

58 Get rid of that Social Conditioning, it's doing you more harm than good. If you don't see it now, then I honestly hope it will "click" for you one day. How is anyone (male or female) going to know anything about you unless you open your mouth?

59   If you can't accept this part of the Mack Game, you'll never be an extraordinary Mack. Your Game will always have a Game Leak (weakness).

60   Honestly this goes beyond Macking. It should be a Standard and Principle for you. What real man will just let any person run over him or treat him however they choose?

61   As far as women are concerned, be the transmitter of what you want so they receive it. You're not forcing anything. Always leave them the option to continue with you or leave you alone.

62   Now let's look at the inevitable and how to prepare for it so you can handle it when it surfaces.

Keeping a Woman Focused on Your Program

63   It's going to happen eventually so just accept it and prepare for it.

64   A woman is going to be functioning quite well in your Program at first, then something is going to come along and throw her focus off. It can come from anywhere.

65   Suddenly she's going to bring something to your attention that seems to go against everything you both agreed on – or so you thought.

66   This is just part of a woman's nature; nothing to get upset or frustrated about. That's why I'm going to give you the Game on how to handle this; just more tools to go in your toolbox. A Mack is always as prepared as possible.

67   When a woman loses focus on the bigger picture (your Program and systems) you have to check her about it and bring her back in line. That's simple means you need to help her refocus.

68 This isn't done through arguing, raising your voice or stomping around like a spoiled child. It's done with your mouth-piece – the way you talk; your communication skills.

69 When trying to get a woman on board with your Program you have to always remember that women have some child-like qualities.

70 What this mean is that just telling them about your Program isn't enough. It has to be broken down in a way to where they can understand why the system you assigned to them is important.

71 You have to take Responsibility. Don't leave it up to the woman to figure it all out; because she usually won't. You have to break down what you need (or want) and why you need it (or want it) in the simplest way possible.

72 Using this effectively includes two things:

(1) Using stories to help drive home your point.
(2) Making sure she sees a benefit for herself in what you're asking her to do.

73 So let's say you come upon a **Domestic** minded woman (one of the four women types). It's not enough just to tell her, "I would like for you to cook for me every once in a while. It will really help me."

74 This is indirect and vague. She'll hear it but she won't really take that and suddenly do what you asked. Why? Because she can't see herself in it. Woman translates things in terms of themselves. A woman's favorite subject is herself – you didn't forget that did you?

75 To break this down to her she needs to understand the bigger picture of her cooking meals for you. She also needs to

understand the benefits as they relates to *her*, not you. I know this might sound confusing so let's get into it.

76 Although her cooking helps you, she needs to understand the benefit of it for herself. She needs to know what she gets out of the deal. I'll give you an example:

77 Let's say, as part of your current Program, you're working on a project to help you get a promotion on your job. There's really no deadline for this project but you really want that promotion so you want to get it done as soon as possible.

78 So instead of just throwing it out there that you would like her to cook for you, you could explain it something like this:

"Hey baby, you know I have a hectic schedule already. Plus I'm working on this project to help get me that job promotion. My schedule goes like this,"

"I wake up at six in the morning and I leave the house by seven. I get to work about eight. I work from eight until five and it takes me an hour to get home,"

"So by the time I get home it's about six. I have to cook, take a shower and work on my project. But cooking takes up so much of my time. So after cooking and showering by the time I get into my project it's already eight at night. To get a good night's rest I try to get into bed by about ten-thirty. That only gives me about two hours to really do what I need to do on my project,"

"If you cooked for me I could save almost an hour a day. About 5 hours a week. I can give some of those hours to you and use some to work on my project. The more time I'm able to put into the project the faster it'll get done. And the faster it gets done the more time I'll have for you,"

"And when I get that promotion just think of how much we'll be advancing. We can go out more and even take that vacation out of the country we've been talking about. More money will be coming in so that's just more money to save. So can you help me out and cook during the week?"

79   If you missed it, read it again.

80   What you just asked her to do is cook for you. But you explained it in a way where it gives you more time for her. You benefit and she benefits.

81   You'll also be able to do bigger and better things together once you get the promotion on your job. Again, you benefit and she benefits. It's a win-win proposition.

82   I'll give you another example to help make this concept even clearer for you.

83   In this scenario let's say you're trying to open up a tobacco shop as part of your current Program. This is your first entrepreneurial endeavor and it's taking up a lot of time. Much more time than you originally thought.

84   You have a woman with a **Confidant** personality type. You have been living together for a while and she's been eyeing a new car she wants to buy.

85   Since most of your money is being invested in your future business, taking on a new monthly car payment and a higher insurance payment is going to work against your current Program. More money going out with no more coming in.

86   It's your Responsibility to explain to her (in simple terms) why she needs to hold off on buying a new car. You can't expect her to figure it out. With her child-like nature, all she sees is something new and shiny. It's like the kid who really wants a new toy.

87   Because women can sometimes get caught up in the emotions of what they want, they'll only use their logic and reasoning to justify why they should have it.

88   In this example your woman hasn't really thought about the financial strain she'll be creating if she buys a new car.

89   Instead of just telling her that buying a new car is a bad idea, you need to explain to her the "reason why". She has to see the benefit for herself in it, although you're asking her to put-off something she really wants. The way you break it to her may go like this:

"You know I've been working hard to get this tobacco shop open. I know you've eyeballing that new car and I see how excited you are about it. But between the two of us I don't think we can afford it right now,"

"We work hard on our jobs. Our house mortgage is $1,000 a month and all our current bills add up to about $350. Then we have to still put gas in our cars, pay car insurance, buy food and basic necessities,"

"Have you done any research about how much buying a new car will cost per month? I did, and it'll probably be around $550. And with a new car that means our car insurance will go up too,"

"Over a year we'll be looking at well over $8,000 going out. That $8,000 dollars can be put into getting this business off the ground instead,"

"I know you want this new car but if you can just hold off for another year we'll have a business that will be bringing in extra money. We won't have to cut back on things; we'll be able to actually have more things,"

"I want you to have a new car; you deserve it but don't forget the big picture. We both want to stop slaving away at our jobs and the business is going to help us with that. The faster we can get this business off the ground, the faster we can both stop working; we'll have more time with the kids too,"

"You have to think long-term. Think about where you want to be in two years from now. Sacrifice now so we can have greater, later. Let's stick to the plan. Are you with me?"

90   Guide her step-by-step-by-step. The mind works best when large amounts of information are broken up into smaller bits. This is essentially what you're doing here.

91   You have to walk your woman through what you're thinking. "Thinking out-loud more" doesn't just apply to flirting and dating. It also applies to making sure you and your woman are reading the same book and are on the same page.

92   When keeping your woman focused the more logic and reasoning you use the better. Women are more emotional than men, so polarize to her opposite and explain things with logic and reason.

93   When you're keeping a woman focused, this can also be a form of checking her. You want to do it in such a way that you're not checking her nature but her behavior. The behavior of getting too wrapped up in thoughts and feelings that may bring more harm than good.

94   Bring her out of her world and into yours by giving her your logical Perspective. What you say has to make sense and she has to see a benefit for her. The more benefits you can provide the better.

95   If a woman is really down for you and your Program, she will come around and see things your way.

96   Like a child she may whine and pout about it, but once the emotion passes she'll see the "reason why" behind what you're explaining to her. This will lead her to getting back focused on the Program.

97   Knowing this is important. Many males, some men and even some Macks fail here. They get frustrated because their woman is getting off-track and "forgetting" what she agreed to do.

98   Check her, but without the emotion. A woman is emotional so she can deal with an emotional male. Don't play yourself by putting yourself into the familiar territory she knows. Bring her back into your little world.

99   If you have to explain this in different ways every single day, then this is what you have to do. It's your Program in place so it's your Responsibility to make sure your teammate is still playing for the team.

100   Think of it like a basketball coach giving a pep-talk before a game. Players on the team have heard similar pep-talks before, but there's nothing wrong with being reminding of the "reason why".

101   We all need that. Good companies do it often with their employees. They might meet every morning (or once a week) and make sure everyone is still on the same page and playing for the same team.

102   As a Mack, the owner of your company (king of your kingdom), your duty is no different. So Mack responsibly – always be playing.

Praise in Public & Criticism in Private

103   Males, men and even some Macks don't praise their women enough. No one like to feel underappreciated – especially women.

When I use the word praise don't confuse that with kissing her ass. Only give credit when it's due. And if it is due, then let it be known.

104 Imagine working at a job where you never hear, "Thank you," or, "You did a terrific job!" every once in a while.

105 When you give praise to your woman, do it out in the open whenever possible. It can be in front of her family or friends, her children, her co-workers or even your family or friends.

106 Think out-loud; say how proud you are of having such a strong woman with you. Say out loud that you're glad that she chose you because together you're a strong team. Make it known that you'd rather have 50% of her than 100% of a lesser woman.

107 Women are creatures of sound. These compliments, especially when done in the presence of others, will make her feel like she should be feeling with a Mack – valuable, desirable and precious (the plus 1); in other words, cherished.

108 You're not less of a man for doing this. In fact you're more of a man in her eyes because you're making her feel like a woman.

109 When the time comes to check your woman on her behavior, you want to do this in private – some place where it's just you and her. It's not always possible but if you can manage it, do it.

110 Women are very social conscious. So if you check her in front of friends, family or her children she will either bury her pain or react in defense of her pride.

111 You made her look foolish, and however she reacts, this will leave a scar; especially if she really respects you and cares about you. She'll be deeply hurt and this may cause unnecessary problems. Why make unnecessary problems for yourself?

112   And when you do criticize her, remember to take out as much emotion as possible when you check her. You shouldn't be yelling or screaming, and don't let this turn into an argument.

113   Explain to her *logically* why you don't like her behavior. Make it simple and make sure she understands the "reason why" you don't like it. Think out-loud.

114   If the woman questions you about being checked, don't get upset, take a moment and think of another way to explain it. Put in into the form of a story or analogy if you can come up with one.

115   You could use a movie, something you read or even something from your own experiences. Just make sure she understands. She doesn't have to agree, you just want her to understand. Then leave her to make the choice on her own.

116   And what happens if she does the same thing again after she said she understood your first conversation? Don't allow yourself to get upset, just tell her that you're disappointed and walk away.

117   If she has respect for you and cares, this will sting. It's like a father telling his child that they're disappointed in them. That he knows they can do better but they refuse to.

118   If she plays the "innocent role" like she didn't realize what she was doing (don't fall for this childishness), calmly remind her of your previous conversation.

119   Tell her that obviously she doesn't understand and that's the most disappointing thing of all, because you're supposed to have a stronger connection than that.

120   When she sees that you're serious (and you should be), she'll want to fix what was just broken. Take this opportunity to have a second conversation about it.

121   Again, keep emotion out of it. Don't allow this to escalate into an argument. If she starts to raise her voice or argue, just walk away. Don't allow yourself to get pulled into her emotional world.

122   If the conversation goes smoothly, ask her again if she understands. Also tell her there will not be a third conversation. And when you say that, mean it!

123   If she does it again (which is unlikely to happen with a high caliber woman), you must be prepared to tell her to get out of your life.

124   That's a hard pill to swallow, I know. But this is the coldness of being a Mack. You can never compromise your Standards and Principles. You can't allow your feelings for her to override what you want. You and the Value of your manhood come first.

125   You shouldn't want any woman around you that can't behave in a manner that is acceptable to you. There's no Macking in that anywhere. Respect the Game. Your Game! The rules that you've established. You made them, why break them? That is what males do, not men and especially not Macks.

126   There is one exception to this rule, and that's if you're dealing with multiple women. If it's just you and your women, and you're all not in public, you want to check the woman with the unacceptable behavior in front of the other women.

127   What this does is help keep the other women in check because they can see the results of certain types of behavior. Basically you're training them all at the same time.

128   This is also effective because it keeps everything "out in the open" amongst your women. This is extremely important when dealing with multiple women. We'll cover that subject in detail later in Book 6.

129   As you spend more time with your woman and train her, she is going to be more than ready to give you her body.

130   It's at this point that you can finally give in to that natural urge. You have a woman committed to your Program and she's sincerely doing her best to be a good woman to you.

131   It is only this high quality of woman who deserves your sex. To a Mack, his penis is golden. He places a high Value on it. He only gives it to women who are really with him and what he represents.

132   SEX is an important need of a woman and it's important that you be good in this department. You don't have to be great, but you do have to satisfy her.

133   There's much more Outer Game to learn. Next we'll explore the overall lifestyle of a Mack – what composes the day-to-day management and how you should approach the many ups and downs that come along with it. Macking ain't easy because the kingdom doesn't run itself.

BOOK 6 – MULTIPLE WOMEN, MANAGEMENT & LIFESTYLE

CHAPTER ONE

The Understanding Behind Having Multiple Women

1   Once you get that first woman that's fully invested into your Program, that's it! You can now proudly claim the title and call yourself a Mack.

2   Although this chapter is about the mystery of having multiple women in your life, I first need to make a point.

3   Not every Mack (or man) should have multiple women. It's not a requirement to be a Mack although a Mack will always keep women around, even if they're just friends.

4   If a Mack does have a dedicated Lady, he'll still go out and meet new women. The truth is, you never really know when you'll "blow" the woman you already have. If it does happen you'll have one or two more already lined up to take her place if they're qualified.

5   The lifestyle of a Mack is very unconventional and he needs to make sure any woman that deals with him knows that. She needs to be accepting of the fact that other women will be around in some capacity. He doesn't need to be sleeping with them, but they need to be around somewhere. Just this fact alone will help keep the woman he does have in check.

6   In the Mack Game, having multiple women all contributing to your Program is called having a "stable". Just like a stable full of horses that run races for their owner; a Mack has a stable of women who "run the race" within his Program and systems.

7   If you've been following along closely you're probably wondering how a Mack can have a woman completely into him, have sex with her, be romantic and still have other women he

treats in a similar way? And to top it off, all these women know about each other and they all accept the situation.

8   It baffles the mind, doesn't it? If you choose to have multiple women all contributing to your Program, there's some Game you really have to know.

9   In order to even attempt this, your Value has to be extremely high. Every Game in the World spins around Value. When the right Value is placed on the table, the impossible becomes possible. In the Mack Game, your manhood is the real Value.

10   Every woman knows that a man desires women. A wiser woman has already accepted the fact that a man cheating on her is not outside the realm of possibility.

11   Women worry about this quite often; more often than you can probably imagine. They already naturally fear being abandoned by a man. And if her man leaves her because of another woman, that's ten-times worse.

12   Women are very territorial. What they consider theirs *is* theirs. They will fight to protect what's theirs if they're pushed that far.

13   The average woman will hit "psycho-mode" if she discovers that her man is cheating on her. She'll be ready to fight, flatten tires or even worse. A huge reason this happens is because he shatters the image of who he was *pretending* to be (a good faithful man). Now he becomes the liar and the deceiver and she feels foolish for trusting him to begin with.

14   It's one of her worst fears come true and despite her doing her best to be trusting and loving, somewhere in the back of her mind, she knows this is a reality – males are weak for sex.

15   She may verbally deny it, but she sees and hears about it so much that she figures that eventually being cheated on could happen to her.

16 The funny thing is some women were the "other woman" at one time or another. They dated or just slept with a male who had a girlfriend or was even married. But when it comes to *their* man, they'll be damned if he has a woman on the side.

17 These seemingly contradictions in her nature stem from the fact that a woman will accept a lot from a man she Values.

18 A woman would honestly consider sleeping with a famous actor, musician or sports figure even though she knows that man is married, just to have the experience of being with a high Valued man; valuable from her Perspective.

19 But if this happened to her, if she was married to this famous man, she'll hit "psycho mode". Again, this appears like a contradiction but it's really not.

20 Once you understand *why* it's not a contradiction, you'll possess the secret to having multiple women. And let me clearly define what I mean by multiple women:

21 Everything is upfront and honest. All your women will know you date and sleep with other women. They may even meet each other – or hang out together. A Mack is a real man; he doesn't hide behind deceit and lies. That's shows weakness of character.

22 Here's some Game for you: **Women are more attracted to men that have other women attracted to him**. How does that work? Because *socially* he's a high valued man. This male (or man) could just be attractive, have no real personality and nothing else going for him.

23 But because other women find him attractive, most women will also see him as attractive. Obviously there has to be *something* about him, right?

24   This may be crazy to read if you don't have a lot of experience with women, but the more women you have around you, the more women you'll attract.

25   This works because the average male (and even the average man) doesn't have a lot of women around. It's an anomaly; a puzzle. To a woman, a man that has many women around that find him attractive is intriguing.

26   As usual, this has little to do with the actual man and more to do with the Perspective of the woman. She honestly figures that if a man has many women attracted to him, then he *has* to be good with women.

27   Since this is usually the case, they'll find themselves curious about *what* makes this man so good with women.

28   If many women find one particular man interesting then his social value goes up and with it, his overall attractiveness.

29   This is challenging to a woman because she wants to know if she can be the "one" to have him. She wants to know if she's enough woman to knock all the other women "out of the box". Does she have what it takes to garner his time and attention?

30   For a male (or a man) this is very similar. You can easily accept that an attractive woman probably has a few males around her just because she's physically attractive.

31   For women, it's not completely about the physical attractiveness. For them it's the fact that a man appears to be good with women because many are around trying to get his attention.

32   A women's social value is based on her attractiveness. A man's social value is based on his overall manhood. And with manhood comes effectiveness with women. This screams extreme confidence, and this radiates in his Aura – women can literally feel it.

33   Since women translate things into how they can benefit themselves, why wouldn't they want a real man with confidence that's *already* good with women?

34   Wouldn't you prefer to have an attractive woman over an ugly one if given the choice?

35   Another matter that needs to be addressed is the Plus 1 (of the 5 plus 1 important needs of a woman). The Plus 1 states that: A woman's greatest need is to feel more valuable, desirable and precious than other women – she needs to feel cherished.

36   If this is true, then how is it possible that this need can be fulfilled by a man that's intimately involved with multiple women at the same time?

37   The "secret" lies in Value of course. But we have to go a level deeper for the complete understanding.

38   Let's say for a moment you want to buy a house. You already have in your mind certain things that the house *must* have. You may need a certain number of bedrooms; or you may need it to have a full basement; the right neighborhood may be an important factor.

39   So you talk to your realtor and tell them your requirements. At that moment it's their job to shop around and find homes that fit those requirements.

40   When your realtor comes back with a list of homes to view what are you doing mentally? You're checking off that list of requirements you have in your head.

41   Does the house have a large backyard? Does the house have a large kitchen? Is one of the rooms going to have enough space for a home office? Is the neighborhood a safe neighborhood?

42   The less this house has of what you want (and need); the less likely you are to buy it. The house loses Value to *you*, but the house may be the perfect fit for someone else.

43   Let's say the house you're looking at has 15 of the 20 things you want. You would still consider buying the house because you know you have to compromise on a few things.

44   At that point, it's just a matter of does it have the most *important* things.

45   Human beings (generally speaking) have a list of qualities in their head about what constitutes a good "catch" when it comes to choosing someone to date.

46   If a woman sees that a man has 15 out of the 20 qualities she thinks and feels she wants, she'll compromise on the rest. The man may not be perfect but damn near close.

47   To *her*, his Value is high enough to sacrifice a few short comings for.

48   The **First Key** is finding the women who will be so infatuated with you that they'll compromise on you having other women. The higher the overall Value of your manhood and social Value, the less difficult this becomes.

49   The **Second Key** is that you must make each woman feel like they're the *only* woman when it's just you and her. You have to place them in a "bubble" – where the rest of the world doesn't exist when you're together.

50   Realistically she knows there are other women around, but she is getting most of her needs fulfilled by you and she's satisfied with just having that.

51   Many males, in their silly way of thinking, would like to reason that only women who are naïve or have low self-esteem would

accept a situation like this. They think, 'Shouldn't a woman have enough self-respect to be a man's *only* woman?'

52   It's this same male that will ignore the reality all around him and refuse to see it.

53   When a woman sees real Value in something that benefits herself, she'll go after it (most of the time). This goes beyond men; she'll do it for anything – a house, a car, a new pair of shoes, a new piece of jewelry, a new job, etc.

54   As far as men are concerned, when they see the Value that benefits herself, she'll go after him. He could have a girlfriend, or be married. Her Perspective of his Value is worth more than her socially conditioned morals.

55   Although women are generally more loyal then males (because they take relationships more serious), when she does cheat, she'll cheat with a male that does what? Gives her what her current boyfriend isn't giving her.

56   What is current boyfriend not giving her? The 5 plus 1 – COMMUNICATION, SECURITY, PROVIDING, SEX, ENTERTAINMENT and making her feel like she's more valuable, desirable and precious than other women… even if it's just when he's around her.

57   A woman will make compromises for a man that has three main qualities. And this can include accepting that he is intimate with other women. A man of this caliber must possess:

(1) A High overall Value of manhood;
(2) High *social* Value (appears to be good with women) and;
(3) The ability to touch her at the deepest levels (the 5 plus 1).

58   This understanding is vital if you want to have multiple women because asking a woman to accept this directly will usually be met with a strong, "No!"

59   But bringing a woman into your Program where dating other women is already a part of your lifestyle leaves her the option to continue forward with the Mack or leave.

60   And this is the option she wants. She wants to be able to make the final decision for herself. She'll respect a Mack who gives this to her.

61   Having multiple women starts very early when you're getting to know a woman. This should be made known usually during the first date – avoid this topic during the social outing. See if the woman is even worth the trouble first.

62   Also, you want to build mental attraction first so she is more "open" to at least hear what you have to say later.

63   This upfront honesty will keep you from ever being accused of being a liar and a deceiver. You're letting her know the reality of how you live and giving her the option to accept it or reject it.

64   The way you start with a woman has to be the way you continue. She may not like what you have to say, but she'll respect you for not lying to her.

65   It's much worse when she finds out later down the line that a male (or man) is a liar. Especially when he has her heart. This is what puts a woman into "psycho-mode".

66   You have to be a man and explain to her that you'll be dating other women while you're also dating her.

67   If she understands your "reason why" and she sees your Value of manhood, she'll accept this. She won't like it, but in her mind, a man like you with high Value (and high social Value) might be worth making the compromise for.

68   This is yet another reason why a Mack keeps a good number of female friends. They add to his social Value, especially women he has personally "friend-zoned" because they may be still attracted to him.

69   He's desirable to other women, confident and charming; therefore he must be good with women in general.

70   So what exactly is your "reason why" you want to date multiple women at the same time? If it's just for sex then you're not really Macking. Your reason has to be deeper and more meaningful than sex.

71   If your reason is just sexual gratification then you'll lessen your overall Value of manhood when trying to explain this to a woman.

72   Trust me, they'll ask a lot of questions and you should be prepared for every single one of them. Answering, "Just because," or, "That's what I want," isn't going to cut it.

73   A Mack rules his kingdom (company) with logic and reason, not based on how he feels.

74   So be real with yourself. What is the "reason why" you want multiple women in your life?

75   Only you can answer this question for yourself so think long and hard.

76   If you can't see past sex, then having multiple women may not be a good move for you if you call yourself Macking. You'll end up looking like every other average male that has a hard time keeping his penis in his pants. Many women despise that trait – they'll lose respect and you may turn them off completely.

77   A real Mack is levels above the average male in everything he does. He's almost super-human; this is part of what makes him a Mack.

78   A woman who asks questions about your motives is a good sign because she's really saying, "Convince me why I should accept this?" She really wants to understand it so she can wrap her head around it.

79   When you can logically explain your "reason why" so that it makes sense to *her*, this gives her the option she wants – whether to accept it or reject it.

80   The higher your Value of manhood (and social Value) the easier it is for her to accept it. To her, you'll be worth the compromise. You're the "house" that has the 15 out of 20 things she's looking for.

81   Here's some more Game for you: If you can find just *one* woman that comes into your Program and accepts you having other women – as you meet these other women, convincing them to get on board is even easier.

82   Women are social creatures. They have a pretty big influence over other women. If a group of women are against sleeping with strange males, then that whole group will take on that mentality.

83   If a group of women consider themselves "sluts" and don't care about who they sleep with; almost that entire group of women will take on that mentality.

84   It's just like meeting women at a club or bar. If the group of women all agreed to leave together, then every female in that group will generally not leave with a man under any circumstances.

85   No woman in the group wants to break the group's "social rule". So they'll all follow the rule. Breaking the rule is frowned

upon. No female wants to be looked down upon by the rest of their "girls".

86 So if your "main" woman accepts you being with other women then the next woman you present the idea to will view it differently. Instead of thinking, 'This guy must be out of his mind!' she'll think, 'Why is this other woman OK with this?' Her inquisitive nature will cause her to start asking questions and this is what you want.

87 Think of an antique merchant balance scale. When you already have a woman that's accepting, you have a "weight" already on one side of the scale; it's "tipping" to the side you want.

88 Not all women will accept a man being with her and other women at the same time. It won't matter how high his Value is. Like I mentioned earlier, if she starts asking honest questions (not asking because she's offended and trying to belittle your Perspective), you can usually convince her to at least give it serious consideration.

89 While she's considering, keep on Macking her. Keep doing everything you would normally do. Tease, flirt, take her out on dates and converse with her.

90 Just make it very clear that once she accepts you and your Program, she's also accepting that you'll be dating and possibly intimate with other women.

91 This is where some men get scared. They found a woman who says she can accept everything but they get scared to continue looking for the second woman because he thinks he'll blow (lose) the first one.

92 Is it possible to blow (lose) the first girl? Of course it is. She may mentally make peace with the idea at first but, once it's in her face and becomes a reality, her feelings may change.

93   You have to accept this if this is the type of Macking you want to do. There's no magic trick to keeping a woman around who can't handle her man being with other women. The best you can do is to keep Macking, keep giving her all your "reasons why" and keep fulfilling her most important needs.

94   When you're around her, make it just you and her. Tell your other woman you're going to be busy that day. If your other woman (or potential woman) asks why you're going to be busy, be honest. If she respect you and recognizes your Value, she'll wait her turn.

95   Another fear that arises: If you have a woman that knows you're intimate with other women, won't she end up "cheating" on you?

96   That's also a possibility. But a Mack is more concerned about his women contributing properly to his Program over one of them "cheating".

97   Trying to prevent any woman from sleeping around has no business in the Mack Game. A Mack must accept that this can happen and make peace with it. This isn't something some of you want to hear but let's step out of fantasy land and live in reality.

98   Males (and some men) cheat because they *want* to cheat, for their personal reasons. Women cheat because they *want* to cheat, for their personal reasons.

99   Constantly worrying about what "might" happen places you on the same emotional level as a female. This is a place where a Mack shouldn't want to be.

100   Is it possible to have multiple women and none of them "cheat" on you? Of course it is but, you don't make that decision, the women do.

101 If you have Tight Game, even if a woman does "creep" for awhile, she'll usually come back because that other male doesn't understand how to fulfill her deeper needs.

102 You'll have her mind, heart and body (maybe even her soul). What does "the other guy" have? Probably just her body. A Mack knows that you can't *hold* a woman with sex alone. The other guy is just a diversion – amusement.

103 Your woman sleeping with another man may be new and exciting at first. However, when the rest of the substance isn't there, she'll usually remember what she's missing with you. She'll realize something is broken and she'll want to fix it.

104 Holding a woman for a long time doesn't mean that she'll never leave. Some women will leave (or sleep with another male), realize there isn't anyone of higher Value, then come back to you.

The spell of Value can only be broken by someone of equal or greater Value.

105 When a woman leaves or "cheats" and comes back, make sure she understands nothing has changed about your Program and lifestyle. If she can accept that, then welcome her back with open arms; at least the first time. If it happens again you should cut her off completely. Forgive but don't forget.

106 Women who leave or "creep" with another male and come back to you are usually some of the most loyal and dedicated women you'll have. Your Value to them will be exponentially higher than it was before. Funny how that works, isn't it?

107 One thing to realize is that when you add just one additional woman to your stable (team), the problems that arise don't double, they triple.

108 This is why. When it's just you and one woman the relationship's dynamic is this:

(1) You and that woman have a relationship (the way you both choose to relate to one another).
(2) You have your own personal matters to deal with.
(3) She has her own personal matters to deal with.

109   When you add just one more women into the mix, the relationship's dynamic changes into this:

(1) You have a relationship with the first woman.
(2) You have a relationship with the second woman.
(3) You have you own personal issues to deal with.
(4) Your first woman has her own personal issues to deal with.
(5) Your second woman has her own personal issues to deal with.
(6) Your two women will also have some form of relationship.
(7) You'll have issues with your first woman because of the second woman.
(8) The second woman will have issues with you because of your first woman.
(9) The women will have issues amongst themselves.

110   As the Mack, it's your Responsibility to handle all these issues and solve all these problems. They'll both be constantly looking at you and waiting to see how you handle things.

111   You're the one who created this situation to begin with after all, correct?

112   It's not enough to just have a stable of women. A Mack must help them manage their daily life problems and help manage their emotional issues as well.

113   This is why I said earlier that not every Mack (or male) should have multiple women. It can be mentally exhausting if

you're not prepared for it. And it can be physically exhausting as well.

114 You'll not only be spending time with your women, romancing them and helping them, but you'll also be having sex with them.

115 Add-in spending the holidays and their birthdays with them; plus attending social functions together. You'll also be expected to attend their children's birthday parties, sports games and graduations.

116 You have to be their man in every capacity you possibly can. A Mack is a man that's almost super-human. These are the sacrifices you must make for the lifestyle you want to live.

117 As you can imagine, this eats up a lot of your personal time. Some of that time is replaced however because these women are assisting you with your Program.

118 If you haven't built yourself up enough (mentally and emotionally) to be pulled in many directions at once, then think long and hard about having a stable of women.

119 Macking ain't easy because the kingdom doesn't run itself. You have to be available and on duty 24/7/365.

120 I don't write all of this to discourage you if this is what you want. I'm just presenting the reality.

121 Achieving a successful stable of even just two women is a thrill that most males (and even some men) will never experience. It can be a beautiful situation.

122 Image having just two women in your life that are both down for you. Since everything is upfront in the open, you don't have to hide, sneak, connive or lie. You can just keep moving and shaking without that added stress. Just like how a Mack should be.

123 Something else to consider: Each of your women will be keeping a mental count of how much time you spend with them and what you do or don't do for them.

124 You can place "controls" in your Program so that they shouldn't expect you to be with them for everything. A Mack must have boundaries. But you must have the ability to help them solve their problems.

125 If you don't do anything else, you *have* to PROVIDE this. Otherwise, why are they with you? Because you're charming and you make them feel good about themselves?

126 Don't forget the 5 plus 1. SECURITY and PROVIDING are more than just talking and romancing. These require hands-on action sometimes.

127 In the lifestyle of a Mack, solving problems and keeping every area of your life and their lives running smoothly is called management. We'll cover this in the next chapter.

128 I've given two keys already (verses 48 and 49) that will help boost your Value so that women will give your offer serious consideration. Now let me give you two more keys that are just as important to have.

129 The **Third Key** is that every other woman you bring into your stable must be around similar Value to your main woman. A Mack's main woman is the woman who's contributing the most to his Program. This is usually the first woman he brings in.

130 These women's personalities can be different, their backgrounds can be different, their career paths can be different, their interests can be different; but they must be at a similar station in life. They have to be social equals (or very close) and be able to connect mentally.

131   Oil and water don't mix. If you're first woman is a marine biologist and your second woman never finished middle school, this is going to make the situation more difficult to handle.

132   Its like trying to hammer a nail into concrete. You're going to get a lot of resistance.

133   Mainly what's going to happen is the first woman will look down on your second. She'll look at you and think, 'How did he get me with the Value I have, then get a woman who is nowhere near my level?'

134   This works the opposite way as well. If your first woman is a wild party girl and your second woman likes to stay home all day and read books, the second woman will feel as though she doesn't have a place in the equation; she doesn't "fit in" and therefore doesn't matter.

135   The second woman might *think* she's intellectually superior to your first. And then she'll start *feeling* that she actually is. Because she thinks and feels that way, she'll *act* that way. It will come out in her behavior. She'll question your choice of women because she'll be the odd one out. She won't feel like she belongs.

136   When putting together a stable, your women are going to have to meet eventually; even if it's just briefly a few times.

137   Since both of these women are kicking into your Program, the situation usually comes up where they'll have to work together to help you out in some capacity. Or they may need to help each other.

138   If they feel too different from one another, they won't question each other, they'll both question **you**. You created the situation so you're the Responsible party. That's how it should be.

139 On a few levels, the women you add to your stable have to see some of themselves in the other women. They have to be able to relate to them. Let me explain why this is important.

140 The key-word here is: **FAMILY**. Your stable needs to function together as a family unit. They not only need to have your back, but they also have to have the other women's backs too.

141 This can be something small, like helping you shop for a birthday present for your other woman's child. Or having them pick up a prescription for your other woman because you don't have time to.

142 It can also be bigger things like pulling together your own resources and the resources of all your women, to purchase a piece of land or start a business.

143 They need to think of this situation as a family. Families *do* for one another. Yes, families also fuss, argue and fight, but at the end of the day they learn to forgive and look past certain things (most of the time).

144 I urge you as a Mack to stop looking at having multiple women as just sex, or a way to feed your ego. There is so much potential **power** contained in a group of people working together.

145 Everyone involved can help each other reach their individual goals faster and help out in areas where another person can't.

146 It's like a basketball team. Each player on the court has a certain position. When everyone plays their position, the team can function like an actual team; everyone in harmony working together for the goal of winning.

147 By functioning in a family capacity, you should possess the policy of "openness". Nothing should be hidden. There should be no sneaking around because there's no reason to.

148   You should be able to be completely open and honest with your women and they should be able to be the same with you.

149   If your women do become friendlier with each other, they need to be open with each other as well.

150   There should be few secrets amongst everyone. Secrets create doubt, confusion and distrust. Doubts, confusion and distrust are like razors taken to the skin. With enough cuts, you'll eventually bleed to death.

151   In other words, letting things like this exist in your kingdom (company) is a major Game Leak that will destroy everything you're trying to build.

152   The **Fourth Key** is that your main woman must know, beyond a shadow of a doubt, that you can handle her. If she feels that you can't handle her, then how are you going to handle both her *and* another woman?

153   By "handle" I mean that you're firm but fair with her. You check her behavior often but never her nature. She must recognize and respect you as being a real man.

154   You don't accept anything less than the best of what you know she's capable of. You must build her up through "tough love" and never tear her down. Tearing down a woman is what weak males do because they're insecure and childish.

155   Example: Let's say someone asked you for a million dollar loan. But the person asking for the loan is a habitual gambler. Money runs through their fingers like water.

156   Would you give a million dollars to a person like that? No you wouldn't. Why? Because you know they couldn't handle that amount of money. Giving that to them would be a waste; like flushing it down a toilet.

157   And this is my point. If your first woman feels you can't handle her, she'll think that you can't handle any other woman you bring into your life.

158   She'll resist you and even try to undermine your efforts just to prove to *herself* that she's right. During the process she hopes to prove to you that she's right too.

159   If this is the lifestyle of Macking that you want, your Game has to be air-tight.

160   A few other questions come up like, "Should my women meet?", "Should I let them hang-out together?", "Should I take them all on a date at the same time?"

161   As a bona fide Mack, at the very least I would recommend introducing your women to each other. They might not admit it to you, but they do want to *see* what your other women look like – they want to know how physically attractive they are. They also want to analyze each other's behavior.

162   I wouldn't do this until you are 100% sure both women are handling the situation well and both are involved in your Program as they should be.

163   As far as taking them out together or letting them hang-out together by themselves, that's your decision to make. It's your world. But keep in mind the magic word, FAMILY and what it means to you.

164   If your women already know each other (yes, this can happen), then you don't want to interfere with their relationship too much. Trying to drive a wedge between them looks weak – like you have something to hide or have a hidden agenda.

165   One more thing you need to keep in mind before we move on. When you present this idea to a woman you need to see it

from her Perspective – not just yours. **Never ignore both sides of the coin because you'll usually miss something crucial**.

166   Even if she considers the idea, she's going to be afraid. She's scared that she'll be looked down upon by other women, her friends, her family and even her children.

167   From their Socially Conditioned Perspective, what female in their right mind would accept being with a man that has other women?

168   Despite what you might think, it takes a very strong woman to commit to a situation like this. They're sacrificing not just having a man all to themselves, but also their social Value.

169   They'll be concerned that they'll look "stupid" to other people. They'll worry about being disrespected and looked at as weak and foolish. They don't want to be scrutinized or have people tell them they're being manipulated. They don't want to be constantly questioned and have to explain why they made this decision.

170   If they consider your proposal, they probably won't tell you any of these fears, but as a Mack you already have to *know* them. You should bring this up to them directly to hash out these fears and address them one-by-one.

171   Don't wait on them! It's your Responsibility to help guide them through their inner turmoil and mixed emotions about accepting this kind of lifestyle.

172   That's what this really is – a certain type of *lifestyle*. A person in the military knows that if they have to go to war, there's a possibility that they can be seriously maimed or killed. The same thing with a police officer and to a lesser extent, a government agent.

173 Those are lifestyles. They're more than just average everyday jobs. Those men and women have to literally take oaths and uphold them.

174 That means that even when they aren't "on the clock" they have certain moral and legal obligations to uphold. They have to adjust their entire lives around that fact.

175 When a soldier is called to duty, they have to go. When a police officer sees a crime committed and he or she isn't in uniform, they still have to take some form of action.

176 These are lifestyles that require standing on the choices they've made. These aren't always convenient and they're often thankless "jobs", but they have to pay the price for the life they chose.

177 With your women it's no different. They have to be willingly to face the rest of the world with their head held high, despite accepting a lifestyle that isn't "normal".

178 As a real Mack, you should give them a "reason why" they should keep their heads held high.

179 You need a strong "reason why" you want multiple women in your life. You must, I repeat, *must* help them find their own personal "reason why" they should accept this lifestyle.

180 Part of this "reason why" should include something greater than yourself. Women need to know there's a better way of living by being with you. That's just good Macking.

181 This is something you have to put together for yourself. It's not something I, or anyone else, can give you.

182 But I'll emphasize again, you have to look far beyond just the sexual aspects and the feeding of your ego. Those are weak

foundations. A house built on a weak foundation will eventually topple over.

183   An important piece of Game here to cap this off: **Never Mack past one woman trying to get to the next**. Solidify things with your "main" woman *first*. Make sure your relationship is well built and strong.

184   This must be done before you take some of your time and attention away to look for the next woman to add to your stable.

185   Now let's take a look at some extremely important concepts so you can get a bigger picture of the overall Mack lifestyle.

186   We're going to dig into leadership and management. We're also going to look at how to handle some of the many problems that will be headed your way.

CHAPTER TWO

The "Mack's Scepter" (Part One)
Leadership Fundamentals

1   A Mack is a leader. And like the literal kings of old, he's the highest level manager of his kingdom. Almost everything going on in his world runs through him. That includes his life and his woman life (or women's lives).

2   Whether a Mack has one woman or several he must lead. Even if he has no women, he still has to be able to lead himself.

3   A Mack lives in a world all his own. It can be lonely because he gives up so much of himself and deals with so many issues that he seldom has other people around to help him with his own. This even includes his own woman (or women).

4   There are a lot of demands placed on a Mack so it's vitally important that a Mack learns to lead and manage his kingdom (company) accordingly.

5   Before we get into some of the problems that will come up and how to handle problems in general, let's look at leadership. Leadership and management are two different things.

Leadership is where you guide people in a direction, course, action or even an opinion.

Management is bringing about successful accomplishments despite difficulty or hardships. Also it means to take care of, or take charge of something.

6   Leadership is like knowing you're going to drive from New York to California – you have a course; a direction (goal). Management is solving every problem that might occur during the

drive – and also having the foresight to prevent problems from happening to begin with.

7   Both leadership and management combine to form the "Mack's Scepter".

8   When you look at images of historical kings, queens and emperors, you'll see them holding a staff or scepter. To some cultures it represented power and authority.

9   In the Mack Game, this Scepter represents your spine – your *backbone* as a man.

10   A Mack must rule with a strong backbone, otherwise his women will see him as weak and refuse to accept his leadership. In truth, that's how almost all Games work so this shouldn't be a surprise.

11   Your Program has already given you a general blueprint to follow. You know where you're going and have systems in place to get you there.

12   You're already halfway a leader and manager so now it's just about filling in the details. We'll definitely be covering management but first let's define leadership. How does a Mack develop leadership qualities?

On Leadership

13   I will be explaining leadership through the Perspective of leading a group or team. Although your team may only consist of you and one woman, I still want to give you the wide-angle view of it.

14   A Mack should have the ability to lead both women and weaker males. The tenets of leadership are universal – they work regardless of a person's sex.

15   Kings are the highest level managers in their kingdom (company). As a Mack, you take the position of king (President/CEO). Being a leader also makes you a manager.

16   You can be good at managing without being a good leader but, you can't be a good leader without knowing how to manage.

17   It's like you can trust someone you don't love, but you can't truly love someone you don't trust.

18   Like everything else in the Game, your Outer Game is only as good as your Inner Game. You must be able to lead yourself, *first*. Once this is mastered, you'll then have a foundation to lead your women. This foundation will be built with experience and skill.

19   Leadership styles are different. Some are indirect and others extremely direct. Some are heavy on delegating the majority of the work to the team; others have each member play a specific role. The latter is more the style of a Mack.

20   In order to understand how leadership works in the modern Mack Game, you need to first understand something about human nature.

(1) People may not try to win but they don't want to lose.
(2) People will perform best in what they like to do, feel comfortable doing and have confidence in doing.

21   The struggles of leadership are firmly rooted in the principle of Responsibility. And here's why:

(1) The strongest of chains will break at its weakest link.
(2) When moving together as a unit, the entire team must move at the speed of the *slowest* person within the unit.

22   People of weak character break easily. Weak character in both males and females is usually due to a lack of Standards, Principles,

integrity, morals and motivation. And no matter how effective your team may be, they will have to pick-up the slack left behind by the most ineffective member.

23 The reality is, some of the slowest moving members of your team will be the most loyal. Unfortunate, but true.

24 Leadership in the Game has been (and always should be) based around a **Family Model**. It can also be called a Household, Clan or Tribe model, although you probably won't hear a Player use those terms.

25 So what is this, Family Model? It all starts with your vision. Your Program is a piece of that vision.

26 Before taking the leadership (and management) role in the Mack Game, you have to have a clear vision. And you will communicate that vision to those on your team – those who you consider your family. You all must working *by* each other and *for* each other.

27 As you should already know, your Program is made up of a goal and might have sub-goals. You cannot be a leader in your own life, or other's lives, if you don't know *where* you're going.

28 Its called leadership for a reason. Where are you leading yourself and other people to? What's the end-game?

29 You never have to share your entire step-by-step plan with your team, but you should share your entire vision with them. The reality is: People respond to a vision more than ideas and plans.

30 If you don't have a solid Program, you'll have huge holes in your Game. Of course this leads to Game Leaks and eventually Game Loss.

31 There are no contracts in the Mack Game. One of the "secrets" to effective leadership is realizing that you don't want

your women completely hooked on you. You want them hooked on the vision – your Program is just a method to see this vision realized.

32   This is how it should be. Why? Because women translate things into how they benefit themselves. So if your vision can benefit them, which it should, you're actually leading them to somewhere they might want to go anyway.

33   For those of you reading this that are more familiar with my work, you know that having a Purpose (Principle number 2 of the 9 Principles) is one of the most important decisions you can make in your life.

34   If you have a Purpose for your life then you already have a vision. Use your Purpose and give your team the passion behind your Purpose.

35   Your vision (or Purpose if you have one) is something that must remain alive. It's something that you should remind your team about almost daily. When they realize how committed and serious you are to it, the "lower" will respond to the "higher" and they'll accept your leadership.

36   Whether your team is moving or not, you're in motion. You're on your path. Your actions alone will speak volumes about your conviction and passion.

37   They say a true leader leads by example and that's a great saying. In the Game we say, "If everyone's eyes are closed then no one knows where to go." That's another way of saying, "The blind can't lead the blind."

38   Whether there is someone on your team or not, you're still working your Program every single day you can. When you're first staring out, *you* have to be your *own* team.

39   Peep the Game here. When you are moving on your goals (and/or Purpose) you naturally, without any extra effort, will lead by example.

40   Your Program should be one of the most important things in your life. There should be no reason why you don't put in time, energy and resources into it every single day.

41   Your team is always watching you – so let that be what they see.

42   As much as possible, try to outwork your team. When they recognize your passion and drive the lower will rise to match the higher. This increases performance and work output.

43   Along with the qualities of being a man mentioned throughout this book, to be a great Mack you also must develop leadership qualities. Here are some important ones:

Leaders must have control over their moods and emotions. Your moods can affect the team. A leader is like a tuning fork, they want the team to vibrate on same level as them. Transmit and they will receive.

What a leader thinks, says and does must always match. There can be little contradiction in his overall way of doing things.

Leaders are optimistic but they don't ignore the potential of a worst case scenario. Always look at both sides of the coin because you may miss something crucial.

A good leader sets boundaries and guidelines, not strict rules. This allows the team to be creative with how they work the systems assigned to them without feeling restricted.

Leaders provide motivation and inspiration toward their

vision. This is critical. They also give knowledge, wisdom and understanding on how to achieve that vision.

Leaders communicate with open and honest dialogue. There must certainly be a high level of respect for the Mack, but the team is encouraged to keep things real.

Leaders are careful not to over-feed their ego. Any person who feeds their ego will make it fat. A fat ego eventually chokes on its own greed. Stay humble.

Expertise and experience are essential, but the mark of a great leader is his human relation skills. The Game helps in this area because you'll have a deep understanding of human nature.

Leaders praise team members in public and criticize them in private. They also give credit where credit is due.

A leader cannot play favorites. He has to be firm but fair. When the team recognizes favoritism, they'll begin to despise both the favored person and the leader. This also plants the seed of distrust with his judgment.

A leader is not afraid to admit to errors and mistakes. Again, you have to have a certain level of humbleness.

A leader knows how to keep secrets but encourages that no one keep them. There will come times however when you will be asked to keep matters private. If you feel that's reasonable, you must keep your word.

A leader knows that loyalty breeds loyalty. Stay loyal to those under you. Fight for them and with them, and they will do the same for you.

44 This was just hinted to above, and we need to examine this because this is an important area of its own. Exceptional

leadership involves an understanding of human nature. The Game itself was designed to work through people. The modern Mack Game is no different.

45 What you'll find often is people don't like too much change. People like to box themselves into a comfort zone. The more aggressive your Program, the faster things are going to be changing.

46 People prefer stability; especially women. You have to know your women up - down, backward - forward, in and out.

47 Usually women (and weak males) that embrace challenges can handle change fairly well. But honestly, how many people actually embrace challenges?

48 You have to assess how each member of your team reacts and handles change. If you mis-manage this, you'll cause dissatisfaction, anxiety, skepticism, doubt and defiance. In other words, fear.

49 To counteract this you must always be open about changes. You must make sure your team is included in the changes and always give them the power to choose whether or not they wish to stay.

50 Change represents loss. But, in order to gain something, you will lose something else. This is the way of nature. When you catch a fish, you lose the bait in the process; when you gain something you lose something else – this is the reality of how things are.

51 Adjustments to change take time. As a leader and a Mack you have to know this and accept it.

52 A rule of the Game is **brutal honesty**; with yourself and with your team. Don't make promises you can't keep and don't give false hopes.

53   It OK to sell a dream. Let's be real, that's what sharing a vision is. You're offering the potential of something that doesn't exist yet. But if things don't start to materialize you're going to be faced with very unmotivated people.

54   This is why the systems that make up your Program should be adjusted often for effectiveness. If you discover a better way to do something, then implement it.

55   Systems are not set in stone. There's always room for improvement and there's always more things to learn.

56   Something you should never forget: When the goal that your Program is based upon is accomplished, it's your Responsibility to make a **new goal** and form a **new Program** around it.

57   Be prepared in advance to handle the emotion of fear from your team, they'll usually not react with logic and reason. And you shouldn't expect them to – it's basic human psychology.

58   It's your duty to your team to provide them with the best tools and resources they need to operate effectively. This includes physical tools, knowledge, guidance and information crucial to the systems they run.

59   You can give a wrench to someone and tell them to go fix a car. That's terrible leadership. Provide your team with all the necessary tools and give them the instruction they need. If you don't have that knowledge yourself, then find someone who does.

60   Don't **send** your team into battle. **Lead** your team into battle. You must be hands-on and accessible. Everyone will be looking at you. A dominant leader pulls a huge stone along *with* his people. A weak leader sits on the huge stone and yells for his people to pull faster.

61 You must represent what you say you are. Lead by example and follow the rules you set down. If you don't, the stronger members in your team will recognize the weakness and leave.

62 A king (President/CEO) is only as good as their kingdom (company). Never carry yourself above the rules and regulations you set in place. A Mack only rules because others accept his rulership. If you constantly violate the Game, and break the rules you set down, you'll find yourself removed from the throne.

63 That's the Game. That is how it's always been and how it will continue to be until human beings reach a certain level of evolution.

64 The best way to build people's confidence is to give them responsibilities they feel they may not be able to accomplish. Keep encouraging, guiding and helping them. When they finally do accomplish the task, they'll feel empowered.

65 A small group of empowered people can accomplish more in a shorter amount of time than a large group of people with little confidence in themselves.

66 Encourage people to focus and use their core strengths. Delegate properly while at the same time giving them tasks slightly outside of their comfort zone to inspire and empower them.

67 It's your Program, your little world and your family. You're Responsible for your kingdom (company) and everyone in it.

68 Always show appreciation and respect toward your family. They will give this to you because of the position you've taken, but to truly *earn* it, you must Reciprocate (Principle number 3 of the 9 Principles).

69 Ask your team for ideas, no matter how "foolish" or "stupid" those ideas may be. Eventually, together, you'll come up with

something solid. You as the Mack of course, make the final decision.

70 Make an effort to stay informed about everything that can affect you and your team. Keep up with technology and the changing times and adjust your Program and systems accordingly.

71 As mentioned earlier, you should be available to your team as much as possible. It's fine to have a team member who weeds out issues that are small and that will waste your time. With that being said, it's important to hear information first hand whenever possible.

72 Information is important, so always keep in mind: **The person that controls the information coming to you is the person that influences your decisions**.

73 Another thing you must develop is a high tolerance for interruptions. Since everything will run from and to you, you will be dealing with situations constantly. And your team will be reaching out to you to get your input and feedback. To repeat, be available!

74 Don't deal with crises indirectly. They need to be tackled head-on whenever possible (and no, it's not always possible). Crises and problems don't take care of themselves. As a leader and Mack you must know how to solve problems.

75 And how do you become a good problem solver? It's actually not hard to learn.

How to Become a Better Problem Solver

76 Every problem is an **effect**. Every effect comes from a **cause**. When you can identify what's causing a problem, and deal with that cause, you can eliminate the problem.

77   There's an old story about a large 18-wheeler truck with an attached trailer getting stuck under a bridge. People gathered around and tried to figure out how they could get this truck unstuck.

78   They ran through their options: They could pull the truck out; destroy a section of the bridge; detach the trailer and just pull it out; they could push both the truck and trailer through to the other side; they could deconstruct the trailer itself; and the list goes on.

79   The problem here is that the trailer is lodged under a bridge. That's an **effect** of something. What's the **cause**? The height of the trailer is too high to make it under the bridge.

80   How do you solve the problem of the trailer's height? That solution was figured out by a young child. His suggestion was to simply let the air out of the trailer's tires. This would make the trailer shorter and solve the problem.

81   Solving problems is like peeling an onion. You peel one layer off and then another and then another until you get to the core of the onion. The core of the onion is the cause of the problem; its root.

82   When you take your vehicle in for repairs, what does a mechanic do? He looks at the problem and then begins to go through everything that may be causing it.

83   The mechanic runs some tests and eventually finds out what is causing the effect. He then determines how to remedy that cause. Sometimes a part needs to be replaced, other times something just needs a little adjusting.

84   As a leader and a Mack, you have to develop this ability. You must be a problem solver because your team will be coming to you with all manner of problems. It's your Responsibility to find a solution to as many as you can.

85   To solve a problem, look for the cause and then deal with that.

86   Every king needs an advisor. A real adviser should be removed from the everyday "business" of the kingdom.

87   They should be able to bring an objective and fresh Perspective on issues. This should be someone with a lot of knowledge, wisdom and life experience.

88   A good advisor (or mentor) can also help you solve problems because they might be able to see what you can't.

89   A good Mack usually has at least one advisor that's good in an area he isn't. This advisor is usually not a member of the Mack's team but they root for your success and understand your vision.

90   With these foundational fundamentals of leadership in place, you can elevate your Macking to the next level. Now let's chop up some Game on management.

CHAPTER THREE

The "Mack's Scepter" (Part Two)
Management Fundamentals

1   Macking ain't easy as you can probably see for yourself by now. It's not something you just do; it's something that you must *become*.

2   We covered how to look at problems and solve them in the last chapter and that knowledge is critical when managing women.

3   It's been said that women are never satisfied. Well the truth behind that is that women crave SECURITY. They just want things to work – they want things stable. They don't so much care how something gets fixed, just as long as it gets fixed.

4   Since this is part of their nature, they're usually very good at adapting and finding a way to survive (generally speaking). But when they have a man, they will pass this Responsibility on to him.

5   As a Mack you accept this Responsibility – its part of what gives you power in your realm (kingdom / company).

6   You have to understand that many things in life *take*. Food, clothing and shelter take money. And that money is usually made by way of a job that takes up time and energy.

7   Family members can take; children take; a woman keeping up her physical appearance takes; friends can take; and this can leave a woman mentally and emotionally taxed.

8   As a Mack, you give. You breathe life back into her. Not to impress her or kiss her ass, but you give structure and boundaries to her otherwise "play it by ear" life.

9   As you become more experienced with women you'll come to find that a woman who is very ambitious and driven is usually the most challenging woman to add to your Program.

10   They're so used to doing everything that they're afraid to give up control. But the truth is, there's a small place within her that wishes she had someone to at least lighten her load.

11   The appearance of her stable life is a mask that hides her inner instability.

12   Taking out the trash, grocery shopping, keeping up the car and the house, advancing in her career, taking care or the children, keeping up social appearances, etc. all by herself is a lonely heavy burden.

13   Although a Mack doesn't come into a woman's life as a "savior" (that what weak males do), he does offer her an added blanket of stability.

14   This happens because a Mack is actually stable. Like the super-human he is, he's on his path and doesn't mind going at it alone. He chooses to bear the weight of his lifestyle.

15   Any woman that chooses to be with him though, must submit to his Program. He isn't going to stop for anyone, not even her. Either she's helping or hindering.

16   Because women desire SECURITY and stability so much, it's totally natural for her to test the boundaries of a male. This is where many males and even some men fail.

17   One of the weakest things you could ever think (or say) is that you can't do what you need to do as a man, because the woman isn't doing what she's supposed to do.

18   You must always keep it moving. Whether the woman is cooperating or not is irrelevant. You keep working your Program.

19   If she's not contributing, don't blame her and stop doing what you know you need to do. Just "fire" her. Cut her off and tell her that you wish her the best.

20   When women test her boundaries with a man, this is what's called a, "nut-check". She's seeing if you have balls. She's wondering if you have a spine or if you're just another weak male.

21   The "Mack's Scepter" is symbolic of a man's spine. It's an extension of his Standards, Principles, Program and philosophy. It's comprised of his leadership and management skills. And he should always wield his scepter of power. This will pass her little tests.

22   Don't get mad or frustrated by this, it's her nature. She needs to know how strong of a man you are so she can determine if you're indeed a real man – what she really wants.

23   There's no need to really check her about this because it's her nature. You do need to recognize when she's "checking your nuts" and let her know that you see that. Then deal with it.

Dealing with Nut-Checks

24   A "nut-check" is a test that women give males to see how much they can get away with. They come in many shapes and sizes. Some are simple, others are outlandish, but they're all about one simple thing: Can she find a weakness and use it as leverage?

25   A woman who has leverage over a male is a woman who will exploit this to get her way. Like a child who uses crying to make a parent second-guess their decision for taking a toy away.

26   Leverage is a form of power or advantage. This is the power struggle that often happens between males and females. They try to position themselves to have certain advantages and power over a male.

27   A woman also nut-checks to see if his Value as a man is real. A male can fake his Value. He can fake his confidence. He can lie, tell extraordinary stories and appear to have Value that he actually doesn't.

28   A Mack invites these nut-checks – he invites the drama. He doesn't run, flinch or back down from his position.

29   A Mack knows that to be tested by a woman is a good thing. It means she recognizes that she's possibly face-to-face with a real man. A woman doesn't usually nut-check a man she's not interested in; unless she has a manipulative agenda.

30   For many males the biggest leverage a woman has over him is sex. If she withholds sex, she can pretty much get him to do whatever she wants.

31   This doesn't work on a Mack however, because sex is one of the last things he wants from a woman. If you can stand on this, you'll disarm one of her most powerful weapon against you.

32   The side-effect is she'll be intrigued. Because checking your nuts is in her nature, she'll find other ways to see where she can gain leverage.

33   If you recall, you want to put files in a woman's mind about you. Passing these tests will place files in the woman's mind that you're not a plaything and that you're not susceptible to her little tricks.

34   The more you disarm her by stripping away any power or advantage she's trying to gain, the more she'll respect you as being a man. And quite honestly, she'll also become more mentally (mind) and emotionally (heart) attracted to you.

35   Here's a scenario: You're out on the first date with an attractive and interesting woman. You picked her up in your car

and decided to go to a drive-in movie. The movie hasn't started yet but the conversation is going well.

36   Suddenly she interrupts the conversational flow and says she wants to go to the refreshment stand for some popcorn and a drink. She asks if you can drive her to the refreshment stand. What do you do?

37   You can often tell a woman is nut-checking (screening) you because she'll ask a question with a certain tonality.

38   It's a similar tonality that your mother used when she kept asking questions to get information to determine if you did something you were told *not* to do.

39   Although the request in the above scenario sounds innocent (most do), she's checking your nuts. If you seriously consider driving her all the way to the refreshment stand and possibly losing the spot where you parked, you'll be a sucker in her mind.

40   She'll see that you're easily influenced by her demands and will inconvenience yourself to please her.

41   So, why would she ask for something like this? If you asked her why you have to drive over there, she would give a reasonable excuse. Probably something like – she's scared to walk over there by herself in the dark.

42   What do you do? Don't think about the woman for a moment, think about yourself. Is this really a *reasonable* request?

43   No it isn't! Put yourself first and tell her, "No. I'm not driving (key-word) you to the refreshment stand. And I'm not walking over there to get you anything either. We can walk over there together though."

44   By saying something like this, you show strength. You show that you have a back-bone *and* you're still a gentleman. Just on your terms, not hers.

45   You have to demonstrate three attitudes of manhood and confidence when being nut-checked:

(1) You're not offended by her testing you;
(2) You're not scared to respond to her test, and;
(3) That you don't really care what she thinks of you.

46   Another scenario: You're on a social outing with a woman you just met. You decided to go feed some ducks at a local park.

47   The overall mood is good and you're slowly unraveling your pedigree about what you represent as a man. Suddenly she looks at you and asks, "So why don't you have a girlfriend? Are you just looking for sex? If you are then you're looking in the wrong place, I don't have casual sex."

48   A male would feel challenged by this. He would then try to prove to the woman that his intentions are "innocent". He's not just some oversexed male looking for his next conquest; he's looking for someone to grow with and live happily ever after, etc., etc.

49   This male would have just failed the test. He's trying to prove himself to the woman and this is a weak position to be in. He's playing himself into what *she* thinks, not what *he* thinks.

50   This gives the woman leverage. Anytime in the near future this male tries to have sex, she can just refer back to this conversation and quote his response.

51   Again, like the first scenario, don't think about the woman for a moment and think about yourself. Put yourself first.

52   As a Mack your response would be something like this, "No I don't have a girlfriend (key-word). Girlfriends are for men that don't know what they need from a woman. I'm not really worried about having sex (key-word) with you either. I want to see what else you have to offer first."

53   Of course your actual response should reflect your personality but I hope you get the idea.

54   Invite the drama! Show you're not offended; not scared to respond; and you also don't really care what she thinks about you.

55   A truly confident man doesn't care what people think about him — he's always himself and lives in his own little world.

You're the Value and this makes you the prize.

56   One more scenario because passing these nut-checks is vitally important to Macking. Sometimes a woman will poke fun at you just to see how you'll respond. She wants to see how you handle yourself as a man and see if you'll back down.

57   Let's say you just approached a new woman. You've introduced yourself and started a conversation. During the talk she looks you up and down and says, "What's up with those shoes? They're so ugly!"

58   A weak male would laugh this off or try to defend himself by trying to explain that he has other shoes and these were the first ones he saw so he just put them on, etc., etc.

59   Here's a Mack's response because he thinks about himself first, "I like these shoes. In fact, I have a whole collection of ugly shoes (key-words). I put on these particular shoes this morning because I knew I was coming out to meet women. They need to see what they're getting themselves into."

60   He could also simply answer, "Thank you!" And from there he would ask her another question and continue the conversation like normal.

61   Said with the right tonality, this comes across as humorous and would probably get a smirk from the woman.

62   What this demonstrates though is the same three attitudes of manhood you want to project – You're not offended; you're not scared to respond; and you don't really care what she thinks about you.

63   You're the Value and you're the prize. You live in your own little world, either she's going to be down with it or not.

64   Another common nut-check happens when you first meet a woman and she immediately throws in that she has a boyfriend. Don't let this stop you from Macking.

65   What you'll often find is that as you build up a mental attraction, she will suddenly admit that her "relationship" isn't *that* serious.

66   Sometimes a woman will claim a close male friend as her "boyfriend" just to fend off weak males from approaching her.

67   If a woman is really into her man and in a serious relationship, she'll let you know. Otherwise keep Macking, this is the only way you're really going to know if this is a nut-check or not.

68   Nut-checks slow down over time but never really stop. A woman will always look for an area where she can gain leverage.

69   As you go through the four stages of dating the nut-checks just change. If you make it to the third dating stage for example, she may start questioning where the relationship is headed. She'll staring asking questions about marriage, maybe having children, etc.

70   It's all about what you want and how you wish to live your life. Be a man and deal with these tests according to what you're thinking and what you want.

Handcuffing a Woman Equals, Freedom?

71   This is a difficult Perspective and mindset that a Mack needs to develop.

72   What makes it difficult is that a Mack allows his women – those contributing to his Program – a large degree of freedom.

73   Handcuffing a woman is symbolism. It represents her accepting your leadership as a man. It involves two of the 5 plus 1 needs of a woman.

74   You constantly need to make her feel SECURE, stable and safe. Also you must touch her ENTERTAINMENT side; keeping her overall mental outlook and mood elevated and positive. You do this by making yourself fun and exciting to be around.

75   These two operate together to limit the "reach" of a woman. This sounds restricting but it's not. It simply means that when she does reach, she is reaching *for* you; she won't want to reach *past* you.

76   When we talk about handcuffing a woman, this has nothing to do with watching her every move, telling her what to do or where she can and can't go.

77   Handcuffing only means that a woman is mentally and emotionally "bound" to you. She is *with* you and *for* you. She wants to cater to you, please you and help your Advancement.

78   This is not something you force on her. If she recognizes your Value and is deeply attracted to you, she'll do it out of sheer respect for you as a real man.

79   She has to do these things because she *wants* to do them. It's her choice based off of the caliber of woman she is. A woman must always have the freedom to choose.

80   You will have to check her behavior and enforce your boundaries through your Standards, Principles and Program; but when she's not around you, you can't expect her to be anyone other than herself.

81   Weak males want to control their women. They want every bit of leverage they can get on them. It even gets to the point where they will tell the woman who they can and can't talk to.

82   They'll monitor her social media posts, find a way to look through her online private messages and check text messages.

83   This insecure jealous behavior is feminine and childish. A Mack can't possess those traits.

84   If a woman treats you like a king when she's with you but "slips up" and has sex with another man, you need to know how you honestly feel about that.

85   A real Mack would accept this. As long as she's dedicated to him and his Program, he won't try to control what she does with her body. And he won't let a woman dictate what he does with his body.

86   This all sounds good, but could *you* honestly accept something like this? It's your little world so you have to make the decision about that. But here's some Game to consider.

87   The more freedom of *choice* a woman has, the more powerful she becomes in her womanhood. This womanhood will often bring out her natural femininity. Why is this important?

88   A woman who has the freedom of choice, is a woman who will usually (not always) use that freedom to do what's in her nature; to be a strong, loving and nurturing person. Particularly to the people she cares about which should include you as the man in her life.

89   Since you're predominantly masculine in your approach and behavior, you want her to be predominantly feminine.

90   This will help maintain a careful balance within the relationship you have both established.

91   Along with the nurturing also come the child-like qualities that are within her. Both the good and bad sit at the same table at all times. You must be prepared to check all outlandish behaviors that come from these child-like qualities if they arise.

92   Remember, check her behavior not her nature.

93   When a woman has been handcuffed by you, you must be confident and rely on the strength of your Macking.

94   She's going to make some decisions you don't like, but overall she will keep herself in check because she doesn't want to jeopardize what she has with you.

95   A Mack doesn't hold a woman through sex, money or kissing her ass like weak males do. A Mack wants *the whole* woman – mind, heart and body. He allows the Game he puts down in those areas to hold her.

96   Be a man and allow your woman (or women) to have freedom of choice. Their requirements to be with you are based on your

Principles, Standards and Program. Let her choose whether she will abide by them or not.

97   Regardless of what a woman does, or doesn't do, just keep Macking.

Staying Ahead of Your Woman

98   Helping your woman (or women) solve problems is probably the most important day-to-day management aspect of being a Mack.

99   You'll have to help them figure out the best course of action when they have an important decision to make. You'll have to calm them down when they're over-emotional about something. You'll have to listen to what happened to them at work that day and who pissed them off.

100   Also they're going to have problems with their home or car or their mirror falling down in their bathroom.

101   If you're Macking properly, your women are going to reach out to you first (or second) – so you're going to hear all kinds of situations where they want your input. Other times, they'll straight ask for your help.

SIDE NOTE: *A Mack does not pay rent, utility bills, cell phone bills or bills of any kind for any woman who's not seriously contributing to his Program. Period! You more than likely weren't there when she acquired those bills; so honestly, you're not responsible for them. You're a Mack, not a charity for women who can't manage their money.*

102   After problem solving, the next most important area of management is staying ahead of your woman (or women). You can't expect women to figure everything out all the time or to understand the Value of things.

103   Take for example the rich man who buys his wife a brand new $100,000 car. To her, it's just another car. And she'll treat it like just another car.

104   She didn't earn it herself, so although she likes going around town and getting jealous stares, she won't really take good care of it. She doesn't fully understand its Value.

105   The Value of the car needs to be explained to the woman. Her husband would need to break down in simple terms, all the hard work and sacrifice that went into getting the money together to purchase that car. It probably didn't come easy.

106   Again this is a part of women's nature. They just want things to work; that's where they place the Value often times.

107   When we talk about staying ahead of your women, this means that you have to accept this and incorporate it into your management style.

108   Let's say your woman really wants a new living room set. This is all she's thinking about. To her, the living room furniture is old and she's tired of looking at it.

109   Although the furniture may still be in good condition, in her mind this is something that's "broke", so she wants to "fix" it.

110   If you're both living together, then naturally it's part of your Responsibility to help purchase the furniture. So you need to figure out the best way to make this purchase, without setting everything else behind financially.

111   You have to figure this out before she decides to do whatever she's thinking. She might be so caught up in the *emotion* of having new furniture, that she'll overlook the logic and reasoning of making that purchase.

112   To her it's just new furniture; to you it should be another bill or financial strain on the household.

113   If you don't figure out all the logistics before she does, she'll just go do what she wants. And what she wants may cause financial damage in the process.

114   A woman doesn't care so much how something gets fixed, just as long as it gets fixed.

115   As far as your Program is concerned, you have to know the best way to keep advancing in life. You must figure it out before she figures it out.

116   If she figures it out first, her child-like nature will kick in and she'll start thinking she doesn't really need your leadership and management – and honestly she may have a legitimate point.

117   You have to explain to her the Value of things as you see it. And you have to get her to see it. Again, you have to figure these things out first.

118   If you don't figure things out first, then you're not leading and you're not managing.

119   As a man, if you're not leading and managing the relationship (or family) then she'll take on that role. A woman needs some form of structure and stability – even if her way will hurt you both in the long run.

120   This happens often because women make emotional decisions. Have you ever witnessed a woman go on a shopping spree knowing that she may be late paying a utility bill or a car note?

121   She was out shopping and got emotionally caught up in the experience. She justified to herself that she deserves those new clothes and that she'll make up for it later.

122   This doesn't apply to all women, but you have to know if it applies to any woman *you're* dealing with. You have to stay ahead of them.

123   To be able to break things down to women so they can see the Value in things refer back to Book 5, Chapter Four – the section on, *Keeping a Woman Focused on Your Program*.

The Open & Honest Policy

124   This is something you must institute in the relationship as early as possible – whether you have just one woman or several.

125   All human beings want to be heard. Whether male or female, we all want someone just to hear us. We want to share our thoughts, feelings and Perspectives without being harshly judged.

126   Women, being the social creatures that they are, express themselves best verbally. They can talk for hours on end about everything going on in their mind and how they feel.

127   A Mack of course knows this, accepts this and uses this to his advantage.

128   Within your realm (kingdom/company) you should have a policy of openness and honesty. No secrets, no hiding things and no topic should be out-of-bounds.

129   This should not only apply to your women but also yourself. You have to be straight-forward and honest as much as possible.

130   Encourage your women to talk about how their day was. What happened and what they did. If a woman seems to be in a bad mood, encourage her to talk about it and be prepared to listen even if it's not that interesting to you.

131   You're just giving her the opportunity to be heard and most times a woman will be content with just that. Not only does she get to express herself, she also gets your time and attention. You kill two birds with one stone.

132   For males, this is difficult because he doesn't really want to know certain things because he's scared and sensitive. A Mack on the other hands wants to know *everything*.

133   A Mack will ask his woman what sexual things she did with her last boyfriends. He won't judge for her answer and just accept what she says. He will take that information and file it away because it might have some use later.

134   A Mack will ask his woman what she feels about current events in the world or the city they live in. He'll ask her every so often if she's happy with their relationship.

135   A Mack will ask his woman about her childhood whether it was good or bad and try to get an understanding of what made her the woman she is today.

136   No topic should be off limits. And if she asks the Mack something he answers openly and honestly.

137   This concept alone will create an extremely strong connection with a woman. She doesn't get a chance to be open and honest in regular life. She's too scared that she'll be socially judged.

138   Yes, you're going to hear some things you won't like. But what can you do about it? It has already happened, just accept it.

139   The key here is that you don't *judge* her. You can speak honestly about what you think and how you feel about what she tells you, but don't judge her. Judging her will only shut her down from being open and honest.

140   If you have a stable of women and they're all on friendly terms, a Mack should encourage open dialogue amongst all his women.

141   He should get his women together and have open talks where everyone participates. A "round-table" discussion if you will.

142   If the women have issues with each other, a Mack must act as a mediator if things get a little "heated". He should remind his women that this is a family and everyone has a history that made them what they are. This is real life.

143   The Mack should let each woman say their piece, one at a time, without being interrupted. Each woman will get the same opportunity to speak and express what's on their mind.

144   The Mack then helps them find a common ground for compromise. Or he makes a judgment about the best course of action. The best course of action should be based on what's best for the FAMILY, not just himself or any particular female.

145   Also if a woman needs to be checked, it should be done in the presence of the other women and *only* the other women if possible.

146   When you check one woman in front of the others, you're actually checking all your women at once. They'll see what unacceptable behavior is to you.

147   Be careful here, you don't want to do this in public unless absolutely necessary. You never want to let unacceptable behavior slide, but a woman will give you more resistance when she feels her social Value is being threatened.

148   Regardless if it's one woman or many, if you checking them brings them to tears, let them cry while you continue discussing your position and finding a solution to the problem.

149   A woman's mood or behavior should never affect yours. Put yourself first – you have something to say and it must be heard and understood.

150   What if a woman brings something to you that she is just "thinking about" doing in the future? And it's something you don't like?

151   Just tell her why you don't like it and ask her questions about why she's thinking that way. Then listen. Don't judge her, and then state your position.

152   Let her express herself and be heard. This is why she brought it to you in the first place. If she wanted to be sneaky about it, you would have found out about it later.

153   In a later section in this chapter, we'll look at an advanced concept of how to *time* your truths and honesty.

Being the Positive Transmitter

154   Amongst all the other Responsibilities that a Mack takes on, he also has to keep the overall mood of his women positive and elevated.

155   As a man, you're the transmitter and women are the receivers. If you start your day in a bad mood, your women will pick this up as well as your children.

156   You should find something that keeps your mood high, positive and energetic. For some Macks, they work-out (even a 10-minute routine done five times a week is better than nothing).

157   For other Macks they meditate or listen to music that puts them in a positive, go-get-it mood. Some Macks study various

aspects of their craft to improve their skills. Doing something you enjoy is a good way to keep your energy and mood up.

158   You should never allow the mood of your women to affect yours. You should always be positive and optimistic about life as much as possible.

159   There will be some days where you aren't; that's just human nature. But the better you can keep up your mood the easier it will be to manage your women.

160   Remember the very core of the Game itself is self-empowerment. Even in the Mack layer of the Game, this is no different.

161   You should want to be slightly better than the day before and you should encourage your women to do the same.

162   When you learn something new, share it with your women even if they don't fully understand what you're talking about. By doing this though, you indirectly encourage them to learn new things as well.

163   If you had a good day, share it with your women. If something funny happened that day, share it. If you heard a funny story, share it. If you saw a movie or heard a song that moved you, talk about it.

164   Your little world is where you and your women live in, remember? Your world should be uplifting, adventurous and fun. ENTERTAINMENT is a very important need of a woman, so give that to her.

165   If you're good at telling stories, tell stories often to keep your women engaged. If you're good at cracking jokes, then constantly keep your women laughing.

166   If you're flirtatious, flirt with your women a lot. If you're more hands-on and like kissing and caressing your women (feeling on breasts or buttocks), then do it every day, multiple times a day.

167   Once you get a woman that's only the beginning. You have to continually Mack her. The way you start with a woman is the way you must continue with a woman.

168   In other words, be you. And be the best you, you can be at all times. Showcase your manhood and your Value.

169   If your woman has low self-esteem (the way she feels about herself) or a low self-image (how she feels about her appearance) then take it upon yourself to help her improve them.

170   Talk to her and encourage her. Let her know that she's with you now and that you know she has the potential be greater and better. All it takes is a little effort every day.

171   If she's very insecure about her body and physical appearance, go shopping with her. You don't have to buy the clothes; just help her put outfits together that you think make her look more attractive.

172   If fashion isn't your strong suit then just ask the workers at the clothing store to help her.

173   Women with a Mack should be "upgraded". This can be through clothes, diet, environment and/or attitude – their mental and emotional states.

174   The 5 plus 1 needs of a woman are crucial here. You should be touching at least one of these every day.

175   Some women will have never experienced anything like this from a man before, so they may take some time to come around. But don't let that stop you. Always be Playing – keep Macking!

176 In your world you set the tone. That tone needs to be positive and upbeat, not negative, boring or dull. A woman can find that almost anywhere.

177 Yes you're going to argue, fuss and disagree but once that problem gets handled, then bring back the positive tone.

178 If you need to leave or step away for a few hours (or even a day) to cool off, then tell her what you're going to do. She's going to ask why, just tell her you need to cool off and then leave immediately.

179 When you come back she's going to want to talk about it, so talk about it. She wants to know if what was broken can be fixed. Once it's fixed then reset the positive transmitting.

180 There's no need to dwell on the negative. It's like planting weeds in a beautiful garden. Why would you purposely destroy something beautiful? That's not part of The Game.

181 Remain the transmitter, always. This is a requirement of being a good leader and manager of your realm (kingdom/company). This is part of wielding your Mack's scepter – use this power properly.

182 Don't be lazy here, it will create Game Leaks (weaknesses) and lead to Game Loss (losing things you've gained).

A Woman's Fear of Getting "Too Attached"

183 There will come times when a woman will tell you that she may need to "back-off" because she's getting too attached.

184 Or she may say she's falling for you too fast. She could also say that being with you has a lot of conditions. She may even say she feels guilty or "bad" for liking you so much because you still date other women.

185 All of this boils down to her fears; and to a lesser extent her insecurities. What she's often saying here is that she wants more from you; more time, more attention and to be emotionally closer.

186 But what she's really afraid of is ending up hurt or abandoned by you.

187 Sometimes included with this is that she's worried about becoming a certain kind of woman because of you. A woman who is not the woman she's "supposed" to be. What's she's really trying to figure out is if you're worth it.

188 If a woman ever brings something like this to your attention, you'll know that you're very deep into her heart. While this is what a Mack wants, you have to treat this situation delicately.

189 This matter can often be resolved with a serious heart-to-heart conversation. No texting. Either get with her face-to-face, over the phone or on a video call.

190 Tell her you want to talk so you can put both of your thoughts and feelings on the table; this way you can both examine them.

191 During the conversation you need to be honest with what you think and how you feel. You also need to let her express what she thinks and how she feels without judging her.

192 If she's being sincere, she'll be in a very vulnerable state here. And she knows it. But something is broken and she wants to fix it. Help her fix it!

193 Explain to her that every relationship has to encounter some difficulty. But if both of you can come out on the other end together, it will only make your relationship stronger.

194 And that's the truth – a truth she will recognize.

195   Take this time to redefine your relationship to one another. Remember the root word of relationship is the word, *relate*.

196   A relationship can be anything the people in it agree to – their choice of how they *relate* to one another.

197   Bring her out of thinking about the future and define where you want your relationship **right now**. The past is gone; the future doesn't exist yet, so deal with what's in front of you – now.

198   If you want to keep the woman then your agenda should be to do that. If you don't want to keep the woman then break the relationship off and explain to her why just being friends is probably the best thing to do.

199   If your agenda it to keep the woman, then while you're re-defining your relationship, you need to have at least one "hook-point". This hook-point will serve as the "reason why" she should stay.

200   The more hook-points you can implement, the better.

201   Keep in mind that a woman will only bring this to your attention because she really wants a "reason why". If she was just going to back-off and leave you alone, she would do that just to avoid the Responsibility of confrontation.

202   At the risk of sounding repetitive, she sees something broken and she *wants* it fixed, so help her fix it.

203   Let me give you some examples of hook-points so you can come up with your own when the time comes:

If you feel a strong connection and she feels it too, ask her why she's willing to throw that away? Isn't it hard enough to find something like that? Why let it go so easily?

If your Mack game is tight and you've been touching her 5 plus 1 needs and she seemed overall happy, then get her to think about all the good times you've had so far and it will only get better as you both get closer.

If you and/or she have made noticeable life Advancements together, then explain to her how great of a team you are. Not many couples can achieve greatness together but you're already on that path. Why break that apart now?

You can explain to her everything changes. There are four seasons in nature. Just because you all may have hit a rough patch, that doesn't mean that will continue. If you keep striving and working together for the best, you'll both eventually reach the "spring" and "summer" of your relationship.

If she has a young child (or children) and her child has grown fond of you, remind her of that. If you honestly care about her child (or children) explain to her that you care about them and breaking off the relationship so quickly isn't the best move for everyone involved.

204   With a little forethought and creativity, you can come up with your own hook-points based on your actual relationship with the woman. A Mack uses everything he can to his advantage. Remember to be sincere and honest.

WORD OF CAUTION: *Don't bring up great sex as a hook-point unless she brings it up first. Although it may be true, in her mind she will see that maybe sex is the only reason she's sticking around. This might make her feel even more skeptical about her reason to continue with you. If you've been Macking properly, she shouldn't be thinking along these lines but it is a possibility.*

205   Your agenda is to simply redefine your relationship so that it works **now**. But she has to see a "reason why" she should. This is what she's indirectly asking from you.

206   Like I previously mentioned, it's not about lying or being deceitful. That will do more harm than good in the long run. All you're doing is giving her the true, honest reasons why *you* want her to stay and why she should.

Timing Truths & Honesty

207   To put Macking aside for a moment, the Game itself is brutal truth and uncompromised honesty. But the use of direct honesty is best applied at certain times.

208   Largely due to Social Conditioning, the average person will back down when confronted by a truth they're not prepared to hear (or don't want to hear).

209   As a Mack, timing your truths and being brutally honest is a skill that can only come from experience, all I can do is point you in the right direction.

210   Honesty is direct and dominant; lies are weak. People only lie because they're afraid of the response they might receive if they tell the truth.

211   The uncommon sense is – being brutally honest (direct) upfront can work against you. Just like trying to hammer a nail in the dark. It will take way too many tries to successfully get the nail in.

212   It takes much less effort, time and energy to first turn the lights on so you can see what you're doing. This is what timing honesty and truths are – it's seeing where you need to aim before you deliver your blow.

213   A well timed and well placed truth will be of more benefit to you than any lie. It helps your reputation, makes you trustworthy and greatly increases your Value as a man.

214   To get a better understanding of how this works in the real world, let's look at a situation.

215   A skilled salesperson knows that he or she must sell the "sizzle", not the steak itself.

216   A salesperson knows that they should concentrate more on the benefits and Value of a product. What is beneficial and valuable? That is determined by the person they're selling to – the buyer's Perspective.

217   Let's use the "buying a new house" example again, but this time from the Perspective of the real estate agent; not the buyer.

218   A skilled real estate agent will first find out what their client wants and needs. Then they'll find properties that match their wants and needs.

219   As the client is walking through different properties, a skilled salesperson will then start the sales process. They'll explain why a particular property fits the client's wants and needs.

220   They'll push benefits and Value first, but are they telling the client the *whole* truth about the property? Most of the time, no.

221   They usually know the negatives of a particular home, or maybe where the property is located has some negatives. The client won't learn these things from a skilled agent unless they ask specific questions.

222   Is this being dishonest? Not necessarily, they're just timing their truths and honesty. If the client asks for specifics, a sincere agent will be honest with them. But if the client doesn't ask, they usually won't tell.

223   Again, they turn the light on first before they try to hammer nails into the wall. They know their client's wants and needs and

they attempt to deliver. They'll time their truths and honesty to prevent a sale from slipping away.

224   If the real estate agent can get the client emotionally tied into the property first (by playing on their wants and needs), any negatives that may come up should only be a shadow – the benefits and Value should outshine them.

225   They give their client the benefits and Value first; the "shadow" areas come in second, third or fourth.

226   If we go back to the history of many criminal organizations, they had rites of passage or initiations. What was the purpose of these things? They wanted to test both loyalty and commitment but this also allowed the initiate time to discover, for themselves, the "shadow areas" of the organization.

227   Yes, they were told everything that was involved upfront, but to actually live through it is another matter. When you live through something, that's when it becomes real. Everything else is usually just an assumption (fantasy) made up in a person's mind.

228   The initiate is "sold" on the benefits and Value of the organization, they're told about the negatives but the negatives don't become real until they're experienced.

229   This is another example of timing truths and honesty – being both direct and indirect at the same time. This is Contrast (Principle number 8 of the 9 Principles).

230   Like some 9-to-5 jobs, after the initially training period is over and you really begin to work, your co-workers are usually more than willing to tell you that some of your training is not the best way to get the job done.

231   The training however is necessary because you need to know the basics, but practical application will serve you much better.

232 When you sign a contract for anything, the terms and conditions are laid out directly. But most of it is "legal speak". If you don't understand legal jargon you may miss something important in the contract.

233 If you don't ask specific questions, does the person asking you to sign the contract go into excruciating detail, point-by-point? 9 times out of 10, no they don't.

234 The point here is that when you time your honesty and truths you are direct but the details come when the person you're speaking with asks the right questions.

235 You're also not lying or deceiving your women either. You can tell them everything and elicit their agreement (which is Macking correctly), but the finer details come over time. Sometimes the finer details are best learned and/or told over time.

236 When you take a math class in school, you don't start at the calculus level. You start with basic arithmetic and then you move on to geometry, algebra, etc.

237 Education has its stages and timings. So do truths and honesty. Were you "deceived" because you didn't learn calculus first?

238 As usual, I must give a word of caution. Your name must become synonymous with strong character and integrity (real manhood). Stand behind what you say because as a Mack you must deliver.

239 So when you're Playing, timing your truths and honesty, do it properly. Do it without misleading or taking advantage of women or even males.

240 To sum all this up: **Explain the big picture upfront – reveal the finer details later or when the proper questions are asked.**

241   This concept may seem foreign to you now, but once your Mack Game begins to expand, you'll find it an important management tool.

How to Handle Blowing a Woman

242   Despite your best efforts you're going to "blow" women. Meaning, they're going to leave you or you're going to have to cut them off.

243   I urge you to not waste too much mental energy trying to figure out why they decided to leave and instead leave the door open if they decide to come back.

244   The exception to this rule is if they did something "foul" or harmful to you or another one of your women.

245   If a woman slices your car tires or cuts up your other woman's clothes, then she shouldn't be allowed to come back under any circumstances. She violated her man (or the family unit) and that's a big deal; completely unacceptable.

246   I advise you to completely cut-off any future contact with a woman like this. If you allow her back she will only cause more problems down the road.

247   If a woman leaves just because she's "unhappy" then ask her why she feels that way and let her leave. Don't try to hold onto a woman who has gotten up enough courage to make that decision.

248   If she brings it to you then trust me, she's been thinking about it for quite a while.

249   The open and honest policy can help out here because if you're listening closely, you can spot when a woman is beginning to feel dissatisfied.

250   If you catch it early enough, you can do things to help hold her. Sometimes there's nothing you can say or do.

251   You're a Mack, not a prison warden. If a woman really wants to leave, put your emotions away and let her leave. You need to tell her all the positive things you saw about the relationship and honestly express that you hope she finds what she's looking for.

252   That was your woman, and although she has chosen otherwise, you still want her to be happy. If you honestly don't feel that way, don't say it. But if you do, then say it with no hesitation.

253   As much as possible, you want to end a relationship on a positive note. If nothing else, this woman will still contact you every once in a while and her presence can be used to help keep your other women in check.

254   Since she's no longer your women, she's no longer entitled to everything that a Mack provides. So you need to cut out the sex, the dates (occasional social outings are fine), long phone conversations, accepting her sending you nude pictures and flirtatious text messages.

255   Check her behavior and explain to her that although you still care about her, she can't ride the fence. Either she's with you or not.

256   She chose to leave, so to you she is just a friend. Treat her as such. But the door is open for her to come back as long as she can accept that nothing has changed. You still have requirements and you still have a Program that's in motion.

257   This can be difficult, especially if the woman was around for many months or even a year or two but if you're a Mack, then you come first and the lifestyle you live shouldn't change for anyone.

258   If you're really Macking, you won't have a lot of time and mental energy to give her anyway. You have a Program and a kingdom (company) to lead and manage; eventually you'll find a replacement for her anyway.

259   Sometimes a woman will leave you and never come back. Others will leave and come back when they realize they were better off with you. Still others will leave but still care so much about you that they'll still campaign for your Program.

260   They don't want to be with you, but they still want to see you win. How do you handle that situation?

261   Under normal circumstances, you would give a good portion of time, attention and have sex with a woman who campaigns for you. But when a woman you used to be with leaves, you still have to treat her like just a friend. This isn't a normal circumstance.

262   Be appreciative of her efforts and the time she's taking helping you, but still treat her like a friend. The only reward you may consider giving her is slightly more of your time, birthday and/or Holiday gifts and that's all.

263   Don't let an "ex" take you off of your overall Game. Yes, she's spreading the word about you and assisting, but that's her choice.

264   You shouldn't need her to do it at all. Like I said before, if you're really Macking she'll eventually be replaced anyway.

265   This book is tightly packed with information that will benefit the novice and the more experienced Mack alike. However for the novice you may be wondering, "Where exactly do I *start* with all this information?"

266   In the next chapter we'll answer that question and bring all this together.

BOOK 7 – MACK GAME MANIFESTATION

THE FINAL CHAPTER

The Path to Mackhood

1 If you've read this book thoroughly up to this point then you need to congratulate yourself. Give yourself a pat on the back, seriously!

2 The average male will never finish this book. Then there's another group who will read it once and put it down. Then there's another group who will get a few tips and leave it there. But the most successful man will be the one to *study* this information and actually *use* it; he'll break it apart and figure out how it works with him and the lifestyle he wants.

3 You now have more Game and wisdom about manhood, womanhood and relationships than 95% of the male population. Don't forget that your Outer Game – you're overall effectiveness with women, is only as strong as your Inner Game.

4 Certified Midwest Player, *Jackpot JPeezy* (aka *JP*), once told me an acronym for the word Mack. He said that M.A.C.K. means: Master Applying Correct Knowledge. This book has given you the correct knowledge by clearing away many misconceptions that have built up over the years. Your Responsibility now is to **apply** it so you can **master** it.

5 To really become a Mack, you have to do the work. You should do every exercise presented in this book and practice them daily.

6 I wrote this book in a specific way that requires it to be *studied*. After you study and learn its contents then it can be used as reference guide. When you find yourself approaching a specific event, you can refer to a specific chapter or section to have some Game going in.

7   A Mack is always as prepared as possible. He's **pre-emptive** not **reactionary**; he plans, plots and executes instead of waiting to see what happens *then* deciding what to do.

8   In reality being pre-emptive isn't always possible, but you should do it as much as you can.

9   To become better with women requires you to get in the Game and get experience. Would just studying a sport suddenly make you good at it? No it wouldn't – you have to get off the bench and actually play to improve and understand the intricacies.

10   There's only so much a book can give you. To become proficient you have to intentionally place yourself into situations so that you can gain experience.

11   The Game is about self-empowerment. That is you empowering yourself. That means *you* have to do it. No one else can because no one knows you like you should know *you*.

12   Whose a better guide for you other than yourself?

13   You'll make mistakes, you will mess things up but you shouldn't fear any of those things. As long as you recognize where you messed up, you'll be able to handle that situation differently when it comes around again.

14   If you developed your Standards, Principles, philosophy and Program, you're a man now. You've learned yourself and have a set direction for the life that *you've* chosen. It may sound simple in theory, but only 5% of the world's population does it.

15   You have to be fearless but not foolish. Stop being scared and worried about not doing everything perfect at first because that's not living in reality.

16   You must monitor how you talk to yourself. Those little conversations you have in your head should be uplifting and empowering.

17   If you constantly beat yourself up over things, you're going to have a difficult time being the best man you can be.

18   The greatest enemy of a Mack's Game, is the Mack himself. That's right, read that again.

19   The lifestyle of a Mack is like an ocean wave. It rises, falls, crashes sometimes and other times it's smooth and calm.

20   The Game you've received from this book will help you ride those waves with ease and even find the calm spots so you're not subjected to what's going on around you.

21   Macking is about manhood and a man needs to exhibit control. Control over what he says and does. But most importantly, control over what he thinks.

22   There is no magic formula that will make you better overnight or in a month, but there is a formula. And you've been given that formula.

23   I used to have a Mack friend that had a shocking opening line. For 70% of the women he approached he used the same line. It didn't matter if they were "hood-rats" or corporate professional women. You know what his line was?

24   "Hey, ho!" (and that's "ho" as in, whore or prostitute)

25   That's crazy, right? In my mind I could never see myself calling a strange woman a ho. Especially a woman I wanted to Mack to.

26 This "disrespectful" opening line directly reflected the man he represented himself to be. He considered himself very "street" and acted accordingly.

27 I once asked him why he used that line and he told me that all he wanted was a reaction. He didn't care if the reaction was good or bad, he just wanted a response.

28 If the woman cut him an evil look or ignored him, he accepted it. But if the woman said anything, good or bad, he then stepped right up to her and introduced himself.

29 What this taught me, and should teach you, is that you need to remove the limits from your thinking. Always represent the man you are and don't give a damn about how a woman really thinks about you.

30 Would I ever use a line like that? No, because I represent my manhood differently. But the point is, even an opening line like that can be effective. And it was effective.

31 The women who "let him in" with that line are the type of women *he* wanted. He just cut out the fluff and went straight for the jugular vein.

32 In the modern Mack Game, the limitations are only set by you. When real Value is placed on the table, what's considered impossible becomes possible.

33 You'll be your own worst enemy and most skilled opponent in your own Game. You'll be mentally and emotionally battling with yourself.

34 What you'll really be fighting against are the Socially Conditioned morals and standard that were programmed into you. These will battle against what you really want.

35 Who are you really? And what do you really want? Do you know?

36 A better question is: What do you think and feel you deserve as a man?

37 A man only accepts what he expects. Your expectations are usually based on what you believe is possible. And if you're thinking is limited, you'll be limited.

38 At one time human beings believed that a person flying was impossible. Until someone questioned that logic and tried it. Now we can't imagine life without air travel.

39 At one time human beings couldn't fathom the idea of being able to verbally speak to someone clear across the globe. Now we have phones and the internet, you can reach people across the world in mere seconds.

40 What old antiquated ideas and beliefs are you holding on to? And why?

41 I'm quite sure that many of you questioned many things while reading this book. You want to know are the things you've read actually possible? Do they work?

42 All I can tell you is, "Yes, they do." But I have many years of proof to back that up based off my own experiences.

43 I got those experiences by trying and failing, re-adjusting a few things and trying again until I got it right.

44 This book is based off **Real Game** that has existed for literally hundreds of years; long before the pick-up artists and "seduction community" ever existed. It will continue to work because the basic nature of women and men will not evolve for a long, long time.

45   The Game itself doesn't change but the layers of the Game adjust every four to five years. You have to keep this in mind as you continue with your Macking.

46   Just as an example, there are many more ways to meet women than there was 10 years ago from the time this book was written.

47   In four to five more years, there will be other new ways to meet women. Some will open new doors and close others. A Mack does his best work face-to-face but don't limit yourself when meeting women.

48   You should want to master both the online world and the face-to-face world. In our modern times, some males have become great pretenders when they're online. But let them get in a woman's face and they'll freeze up and be awkward.

49   Their face-to-face behavior won't match the "internet image" they presented. Most women will quickly lose any attraction they've built up when they see this. There's no consistency and therefore there's no SECURITY and stability.

A Powerful Tool of Manhood

50   Once you begin to unravel your self-imposed limitations, you need to add another tool in your toolbox. This is a tool you'll need to pull out and use quite often.

51   You need to always know what your **intentions** are before you do anything. What you do needs to be because it's what you want to do; and represent the type of man you want to be.

52   Let's say you were walking down the street and passed a male and female couple. An elderly woman near them trips and crashes to the ground. The bags in her hands hit the ground and the items inside roll and tumble in different directions.

53 The male runs to help the elderly woman back to her feet and gathers her items back into the bags. He ensures she's alright and then goes back to his woman who has a smile on her face.

54 Looking in from the outside that seems like a very gentlemanly and chivalrous gesture. But what's happening on the *inside* of this male?

55 What was the male's true *intention*?

56 This male could have only helped the elderly woman to look good in front of his woman. That was his intention and that was the only reason he did it.

57 But the male's intention could have been that he honestly wanted to help the elderly woman because that is who he is as a man. Whether his woman was there or not, he still would have helped.

58 Part of being a man is recognizing your intentions. Are you doing things to be impressive to other males or females? Or are you doing things because this is the person you are, or want to become?

59 You have to be *you* as much as possible at all times. You must learn to act (or not act) based off your true intentions as the man you want to become. You must learn to be more sincere.

60 No one else should have any effect on that because you shouldn't really care what anyone thinks about you. A Mack lives in his own little world.

61 Beyond your Standards and Principles lie your intentions. Your intentions are what, over time, will help you become super-human. The reason is because you'll be content with who you really are.

62　While average people run about their lives trying to fit-in or please others, you will "move and shake" through life knowing not only *why* you do things, but also do them with unshakable confidence.

63　This confidence will radiate through your Aura and will literally attract women to you. Your manhood will be showcased by doing nothing more than being the best man you can be and always striving to be better.

64　Own your manhood! Do things because they feel right for you as a man. You should be able to say, "I did that (or didn't do that) because it's the man that I am."

The Process

65　To manifest yourself as a Mack takes work; more inner work than anything else. Whether inner or outer, you have to do the work if you want to be successful.

66　There aren't any shortcuts. You can take shortcuts if you want to but I can guarantee your overall Game will be lacking. You'll run into problems that can simply be solved by knowing who you are as a man.

67　*The Mack's Bible* contains **a ton** of material. Depending on how much experience you currently have with women will determine where you need to start.

68　The following steps are just large "brush strokes", not in full detail. These steps are just enough to give you a framework to start your path to Mackhood.

69　(1) Whether you've never been on a real date before or whether you've slept with many women, the first place to start is re-learning what you think you know about women. Studying Book 1 will help you with this.

70 (2) From there you have to take the time to define your Standards. This can take a while because it requires a lot of thought and consideration.

For most people this takes a couple of days. For others it might take a week. How long it takes doesn't matter. You're building a foundation that you're entire Game is going to stand on.

Don't rush through it! If your Inner Game is weak, your Outer Game will reflect it.

71 (3) After your Standards are in place, then move on to your Principles. Don't rush through these either. Defining these can be a little tricky and they can take longer to develop than your Standards in some cases.

Don't get frustrated, do the work. You'll be glad you did later, trust me on that.

72 (4) Next is solidifying your life philosophy. This usually doesn't take much time because you've already spent a lot of time discovering things about yourself.

It becomes just a matter of taking all the pieces of your Standards and Principles and putting them into a small powerful Perspective on life.

I've found that most people don't get their philosophy quite right the first time. So if it doesn't feel right to you, keep working on it until it does.

Another interesting thing to note here is that while you're working out your life philosophy you'll also discover better ways to define some of your Standards and Principles.

If this happens then make notes of them. The clearer everything is for you, the better.

If you're a detail oriented person you might find yourself feeling overwhelmed at this point. All of this doesn't have to be perfect, just clear.

73 (5) Putting together your Program is next. This can be a tough one for most people because they realize they don't have any real concrete goals or ambitions.

Like the average person, they're just living their life day-to-day. They function and think only about going to work or school and having fun.

To help with this, you need to think of how you want your life to look in five years. Then think about what needs to be done to get you there.

With careful examination and introspection you'll be able to find at least one or two goals – things that you must work toward to create the life you want.

Designing your Program is a long process. Just work through it, step-by-step. Think long and hard about all the pieces you're going to need and how they fit together.

Once you're done there then you can create your weekly or monthly schedule. Don't forget to leave room for approaching and taking women out.

74 (6) During all of the above processes, you want to put a look together. Shop for clothes and jewelry because the new you is coming together. Wrap that new you properly. Reflect on the outside the greatness on the inside.

75 (7) Once your Program is completed, then depending on your level of comfort, you may want to practice just starting conversations with women.

This can be women you already know. But you should want to really test yourself by starting conversations with women you don't know.

The conversations don't need to be stellar. They can be mundane things like talking about the weather or how crowded a store is while you're both at the check-out line.

You're not Macking yet so don't put so much pressure on yourself. You're not trying to flirt and you're not trying to get phone numbers.

All you're doing at this stage is getting your mind comfortable with speaking to women; lessening the anxiety and building your confidence.

At the end of you day, mentally review your conversations. Think about where you can improve or what you could have done differently.

Don't beat yourself up over making a mistake, running out of conversation or saying something "stupid". This is all a learning process. You can't do calculus if you don't know basic arithmetic.

Use the, *"How to Install New Mental Files"* routine (in Book 2 – Chapter Three) to positively reinforce the success you're after. This also sets your mind up to become better at pulling the "files" that will make you better overall.

How long does the process of getting comfortable talking to women take? It varies from person to person.

I would suggest starting at least three conversations a day with women who are strangers. You don't have to break your daily routine to do it.

This can be done while you're pumping gas, waiting on a bus, ordering food at a restaurant, in line at a store, etc.

On average, 30 days of this along with properly "installing" new mental files will get you through the door.

When it's all said and done, the time frame isn't important. You want to have opened conversations with 90-100 women. If you have the motivation and the time, this could actually be done in a week or two.

If you're already comfortable with this, then skip this step.

76   (8) Once you have a handle on conversing with women, you can start flirting more with random women. Give them compliments, think out-loud and expect nothing more than to hear, "Thank you."

If this leads to a conversation then so be it, have a conversation. If not, then this is acceptable. You're just "flexing your muscles" at this stage.

If you're really advanced then you can move on to the next step.

77   (9) Now that you have built up some comfort and confidence, its go time! Work on your approach. Prepare some designed pre-planned responses.

You should have gained enough experience speaking with women to where you have a strong idea of how they respond to certain things. Use that experience to help you.

Get in front of a mirror and practice. Work on your facial expressions and your tonality.

78   (10) Go back out and approach women – women that you actually find attractive.

Like before, you're implementing new skills so you're going to make some mistakes. That's OK. If you say something "corny" then own it. If you're stumbling over your words, tell her that she has you so nervous you can't get your words straight.

Make this process fun. Be the best of yourself!

At this stage you want to actually ask for phone numbers. Don't gauge your success on how many you get. Measure your success by how many you actually *ask* for.

Every night, review, think of ways to improve, do the new mental file installation routine and implement your changes.

Practice, practice, practice. Keep track of the number of women you approach and when you get to 100, take an assessment.

Review, think of ways to improve and find ways to add in the conversation tools from Book 4 – Chapter One.

Keep practicing and keep expanding your range of conversation.

79 (11) Once you get a phone number then you need to practice talking over the phone and texting. Your overall conversations and texts should be light-hearted and short. All you're really trying to do is get a woman to agree to a Social Outing.

As long as you can keep the attraction and stay interesting, you'll eventually be met with success.

Don't get down about a woman saying no. And don't allow yourself to feel down about a woman who says she'll go out, but then cancels or just simply doesn't show up.

This happens to even the best Macks. It's part of the Game so charge it to the Game.

You should still be approaching women anyway so there's no reason to get hung up on a couple of women who didn't recognize your Value. Stay in motion and keep Macking.

80 (12) Remember your agenda with the Social Outing. You're just building a mental connection with the woman and seeing if she's actually interesting enough to get to know further.

Stay calm, showcase your manhood and have a good time. There are a lot of things to remember, but the main goal here is to get a woman very comfortable with you so she opens up and talks about herself.

Be open and she'll get comfortable enough to be open in return. **Transmit** so she'll **receive**.

After a social outing, review, think of ways to improve and work on those mental files.

81 These steps will get you on your way. This book will serve as a great reference guide once you've studied it.

82 You can always come back and you'll see small details that you've missed before. This will happen because you've changed through your own experiences. New things will stand out and grab your attention because they'll become more relevant.

83 It's the gift that keeps on giving. As you develop yourself and your skills, the knowledge, wisdom and understanding in this book will be right alongside you. It will "grow" with you.

84 Just remember, don't act too serious. Enjoy being the best man you can be. Enjoy the time you spend with women. Make this exciting.

85 When you finally find the right woman for you and months pass – keep igniting feelings into your relationship. The feelings you both had when your relationship started because the way you start with a woman is the way must continue. That's just good Macking.

86 Congratulations! You have now been fully initiated into the world of the modern Mack Game. Get off the bench and get to Playing. Have more women and take back your manhood. You're worth it and you deserve it. Now you know why.

About the Author

W. James Dennis started his first business when he was 17 years old. It failed. He then started his second business in his early-twenties, which failed too. But just a few years later with an example of business success to learn from, his third business did succeed and he operated it for over 10 years. During this time he was a dedicated student of the "Game", something which he calls, *Uncommon Sense*. Realizing his passion was writing and educating, he changed gears in his life and is now an author, public speaker and small business consultant living just outside of Atlanta, Georgia – United States. His favorite quote is, "Keep it moving and keep it simple in the process."

Connect with W. James Dennis

wjamesdennis@gmail.com
facebook.com/wjamesd | twitter: @wjamesdennis

Also by This Author

Unlocking the Small Business Game – *The Playbook for Starting a Small Business from Nothing Using Simple Clear Uncommon Sense*
Holding Magnetic Conversations – *Learn to Be a Master Communicator in Just Hours*
Revealing the Secrets of the Game – *Exposing the Most Heavily Guarded System of Self-Empowerment Ever Designed*

Tighten Your Game With This 2-Hour Audio Lesson!

Learn More At: https://gum.co/almm